D0732749

Fishing by Obstinate Isles

San Diego Christian College
2100 Greenfield Drive
El Cajon, CA 92019

avant-garde & **modernism studies**

General Editors

Marjorie Perloff

Rainer Rumold

Consulting Editors

Peter Fenves

Stephen Foster

Christine Froula

Françoise Lionnet

Robert von Hallberg

821.09
T925f

Dr. Donald Wesling
4968 Foothill Blvd.
San Diego, Ca. 92109

Fishing by Obstinate Isles

Modern and Postmodern

British Poetry and

American Readers

KEITH TUMA

Northwestern

University Press

Evanston

Illinois

Northwestern University Press
Evanston, Illinois 60208-4210

Copyright © 1998 by Northwestern University Press.
Published 1998. All rights reserved.
Printed in the United States of America
ISBN 0-8101-1622-7 (cloth)
ISBN 0-8101-1623-5 (paper)

Library of Congress Cataloging-in-Publication Data
Tuma, Keith, 1957–
Fishing by obstinate isles : modern and postmodern British poetry
and American readers / Keith Tuma.
    p.   cm. — (Avant-garde and modernism studies)
Includes bibliographical references and index.
ISBN 0-8101-1622-7 (cloth : alk. paper). —
ISBN 0-8101-1623-5 (pbk. : alk. paper)
1. English poetry—20th century—History and criticism.
2. Modernism (Literature)—Great Britain.   3. Books and reading—
United States—History—20th century.   4. Literature,
Comparative—English and American.   5. Literature,
Comparative—American and English.   6. English poetry—
Appreciation—United States.   7. Postmodernism (Literature)—
Great Britain.   8. American poetry—English influences.   I. Title.
II. Series.
PR605.M63T86   1998
821'.9109112—dc21   98-35302
                                                                CIP

The paper used in this publication meets the minimum requirements
of the American National Standard for Information Sciences—
Permanence of Paper for Printed Library Materials, ANSI Z39.48-1984.

Contents

Acknowledgments

I want to thank Nathaniel Dorward, Robert von Hallberg, Christopher Knight, Peter Quartermain, and Maeera Shreiber for comments on drafts of parts of this book.

Thanks also to Richard Caddel, cris cheek, Andrew Crozier, Andrew Duncan, Ken Edwards, Clayton Eshleman, Alan Golding, Robert Hampson, Romana Huk, Ann Massa, John Matthias, Marjorie Perloff, Tom Raworth, Peter Riley, Lawrence Upton, and William Walsh for dialogue and assistance, generosity and curiosity, and to Sue Betz and Rachel Drzewicki at Northwestern University Press for work on the book's production.

This book is for Cris Cheek and Tom Raworth in England, if they'll have it, and for Diane Tuma and Allison Tuma, whose laughter and love in Oxford, Ohio, made it possible.

Portions of this book appeared in earlier and substantially different versions in *Chicago Review, Contemporary Literature, Forked Tongues: Comparing Twentieth Century British and American Literature, River City: A Journal of Contemporary Culture, Sagetrieb,* and *Sulfur.* Thanks to the editors of those publications.

I am grateful to the authors, publishers, and literary estates listed below for permission to reprint material quoted in *Fishing by Obstinate Isles:*

"Masters" from *Collected Poems 1944–1979* by Kingsley Amis, reprinted by kind permission of Jonathan Clowes Ltd., London, on behalf of the Literary Estate of Sir Kingsley Amis.

Selected excerpts from *Éclat* by Caroline Bergvall, Sound & Language, 1996, reprinted by permission of the publisher and author.

"Aix-La-Chappelle, 1945" from *Collected Poems* by Edgar Bowers, Alfred A. Knopf, 1997, reprinted by permission of Alfred A. Knopf, Inc.

Selected excerpts from *The Arrivants* by Edward Kamau Brathwaite, Oxford University Press, 1973, reprinted by permission of Oxford University Press (England).

Selected excerpts from *Collected Poems 1952–83* by Alan Brownjohn, reprinted by permission of the author.

Selected excerpts from *The Complete Poems* by Basil Bunting, Oxford

University Press, 1994, reprinted by permission of Oxford University Press (England).

Selected excerpts from *Aimé Cesaire: Collected Poetry* by Aimé Cesaire, trans. Clayton Eshleman and Annette Smith, University of California Press, 1983, reprinted by permission of the University of California Press.

Selected excerpts from *Collected Poems 1956–1974* by Edward Dorn, Four Seasons, 1975, reprinted by permission of the author.

Selected excerpts from *SCRAM: Or the Transformation of the Concept of Cities* by Allen Fisher, Spectacular Diseases, 1994, reprinted by the permission of the author.

Selected excerpts from *Unpolished Mirrors* by Allen Fisher, Reality Street Editions, 1985, reprinted by permission of the author and publisher.

Selected excerpts from "Speak, Bitterness" by Forced Entertainment, Sound & Language, 1995, reprinted by permission of the publisher.

Selected excerpts from *The Man with Night Sweats* by Thom Gunn, Faber and Faber (England) and Farrar, Straus, Giroux (United States), 1992, reprinted by permission of Faber and Faber Ltd. and Farrar, Straus, Giroux.

Selected excerpts from "A Good Read" in *Selected Poems* by Tony Harrison, Penguin, 1985, reprinted by permission of Gordon Dickerson for the author.

Selected excerpts from "The Mystery of the Charity of Charles Péguy," in *New and Collected Poems 1952–1992*, copyright 1994 by Geoffrey Hill, reprinted by permission of Houghton Mifflin Co. All rights reserved. Previously published as *The Mystery of the Charity of Charles Péguy*, 1983.

Selected excerpts from "Sister Midnight" by John James, in *A Various Art*, Carcanet, 1987, reprinted by permission of the author.

"Nothing to be Said" from *Collected Poems* by Philip Larkin, Faber and Faber (England) and Farrar, Straus, Giroux (United States), 1989, reprinted by permission of Faber and Faber Ltd. and Farrar, Straus, Giroux.

Selected excerpts from "Anglo-Mongrels and the Rose" from *The Last Lunar Baedeker* by Mina Loy, Jargon Books, 1982, reprinted by permission of Roger L. Conover on behalf of the Mina Loy Estate.

Selected excerpts from *The Ecliptic* by Joseph Gordon Macleod, Faber, 1930, reprinted by permission of Martin Creegan, Iain Antony Macleod, and Sandra Macleod for the Joseph Gordon Macleod Estate.

"Molecular Power Progressives" and selected excerpts from *The Sway of Precious Demons: Selected Poems* by Geraldine Monk, North and South, 1992, reprinted by permission of the author.

"Starlings" from *In the House of the Shaman* by Maggie O'Sullivan, Reality Street Editions, 1993, reprinted by permission of the author and publisher.

Selected excerpts from *God's Gift to Women* by Don Paterson, Faber and Faber, 1997, reprinted by permission of Faber and Faber Ltd.

Selected excerpts from *Catacoustics* by Tom Raworth, Street Editions, 1991, reprinted by permission of the author.

Selected excerpts from *Logbook* by Tom Raworth, Poltroon Press, 1976, reprinted by permission of the author.

Selected excerpts from *Distant Points* by Peter Riley, Reality Street Editions, 1995, reprinted by permission of the publisher and author.

Selected excerpts from *Poems and Adolphé 1920* by John Rodker, Carcanet, 1996, reprinted by permission of Carcanet Press Limited.

Selected excerpts from *Exactions* by C. H. Sisson, Carcanet, 1980, reprinted by permission of Carcanet Press Limited.

Selected excerpts from "Twenty Words, Twenty Days" in *While Breath Persist* by Gael Turnbull, The Porcupine's Quill Press, 1992, reprinted by permission of the author.

Every effort has been made to locate and contact the publishers and/or copyright holders for materials reprinted in this book. We will be grateful for correspondence concerning materials reproduced here beyond standard practices of fair use.

Introduction

Reading Modern and
Postmodern British Poetry

In the United States, British poetry is dead. It's as dead as Philip Larkin, who survives as a biographical scandal but not as a poet whose work makes much of a difference to the more vital among American poetic practices. It's as dead as the syllabus in those few and increasingly fewer college classrooms where recent British poetry is taught and the reading ends with W. H. Auden, Dylan Thomas, or Larkin himself, or perhaps with a sampling of Blake Morrison and Andrew Motion's *Penguin Book of Contemporary British Poetry* (1982) gesturing at the present. British poetry is dead so long as no British poetry critic seems destined to fill the vacancies left by the deaths of Donald Davie and Eric Mottram, who used to carry the news of recent poetries back and forth across the Atlantic. In a posthistorical era of endless "deaths," each with its special effects, the particular death of British poetry in the United States is produced by a combination of benign neglect, ordinary ignorance, and the casual half-truths of a critical journalism cognizant only of the narrowest field of extant poetry. Even anglophiles out of a bygone era of foppish American professors putting on fake English accents don't care, don't know much about it. For them British poetry is as safely historical as medieval architecture.

Glumly disposed, I wanted to begin thus. I might have begun with some faint signs of interest: this or that journal publishes a selection of contemporary British poetry; the Internet accelerates possible conversations and information flow; bored with local models or intent on a new internationalism, this or that contemporary poet-critic tries to find out what's going on in Britain. But if American poetry once had to labor to become visible against a British background, today Americans have to squint to see British poetry at all. Nobody is to blame, exactly, or the blame might be widely distributed among several generations of poets and a profession of academic literary study which still has some use for historical British literatures as they might be read through the lenses of new critical methodologies, and some use for recent postcolonial writing and the contemporary British novel, but very little use indeed for recent British poetry. The blame might be extended to the British themselves: British poetry has suffered in the United States, as it has in Britain itself, because little serious critical discourse is turned its way and what there is seems perpetually to be discussing the same poets. Without a criticism—and the good news is that several recent publications in England have begun to alter this situation, and that younger British critics such as Andrew Duncan, Drew Milne, Peter Middleton, and others have been working hard to reinvent the critical attention needed—much of British poetry is destined to remain beyond even the margins of British cultural discourse, invisible nearly, and therefore extremely hard to learn about in the United States.[1] Whereas academic literary criticism in the United States has proved itself capable of plundering the margins of poetic production to reconstitute its object of study (if not always its methods)—witness the plethora of articles published on language writing in an academic journal such as *Contemporary Literature*—the margins in Britain have been less a way station than a parking garage.

Still, poetry, as a friend of mine says, is harder to kill than head lice, and it turns out that there is a considerable and diverse body of modern British poetry most of us in the United States know little about—not just "contemporary" poetry but also a British modernism mostly missing from our canonical accounts of literary modernism. In what follows I mean, first, to show why we know so little about it. It is not a surprising story, I think, and so I am telling it backwards, from the near present, where there are only a few signs of life, back into the middle twenties and early thirties, to justify my glum thesis: Americans have lost sight of British poetry. In an era now passing into the uncertainties of a postnational and globalized future, rhetorics of national identity and the construction, by poets and institutions alike, of something called "American poetry" have allowed readers of poetry to become more and more comfortable with their disengagement with recent British practice to the point where a poetry which presents fewer difficulties than, say, French or German poetry, is nearly the last place one goes when reading beyond the boundaries of the nation. The ability of criticism consciously or unconsciously to play toady to the bluntest of national desires has, of course, never been exclusively on show in the United States; historically, certain British poetries have been able to count on influential readers in the United States, but that same support has often cost them at home, allowing cultural conservatives to label specific poetries as derivative of American models or to isolate them as somehow un-English. But my first concern is with the United States: by reducing British poetry to a caricature, "othering" it, or by ignoring it, American poetries have been willing to parade their seriousness and international importance.

In commonplaces few would risk in writing, British poetry comes to mean flip frivolity and Audenesque chattiness, a strangely sentimental cynicism in regular measures, one or another post-Georgian pastoralism. Or British poetry is passed into the hands of one or two "representative" poets, Larkin or Ted Hughes; the former in particular is of whatever small use he is primarily for those Americans already promoting an antimodernist rhetoric. In the space of fifty years British poetry has been crossed off our maps, or relegated to the zones of the quaint and antiquarian; American poets and poetry critics no longer feel the need to read widely in contemporary British poetry. We take British poetry in token bits—if at all—and not as a field of contradictory practices, and certainly not as a body of work that might challenge our own arrogant view of American dominance in the art.

Representational logics link poetry and its evaluation to national identity, or, alternatively, to the identities of groups within the nation. In considering the fate of British poetry in the United States, it makes little difference whether we speak of one complex and evolving "American" cultural nation or, following the multiculturalists, many groups within the state; for British poetry, either way it's a losing proposition. For multiculturalists, as Amy Kaplan has argued, a "new pluralistic model of diversity runs the risk of being bound by the same paradigm of unity if it concentrates its gaze only narrowly on the internal lineaments of American culture and leaves national boundaries intact instead of interrogating their boundaries" (15). Even as the rhetorics of national identity are contested or dispersed, the institutional structures of literary study preserve a unified field of study, a "subject"—American literature or culture, or the "literature of the Americas." The subject has been the site of enough struggle hardly to need those older projections whereby an American literature set itself beside or against something called "British literature." These belong to a discarded Atlanticism, but in the wake of that paradigm a truly transatlantic and global one has yet to emerge.

Many (though not all) of the British and American poets I celebrate in this book understand that cultural and national identities are "produced in specific historical and institutional sites within specific discursive formations and practices, by specific enunciative strategies," to quote Stuart Hall (4). Many of them imagine that one of the functions of their work is to contest these discourses and the identities and identifications they produce and reproduce. But a rhetoric of transnational influence can be complex indeed. Take the case of the Scottish poet Tom Leonard, for instance, writing on William Carlos Williams. Leonard wants to understand Williams's constructivist modernist practice within an international field: "His inclination to see and treat language as an object in itself might have been motivated by the thought that this was a necessary initial process prior to the consolidation of a specifically American poetic mode—but in treating the medium of poetry, language, as an object in itself, he was simply keeping abreast of developments in the other arts of his time" (96–97). Thinking about a materialist understanding of lexis, syntax, and phonology and practices enabled by "attention to language as an object in itself," Leonard can name developments that he takes to be related to Williams's practice in the work of Hugh MacDiarmid (lexis), Ian Hamilton Finlay (syntax), and Bob Cobbing (phonology). There is nothing, it seems, uniquely American about Williams's practice. Nevertheless, because none of these poets has fared particularly well in a Britain where Leonard thinks a "Received Pronunciation" dominates, where "language would be considered the possession of a particular class, a form of property which like other forms of property needed protection," it is clear that, for Leonard, an "American-initiated breakdown in prescriptive grammar," a "message coming out of America," authorize an oppositional practice and critique that will be mobile, transnational, and active in particular contexts like Scotland and England if grounded in or identified first with the United States (99–102). Internationalism with an American origin is used in this context to bash the center of British culture in London and Oxbridge, but even while Leonard's "solidarity" with Williams is evident in poems of his own like "Just ti Let Yi No," a rewriting in Glaswegian slang of Williams's famous refrigerator poem, that solidarity names a poetic practice more or less continuous with international models but also distinctly idiomatic. Portable and mobile in rhetoric, a national identity can enter into different contexts carrying different values. If it can be more or less unstable, it can also be volatile, especially in its more reactive formulations, in those more programmatic or wounded or desperate efforts to shore up whatever against the forces of forgetfulness, dispersal, imagination, and cross-cultural hybridization.

As I begin with British poetry off the edge of American maps and work backward just a few years to see it reappear, I am mindful of the history of resentments and anti-American rhetoric in Britain. An aggressive rhetoric of national identity has been equally—if not more—damaging to British poetry in Britain itself as a rhetoric of American exceptionalism once was to British poetry in the United States—before most of us lost sight of that poetry altogether. Among a "mainstream" in Britain, a wounded rhetoric about American boorishness and cultural imperialism has helped sustain some of the most profoundly anti-intellectual and insular poetries written since the advent of modernism—which, preposterously enough, some British critics claim never happened in Britain, especially in England, as if it existed in a time warp. But a British avant-garde has its national moments too. One way to sort among some of the more challenging poets and poetries in Britain today is to determine the extent to which each is engaged with asserting or inventing continuities with specifically British traditions which would include modernist poetries—an academic enterprise, that, and thus not surprisingly centered in Cambridge—or whether they have more or less neglected that chore to pursue alliances with contemporary innovative writing produced elsewhere in the United States, Canada, France, Germany, and other nations. Such distinctions will be a matter of degree. To say that Allen Fisher is less interested in an English modernism—in the work of John Rodker or Nicholas Moore, for instance—than Andrew Crozier or Peter Riley does not mean that Fisher is not concerned with, say, William Blake or Hugh MacDiarmid, or that Crozier's interests do not also include American objectivist poets, Riley's Samuel Beckett.

Insofar as I am concerned here often with discourse about poetry—which even this late in the century some poets believe to be parasitical or secondary, ignoring its power to create and shape readerships and enable practices—I want to be as fair as possible to poets *and* critics on both sides of the Atlantic. At the same time this book might be subtitled something like "static on transatlantic lines." Those lines are, mostly, the "lines" of criticism. Poets have more reason to find and pursue affinities, even if Americans haven't often looked to Britain lately. They also have an excuse to ignore work that doesn't immediately or especially interest them. They might be forgiven the blindnesses and caricatures which they perpetuate. It is harder to forgive a critic his or her blindness, inevitable as it may be.

Blindly, then, I'll say the following about that which follows in the chapter-essays of this book: I want to present enough poetries not to map the whole field of modern and contemporary British poetry but to erode established caricatures and prevent new ones from solidifying; I want to ventriloquize from enough perspectives to prevent discourses of national identity from emerging, as they have in the past, in a way that inevitably distorts and interrupts the reading of poems, or just makes whole areas of poetic practice disappear. Whether British poetry is seen as a nest out of which American poetry emerged, as a first and important screen against which American poetry projected its own identities, or as a once valued and now smothering relic of a past which needs to be altogether exploded in the name of immigrant poetries and the multicultural poetries of the Americas—determining the proper way of thinking about the relationship between the two poetries is not my primary concern. It is not that I have no interest in the particulars of these national narratives—I will be referring to them in an effort to demonstrate the ways in which they have helped us to imagine the superiority of American poetries. But the proof of my case against recent American insularity is no concrete, positive example of a particularly egregious, chauvinistic rhetoric. My proof consists rather in an absence, in the fact that, for the most part, we have just stopped paying attention to contemporary British poetry. The ultimate insult is the suggestion that there is nothing worth bothering about there. Donald Hall captures the frustration that animates this book when he writes that "it is a received idea that English poets for fifty years (or a hundred and fifty) have been interior decorators unskilled in interior decoration" (24). It is "received ideas" that I am exploring—tracing, trying to understand and then defeat.

One can date the "death" of British poetry in the United States fairly precisely, I will suggest, to the late sixties or the early seventies. In chapter 1 I discuss what Eric Mottram called the British Poetry Revival, a moment when active cooperation between American and British experimentalists seemed possible. In the wake of that period, whatever its successes and failures, a kind of diaspora occurred: poets moving off into their separate endeavors and silences, more British poets keeping apace of American poetry than the other way around. Americans had enough to do, perhaps, paying attention to American poetic production. Or that would be an excuse: sitting on top of the world, we had no need to scrutinize formerly glorious islands now thought to be reduced to molehills of festering decline.

As I suggested above, many (though not all) of the poets I most admire, modernist and postmodernist poets, will be skeptical of discourses of national identity; they are more likely to express their sense of belonging to a transnational republic of letters or—the more adventurous among them—an international avant-garde. But while the limits of parochialism and insularity are well known among these writers, it is not the case that internationalism or transatlantic community has been much discussed or theorized among them. Poets might discuss the international triumph of the commodity or consumerism, but a discourse of globalization seems to have had little purchase except as it might summon a vaguely threatening spectre of processes of cultural homogenization poetry is thought to resist—if only because the inefficiencies of its production and distribution allow some to imagine it as somehow not implicated in something as pervasive as consumer culture. When I read someone saying that "cultural globalization, similar to economic globalization, is more likely to result in generating and upholding heterogeneity as a feature as much inherent in its logic as homogenization," and that "although it would be highly problematic to argue that national or cultural identities are not open to influence by mass communication media at all, this does not mean that they are necessarily shaped or constituted by them" (Artmann, 37) I know that I am probably not reading a poet or poetry critic. Too much probity, too hopeful for poets. Multinational corporations, global communications and technologies—poets too bemoan the ways in which they erode the ability of the nation to take responsibility for what happens within its borders, even as they are critical of efforts to define the nation. That we have failed to imagine possible effects of globalization that would have a positive side, to seize or imagine its possibilities as well as resisting its threats, and that we have failed to articulate the extent to which current conditions are indeed new—was it ever the case, for instance, that the modern democratic nation might control much that obtained "culturally" within its territories?—are signs of the lingering power of representational logics linking poetry to the preservation or construction of national cultures. Poets call themselves internationalists or think of themselves as such but aren't eager to suggest what that might mean. British poets, conservative and avant-garde alike, are more likely lately to insist that poets and their readers recognize the threat to national identities represented by globalization. When I read someone arguing that "globalization theory must account for the continuing role of the nation state, for the reconfigured and less reified cores and peripheries, and for the stubborn grip of western (read: American) cultural imprint on the new globalized world of consumption" (Averill, 209), I find myself thinking now this is something I might hear from some *British* poets, who have been more willing to suggest the extent to which international power can bear an American signature.

It seems foolish to declare oneself for or against the "nation" or "internationalism" once and for all, for or against *any* collective identity, without regard for the contexts in which declarations might function or the nature of the vision of the global, national, transatlantic, or local that might be at stake. It is with internationalists and avant-gardists who seek either to transcend (momentarily) or resist all cultural practices that gather identities too quickly and rigidly into the nation that I align myself in this book, but I don't do so in order to dismiss altogether the value of writing a poetry that would imagine community under the sign of the nation. "National identity" can be useful in challenging the excesses of multinational economic and cultural structures which care little for identities of any variety. But discourses of national identity not challenged by critical practices begin to loom as oppressive. One reason for reading British poetry, and for reading as widely in it as possible, is to combat narrow views of that poetry that emerge in premature and reified accounts of American identity; equally one might contest views of British poetry in Britain that perpetuate nostalgic attitudes and values or produce narrow views of various American poetries. Another, very different reason to read British poetry is to study its own linguistic resources, both those which gather national identity and those which disperse it. Every English-language poetry American poetries lose sight of is a loss that threatens to convert idiomatic American poetries finding their way in and amid a world of "English" and other languages into insular poetries self-satisfied with what is felt to be their own. It is crucial to insist upon the differences of British contexts as they enter into a poetry; it can also be useful to point to affinities. Occasionally one wants to do both, to point to differences and affinities; one doesn't want to be confined to celebrating only that poetry (or idea of poetry) which expresses collective identity, or its supposed opposite, poetry aggressively resisting a prematurely stabilized and coherent ascription of identity.

Eclecticism within and beyond the nation: not only can I read this and that both but I can read this and that for different reasons and in different ways. Situadedness, contextualism: these aren't new words or tactics. One might read a poet such as Basil Bunting, for instance, with an eye toward identifying a Northumbrian difference that would set his work apart not only from American poetry but also from the bulk of English poetry. Or one might read him — as a model citizen within a republic of letters — as a poet whose affective and linguistic structures are eminently transportable and exemplary.

An internationalist perspective in poetry would like to avoid participating in the more exploitative machinery of multinational capitalism, but calls for internationalism in the arts from United States citizens can also ring particularly hollow (or threatening). An "international" perspective must at least remain alert to the importance of local contexts — even as it might seek affinities and parallel practices beyond the nation. Charles Bernstein has noted in his essay "Poetics of the Americas" that, too often, internationalism has "provided models of connoisseurship that have removed poems from the local contexts that gave them meaning" (3). Suggesting that "the problem is how to pursue affinities while resisting unities and how to resist unities without losing the capacity to be poetically responsible," Bernstein proposes that we (all readers seeking to find their way or extend the possibilities of poetry) "pursue the collective and dialogic nature of poetry without necessarily defining the nature of this collectivity" (4). It might be objected that this is the politics of elusiveness — that Bernstein offers no vision of new forms of international community that might be constructed or shored up by poetry but only a means of contesting those identities and collectivities already given, more or less defined. Even the most "avant-garde" poetry these days is largely reactive (I don't mean reactionary), which is not to say that the virtual community shaped by reading across national boundaries, or the solidarities encouraged by identifying with something as nebulous as "an international avant-garde," are without consequence in building collectivities but only that a recognition of the power of all that against which such art competes and the limited audience of poetry tends to discourage visionary and revolutionary postures. For some, a republic of letters names an idealized space apart from the local politics of the nation. For others, even an aestheticist internationalism can proffer an image of freedom critical of tangible unfreedoms and limits. An international "republic of letters" or an "international avant-garde" might name the possibility of a world with fewer boundaries and contingencies, an as yet nonexistent democracy, or perhaps one should say that one hopes it might name such a world.

One point of talking about various British poetries in this book will be to show some of the ways in which "our [American] boasting about the significance of non-European American poetry has deafened us to the newness of English-language poetries" other than our own, as Bernstein honestly admits (3). This is to say that it is not just Walter Benn Michaels's recently redefined "American modernism" that has nativist, exclusionary moments, but also too often—as the British example shows us—"international modernism" itself as advocated by Americans such as Pound or his most influential exegete, Hugh Kenner. Monumentalized narratives of literary modernism have been written contemporaneously with the growth of an increasingly global American power and the rhetoric of American exceptionalism, leaving modern British poetry behind. Is it the common wisdom that, in poetry, a British difference names only the near obsolescence or the difficult nuisance of residual forms of poetic practice? That would be one way to read some of the discourse about poetry this book will discuss, one of the realities which defines the space it enters into.

As its title borrowed from Pound's *Hugh Selwyn Mauberley* indicates, this book understands the resistance to some forms of modernism among many in Britain throughout this century as a form of "obstinance." Aesthetic values shade over into a moralizing language I am uncomfortable with. As an advocate of various American and British modernist and postmodernist poetries, I have little choice in this matter. But I hope that it is clear that I also understand the extent to which British "obstinance" is sometimes bred by American boorishness. Reading across national boundaries in search of both affinities and differences, holding not just British provincialism but also American provincialism up to the light of comparison is a project that might be initiated on both sides of the Atlantic, and from a range of perspectives. The Anglo-American interface—the subject of the first part of this book—offers many examples of a breakdown of communication, of impediments which make for distorted communication in a world in which communication is, "technically speaking," easier than ever and in which the two participants concerned use idioms that bear some family resemblances. Notorious and sometimes devastating static in the Anglo-American interface ironically supports what some postmodern writers have been telling us about the opacity of language, about signs emptying themselves at each iteration. We have first to recognize the possibilities of communication breaking down, I think, in order to learn to listen better, in order to reinvent attention.[2]

Why is it, I sometimes wonder, that anti-Americanism among the French is legendary, having passed into the popular imagination, whereas few speak of anti-Americanism among the British? And what might it mean if, as Americans, we were better able to hear it when it voiced itself? In the United States, anyway, there has been considerably less discussion of the British fleeing Americans than of Americans fleeing the British, and too rarely acknowledgments such as the one quoted above from Bernstein, who admits that those American poets most closely identified with "experimental" or "avant-garde" poetries must share the blame for perpetuating a neglect of British poetry, so intent have they been to celebrate their own accomplishments.

Surely, simple characterizations of British poetry as a monolithic source of all that is obsolete, standardized, and ruled by timid conventionality have outlived their usefulness. The closer view on display here, focused on particular poets and discourses, as well as on moments in the history of Anglo-American relations in poetry over the course of the last sixty years, means to paint some detail into the larger picture of the blind struggles across the hyphen in "Anglo-American" in order to complicate it, without necessarily blotting the picture out. It shows us an older Pound still in dialogue with contemporary British poetry. It shows us a British contemporary poetry which has absorbed varieties of modernism while remaining suspicious of an Americanized rhetoric of "international modernism." It listens to the voices of antimodernism in England and the familiar claim that antimodernist American poets (such as some fifties poets) were Anglophiles. It takes up these and other topics as unsystematically as possible, because I want no part of the power of systematic, "theoretical" language and know I'm lucky even to have your attention for as long as it takes to wind my way into an improbable subject.

As an American reader of modern and contemporary British poetry, I am regularly made aware of the death of British poetry in the United States. Here I am speaking of matters other than the way the death of British poetry enters discourse affecting the production and reception of poetry. At its most basic and frustrating level, this death means great difficulty in obtaining information concerning recent developments in British poetry. It means knowing that even British poets who have been publishing books in Britain for thirty years—Peter Redgrove, for instance—will often not have an American publisher. It means stumbling around in the dark without much assistance from literary journalism and criticism. It means knowing that there must be poetry beyond that which makes it into mainstream anthologies and publications—the work of Ted Hughes, James Fenton, Craig Raine, and others—but being left largely on one's own to find it, or relying on a few friends—more recently, on the resources of the Internet. It means the hassles of blindly ordering books from British catalogs, or relying on the selections of rare and specialized distributors such as Dufour in Pennsylvania and Small Press Distribution in Berkeley, or friends in England. It means feeling lucky when I am able to obtain a small-circulation British journal such as *Parataxis* or *Angel Exhaust* containing intelligent criticism of "alternative" British poetry. It means knowing that your view of poetry in Britain is ever-changing but necessarily limited by an inevitably distanced and haphazard engagement with it, and that the best you can do is to work to defeat some of the more aggressive caricatures that arise when we leave discussion of particular poets behind and start to talk of "national" traditions.

If asked, I am not likely to defend my interest in British poetry as an interest in something *British* but rather as an interest in poetry. Italian philosopher Giorgio Agamben writes of love that it "is never directed toward this or that property of the loved one (being blond, being small, being tender, being lame), but neither does it neglect the properties in favor of an insipid generality. . . . The lover wants the loved one *with all of its predicates*" (2). But in what sense could we begin to think of "nationality" as an important predicate in our reading of poetry we admire enough to want or need to acknowledge? I am aware that critics have worked to identify this or that syntactic practice or quality of diction or form as British—or, alternatively, Northumbrian or Scottish or southron. These claims are usually contested: the same poem by Basil Bunting is read by Donald Davie as an example of standard British syntax, albeit condensed in modernist fashion, and by Peter Quartermain as a synthetic construction resisting this same standard and marking a Northumbrian difference.[3] I am aware, too, of other ways in which the specificity of cultural and geographical contexts enter into any reading of "British" and "American" poetries. But isolating these (and other) predicates is not what gives me the most pleasure in reading British or any other poetry. However important I might think it that we know the history of the rhetoric of nation in poetry criticism, however intent I am on calling attention to the oversimplifications and the destructive nature of a particular discourse about poetry which has unintentionally or willfully foregrounded issues of national traditions and coherent "national poetries," I am not likely in the end to defend my interest in British poetry by moralizing about the harmful nature of such discourse or speaking on behalf of a historical knowledge of its influence. Nor would I limit my pleas on behalf of the British poetry I admire to an insistence that, as good American citizens in an international economy and world, we ought to want to know what's going on in Britain, noting that the poetry would be one good place to try to determine that, one place perhaps to complicate mainstream American film's longstanding obsession with sentimentalized histories of British aristocratic life. Not that one would want to neglect what British poetry might have to offer in its idioms, its subjectivities, its "subject matter" — however broadly one wants to define these terms.

No, I would *want* to defend my interests in British poetry, impossibly, in exactly the same terms I would use to defend my interest in American poetry, even as I might seek to explore differences to be found in reading it. Which is to say that I seek many kinds of *pleasures* in poetry — of story and discourse, of sound and rhythm, of lyric subjectivity and dispersal of lyric subjectivity, of disjunctiveness and discursiveness, familiar and unfamiliar form, heteroglossia and suburban historiography, archival erudition and crude wit, the strangeness of idioms unknown, the commonplace perfectly deployed to re-emerge into value and clarity, the exotic for its own sake, the ephemeral and everyday, the imagination *in extremis,* all that I don't know and don't know I want to, language loping back and forth across the boundaries of sense and nonsense — even sometimes, God forbid, the well-turned phrase. I seek a thousand abstracted qualities beyond that pedestrian catalog, or just one phrase or cadence. I seek not only pleasure but understanding and meaning where I am able to meet it. I would defend an eclecticism in tastes as well as in purposes for poetry against those who argue that

contemporary culture successfully integrates opposition and displays an aesthetics without a normative center. Its ostentatious eclecticism is often linked to a rhetoric of pluralism that allows its defenders to denounce the critical advocates of emancipation as totalitarian. Yet it is postmodernist eclecticism, the consequence of the avant-garde attack on bourgeois normativity, that precludes systemic criticism. (Berman, 51)

It's true—I'm not interested in systemic criticism, as it has a way not just of criticizing totalities but of imagining a vantage point wholly outside our systems, as if it were possible to invent a language altogether asocial and ahistorical. Despite purists who would insist on one or the other, poetry's critical force, such as it is, in Britain and the United States, seems to involve guerrilla raids on bogus clarity *and* willful obscurity *both,* on administered precision and calculated obfuscation. Poetry knows well enough the story of its death as it explores its utopian and critical functions, and knows too enough about the cost of the rhetoric of "emancipation" to be wary of critique uttered too forcefully or finally. Our most "visionary" poets, those invested in systemic critique—Allen Ginsberg, Kamau Brathwaite—are also often self-deprecating poets. In Britain, eclecticism has had a harder go of it, just as, unsurprisingly, national identity has been an issue of some greater consequence: all the more reason to encourage eclecticism there. Just as national identity is of great concern only to those who imagine that, somehow, it has been lost or threatened, eclecticism is of concern only to those who fear that it conceals some more real (and more oppressive) uniformity.

Because few pay attention to British poetry anymore and perhaps assume that the relationship of British and American literatures is a settled question, there is a sense in which this book ends in 1980 or thereabouts. Like that guy you think you know slipping into the party very late through the back door, "nation," insofar as it becomes an issue— the interface of American and British poetry not as a matter of the history of particular influences but rather as a rhetoric which helps shape the reception and (sometimes) the production of poetry—is something one has to decide to talk about these days, not something one takes for granted as important. Particular national identities are most important to those who imagine that, somehow, they have, as it were, "lost" theirs— those who worry steadily about change. Lately, in the poetry world, it has been the British who have been more "concerned" with change, and thus with national identity, across the British-American interface(s). It might not be so bad that Americans now worry less about the British than the British worry about the Americans—the latter at least mostly avoid *articu-*

lating specific polemics—were it not also the case that, as I said, British poetry in the United States is dead. A few American or Canadian voices—John Matthias, Romana Huk, Peter Quartermain, Vincent Sherry, Linda Kinnahan, Donald Wesling—labor on, but few are listening. If we shift our attention to Britain it becomes clear that the need for British poets to assert the independence of their writing from American models, and to insist upon the specificity of British contexts, has not abated, even as we have lost sight of these debates in the United States. Indeed, it is the case recently that "nonmainstream" or "alternative" British poets in Cambridge and London have made arguments along these lines that, at least on their surface, sound very much like arguments made by Donald Davie and others on behalf of specifically British traditions.[4] There are differences—younger "alternative" poets do not often strain after some essential English tradition, are receptive to international models and influence, and so forth—but the anxiety about American cultural hegemony among some younger writers does distantly echo the anxiety of predecessors who dug in desperately around the legacy of Thomas Hardy.

For some who cut their teeth on Poundian modernism as it was defined and narrated in Hugh Kenner's *The Pound Era* and have taken pleasure in a variety of "experimental," "alternative," or "avant-garde" poetries throughout this century—the terms are inexact but their referents loosely agreed upon—British poetry beyond the 1914 Vorticist nexus in London has often been an oddity, as if Britain were the land the "revolution of the word" never knew. Marjorie Perloff mentions the poetry of British writers Jeremy Prynne, Tom Raworth, and Allen Fisher in the preface to her book on radical artifice, but when it comes to the examples of "radical artifice" she wants to examine—in this work and in her work on avant-garde traditions more generally—she turns to the Germans, French, Russians, Italians, and mostly to Americans.[5] She turns to the Irishman James Joyce and the Canadian Steve McCaffery. And she is not alone in her relative neglect of British writers who have been responsive to Continental and American "experimentalisms," nor is she to blame—British literary history and criticism has itself been too often unresponsive to David Gascoyne's surrealism or the adaptations of New York school and Black Mountain poetics in early Raworth and Prynne, or the push beyond these paradigms in their later work and in the work of others. It is also the case that a great deal of British poetry, like much American poetry, too, has contributed to our awareness that, no matter how much we might value a historical avant-garde or postwar neo-avant-gardes, they are far from the full story of poetry in this century. But in the United States we can be perhaps a little more confident that the avant-gardes have had a hearing, while in Britain—and especially for Americans surveying the British scene as out-siders—the issues are less clear, the manifestations of an avant-gardism we might recognize much harder to identify.

The "dominant" critical discourse of avant-gardism in the United States still is the Hegelian-Marxist theory of the Frankfurt school, especially as recently synthesized and revised in Peter Bürger's *The Theory of the Avant-Garde* (1984), a book which originally appeared in German in 1974. Marcel Duchamp and other Dada artists are crucial to Bürger's study of the avant-gardism, which understands an "historical avant-garde" as emerging from but also rejecting an earlier aestheticism (which would have "modernist" adherents) to propose "the sublation of art—sublation in the Hegelian sense of the term: art was not to be simply destroyed, but transferred to the praxis of life where it would be preserved, albeit in a changed form" (49). Whereas aestheticism presumed the autonomy of art from life praxis, avant-gardism sought to "integrate art" into the "means-end ratio-nality" of the "bourgeois everyday" in order to transform it. Bürger's is a sweeping, politicized reading of avant-gardism, and it is not very subtle in its shadings, its attention to particular works and national and local contexts—at one point the entire history of Western art in its relation-ship to patrons and audiences and social functions is reduced to a simple graph. But Bürger's book has done much to encourage a discussion of avant-gardism as part of the history of art as "institution," offering a more materialist reading to supplement earlier readings of avant-garde practices such as those advanced in Renato Poggioli's work, with its more psycholo-gized discussion of avant-garde "agonism" and "alienation." Poggioli's less systematic study has in its favor a greater attentiveness to the plurality of motives driving avant-garde practice; avant-garde practices for him are less one-dimensionally "revolutionary." Poggioli's notable emphasis on the complicity of avant-gardes in their liberal and democratic societies is not denied by Bürger; but one key difference is that Poggioli wants to identify avant-gardism with the most influential and powerful art and literature of the century, and clearly values its ability to challenge again and again the conventions of artistic and social practice.[6] From Bürger's perspective, nothing short of social rupture will do: Dada and other "movements" within the "historical avant-garde" must be understood as failures having achieved the large-scale social change he assumes they even as they transformed the history of art and its institutions fi who would read or write it after them. Neo-avant-gardes are particularly scorned, partly because avant-gardism has "lost [its] shock value" and partly because "the neo-avant-garde institutionalizes the *avant-garde as art* and thus negates genuinely avant-gardiste intentions" (57–58). There are now avant-garde traditions alongside other traditions.

But, contra Bürger, this is neither an intolerable nor a deplorable situation. Nor is it a situation that obtains in the same ways in all locations. By now, "language writing," for instance, has a small but serious audience in American universities; "language poets" are seen at nearly every Modern Language Association convention, their work an irritant mostly to professional creative writing programs and academic poetry critics who would rather ignore it. Via considerable mediations, it leaves its first coterie audiences behind and enters the public sphere. A parallel writing in England is so far from such a setting that it is just now showing up in the public sphere by way of contentious reviews of the Picador anthology *Conductors of Chaos*—one of the few mainstream appearances of such writing, which more regularly lived in performances in London or in xeroxed editions of two hundred put out by Equipage and other publishers. No reader of the book productions of recent experimental British poetry can help but note that, compared to their American peers, British poets have often had to make do with books which are as if stapled together in a garage.

Bürger's rhetoric of genuineness, real avant-gardes and neo-avant-gardes entirely deluded in their ambitions, is troubling. Critics are right to contest his conclusions whether, like Andreas Huyssen, they want to complicate his history by inserting national difference or, like Hal Foster, "to right [Bürger's] concept of the dialectic" insofar as it uses terms like *art* and *life* without sufficient attention to their instability and shifting contexts. Marjorie Perloff, in an essay on John Cage and postmodern genres, has challenged the reading of dada readymades that is at the heart of the theory. Paul Mann, in his book on the "theory-death" of the avant-garde, suggests that Bürger's book, for all its mania for definition and post-Marxist historiography, is best understood as a performative text helping to perpetuate that which it names—the death by recuperation of the avant-garde (mostly after Dada).[7] All such attacks on the pseudoscientism of histories of modernism and avant-gardism are welcome.

In an argument similar in many ways to Bürger's, if finally more Hegelian, Arthur Danto identifies not the end of avant-gardism but the end of art itself—the point in which it turns into its own philosophy—in Andy Warhol's Brillo cartons, which he saw in 1964. With critics like this writing on its works ("with friends like this"), it's no wonder that those who would make any claim on the identity of an "avant-garde" must constantly reinvent its purposes and practices to elude closure. I mention Danto's absurdly pompous and apocalyptic claim because Charles Bernstein, writing from the epicenter of that "language poetry" lately often mentioned in discussions of neo-avant-gardism, has explicitly challenged it (as, elsewhere, the histories of the avant-garde preferred by Bürger and Huyssen). Most poets simply don't bother with such criticism, perhaps because they are bored with the term *avant-garde* itself and tired of the endless effort to frame it and proclaim its death. Bernstein responds to Danto as follows:

> Yet it would seem, from Danto's argument, that it is neo-Hegelian philosophy that has come to an end, or anyway impasse, insofar as it can't account for the contemporaneity of art given its always-already defined conception of what art is. "Progress" is the loaded term (turn), but it may not be contemporary art's most important product. The messiness of the current art scene is at least a progressive critique of the narrowcasting of neoformalist and "postmodernist" criticism; but it's not messy enough. If Warhol brings us to a dead end it's not because art, in its highest vocation, has ended but that we need new maps, new kinds of maps, of the past hundreds-of-years that don't lead to the inevitability of this sort of reductionist closure or conclusion. (1992, 171)

But what will these "messy" new maps be? Postcolonial scholars and critics might help us draw them when they insist, with Kamau Brathwaite, that they will no longer silently play a part in detailing the symptoms of postmodernism in the West without understanding the difficulty as well as the urgency of naming national identities in the Caribbean and elsewhere. Historians of American modernisms might play a part by avoiding "reductionist" or totalizing narratives and staying alert to national contexts, pointing out that art in the United States never obtained anything remotely resembling its status, say, in turn-of-the-century Vienna, Berlin, or Paris, where Bürger's aestheticism became recognized in the pseudo-religious art fervor of a bourgeois public slowly coming to understand its decadence. Historians of British modernisms might draw new maps, too, maps which note the success of British culture in minimizing and marginalizing avant-garde phenomena but also mark the too rarely acknowledged presence of British modernists, poets who have been ignored or insufficiently attended to in Americanized histories of literary modernism and often in Britain itself.

New maps are necessary, too, in imagining how poetry of all traditions might function *within* institutions—naming and in some cases struggling to transform their practices and values, without pretending that radical subversion of institutions or large-scale social change is likely to result. Indeed, with a new map we might even begin to argue that, despite what many view as its recent decline, the study of poetry in the academy still might have value, whether, with Charles Altieri and Peter Middleton, we want to demonstrate that poems can offer more nuanced models of subjectivity than our theoretical discussions of subjectivity can account for, or, with Bernstein and others, we want to imagine poetry and poetics as a mode of cultural studies which can undermine the certitudes and clichés, the "tone lock" and the brain lock which sometimes accompany it, of academic and other discourses, offering new or revised "signifying practices."[8] "Signifying practices have only art to copy from," Bernstein writes (608), yet it must be admitted that for most in the academy today, poetry is the weakling on theory's beach, of little use and unhappy to be so, soaked by the rays of ideology and imagining itself in need of a sunscreen theory's demystifying boutique has for sale.

I defend the academic study of contemporary poetry in what follows, and I think that in the United States we have much to be grateful to for such study, not least in those neo-avant-garde communities which often begin outside the academy and are usually eventually absorbed into it. Universities have not only mediated the reception of avant-garde work; they have funded it and, in the person of critics such as Perloff, Bernstein, and others, actively promoted it. The story is different in Britain, where contemporary writing of all traditions, and especially "experimental" or "avant-garde" writing, remains at some greater remove from academic life; with avant-garde poetry ignored even by academics on the left, contemporary poetry remains only that which can be easily taught at lower levels. With some poets and scholars thinking that contemporary poetry's status in the American academy is in decline now, one good reason to study British poetry, especially British "experimental poetry," is to see what happens to a poetry which more often has had to go it alone, as it were, without being able to depend quite so heavily on the artificial economies created by the academy and other institutions such as grants-awarding agencies.

But this still does not constitute what is for me an adequate defense of an engagement with British poetry. That is a matter of particular poets, and of particular poems. Thus it seems necessary to introduce some of these before I begin in chapter 1 to summarize and comment on the recent history of discourse about British and American poetry in Britain and the United States. I want to celebrate a fairly broad range of British poetry, but perhaps my special burden lies in identifying a modernist and post-modernist British poetry I value. For readers of books on poetry, American and British readers alike, will be quicker to identify the first example below as "British poetry" than the second:

> Having read the promise of the hedgerow
> the body set out anew on its adventures.
> At length it came to a place of poverty,
> of inner and outer famine,
>   where all movement had stopped
> except for that of the wind, which was continual
> and came from elsewhere, from the sea,
> moving across unplanted fields and between headstones
> in the little churchyard clogged with nettles
> where no one came between Sundays, and few then.
> These were marshes of privation:
> the mud of the ditches oozed scummy water,
> the grey reeds were arrested in growth,
> the sun did not show, even as a blur,
> and the uneven lands were without definition
> as I was without potent words,
> inert.
>   I sat upon a disintegrating gravestone.
> How can I continue, I asked?

This is a little more than the first half of Thom Gunn's "A Sketch of the Great Dejection," from *The Man with Night Sweats* (19). The allegorized setting with its traces of Bunyan, the elusive but still recognizably controlled force of the poem's iambic movement, particular phrases such as "At length" and "The wind was *like* a punishment" (my emphasis)—all of this seems to bespeak the weight of British tradition. The subject matter of the poem is easily identifiable—a speaker confronts an allegorized landscape of despair (the book's title and other poems help us to locate the AIDS crisis as one possible source of that despair)—but it is exactly the indirection with which the poem addresses its subject as well as the difference within similarity and the precarious balancing of clauses ("uneven lands were without definition / as I was without potent words") that offers Gunn's poem its powerful restraint. We might speak of the poem's terseness, its reserve—these are clichés, but that's part of the point. Not just the imagery but also the very ethos of the poem will offer few surprises. Its considerable success will instead depend upon its subtle understatement. Later, the poem will emphasize the balancing of its phrases to reduce the psychological crisis the poem describes to its core proposition:

> My body insisted on restlessness
>   having been promised love,
> as my mind insisted on words
>   having been promised the imagination.

Words only against the concept "imagination," the fact of desire over and against the thickly coded promise of "love"—this poet will opt for the real and the tangible, for experience, for the presence of the loved one rather than "love."

These are familiar themes in Gunn's work, and so is the economy of means and precision of syntax. Although Gunn is content with what beginning creative writing workshops call abstractions, his sentence nevertheless suggests their inadequacy; *restless* is the condition of the word with which one struggles. Rarely less than economical even when working in what is for him an atypically narrative mode—English Renaissance poetry is what Donald Davie once found behind more typical Gunn[9]—Gunn's poem will achieve a distinct closure in just three lines:

> So I remained alert, confused and uncomforted.
> I fared on and, though the landscape did not change,
> it came to seem after a while like a place of recuperation.

> (20)

Though Gunn has lived for many years in San Francisco, and even while there is much in his poetry that shows the results of his reading in American poetry in a way that the poetry of W. H. Auden, John Betjeman, and

Philip Larkin rarely does, very few readers would hesitate to call "A Sketch of the Great Dejection" British poetry. It is a matter in this case of what one (or some) recognize as idiom and form, of restraint and decorum.

Could we say the same of Maggie O'Sullivan's "Starlings"?

Lived Daily
or Both

Daily
the Living
structuring
Bone-Seed,

Pelage,
Aqueous,

YONDERLY—
lazybed of need—
CLOUD-SANG
Tipsy Bobbles, Dowdy
wander. Halt upon

grinned jeers, gin's note
someone's in the leading
of small & the pitch meander ears
tune me gold
Dulthie pods,

Lipper
"Ochre harled

ELECTRIC

CONTORTIONS—

(41)

This poem is located in a section of O'Sullivan's *In the House of the Shaman* (1993) titled "Kinship with Animals." Appealing to the trance music and ecstatic subjectivity of "shamans" is not a new tactic in modern poetry, and it is tempting to link the self-conscious primitivism of such poetry with pop cults of wizards and witches and the like, as Andrew Duncan has suggested in a review of this book.[10] O'Sullivan works in the house of the shaman, however, not *as* a shaman, and while she is surely interested in poetic functions we associate with shamanism there is not much that smells of religiosity in her work. For all the animals and animal parts littering her work, the starlings enter this poem only as a lure, occasion for a bravura display of language, the referent for a hyperexpressionistic linguistic excess wherein a "speaker" is altogether diffused among ecstatic sound textures. If the poem remembers the Shelleyan imperative to the nearly divine skylark to "pourest thy full heart / In profuse strains of unpremeditated / art" (602), it does so by *constructing* a language as blithe as birds themselves. This is, as Andrew Duncan also notes, "a radical departure from the ironic, domesticated realism of common bad English poetry: it asks the reader to *get out of it*. The scale runs from reason to suggestibility. The poem as it were shakes the patterns of language apart to impose its own more urgent line. The orthogonal code breaks apart" (1995, 113). It is hard to speak of "identity" in this poem because idiom has been destabilized, set in the whirlwind of visual and vocal production, its "harled" derived from Middle English, its "pelage" (an animal's coat) from Old French, its abundant playfulness ("tune me gold / Dulthie pods") from song and rock music and Stein and Joyce. The Britishisms that appear in Gunn's simultaneously formal and conversational poem are replaced by a synthetic chaos of idioms no one person would "speak naturally," dominated perhaps by those which summon bardic registers with significance to a British past, though rife too with babble and inventive formulations, loanwords, and neologisms which help the poem resist that site of stable middle-class conversation and meditative interiority which Gunn's excellent poem requires and reproduces.

Discussing this "zenith of technique" in which "every element of the signifying complex is mimetic," Duncan notes the presence in O'Sullivan's book of a lorica, a "kind of poem in the form of a protective charm," associated with two fifth-century Romano-Britons, and her persistent use of diminutives and formatives and "noun-string construction" (114; 111). How to speak of syntax where it is not altogether clear that "or Both" in the second line refers to the words "Lived" and "Daily" held separate (as lines three and four perhaps suggest)? The poem unsettles discourse, narrative, and the comforts of "traditional" lyric subjectivity within its first eight lines. And yet the "open-field" visual layout of this performative poetic does help us hear traces of bardic traditions not unknown to English poets such as the Northumbrian Basil Bunting. Lines—and beginning with "tipsy bobbles," phrases within some lines—are often organized as units with one or two stresses, the dominant single stress giving way to two stresses in the middle of the poem. As a whole, the poem depends heavily on its alliteration and assonance as its syntactical disjunctiveness forces us to isolate words and phrases *as* words and phrases. It is as if "bone-seed," "CLOUD-SANG," and "Ochre harled" were fragments from some ur-poem from which all the other bird poems in the canon have descended, except that "fragments" would suggest the absence of some whole text we might then desire. But this poem neither alludes to nor needs such an ur-poem. It merely says, suddenly, "Electric/Contortions." No closure there—unless we read that phrase as referring to the poem itself, or we impose a reading which would really scatter some feathers in its absurd flight.

Perhaps it is significant that I am able to give over an irritable reaching for paraphrasable content or grammatical syntax and everything else that Gunn's poem offers us and that is "missing" here, and accept the disjunctions and juxtapositions, the difficulties, surprises, and discombobulations nearly every word brings, largely because of my familiarity with the work of American "experimentalists" such as Pound, Charles Olson, Susan Howe, Michael Palmer, Jackson Mac Low, and others. In thinking of various among those poetries, I erase the particularity of O'Sullivan's poetry, which seems well-enough described by Duncan as having "to do with fertility—the formation of new bodies (of animals) as looked after by a Mistress of the Wild Things" (115). After wrestling with the book for some pages, Duncan concludes that

> *In the House of the Shaman* works because it is not based in theology or in anthropological field reports, but in physical experiences of growth, recuperation, fertility, and emotional shifts. Subjective experience may be a translation of these physical events. In painting, the expulsion of the object brought a greater concentration on the body, as a set of sensory maps which could be translated into an external (painted) object by direct action; no doubt the same is true of this poetry, violently shaped by sensations too rapid to amount to knowledge. The opposition between true and untrue has been eliminated. There is no point trying to work out what these *stacatto* phrases mean; the reader either grasps the feel from the overall way the text is organized, and starts fantasizing about the same thing the writer is fantasizing about, or the whole thing is like a dry harbour. I think on the whole this is what I want poetry to be like; domestic realists, up against the wall! This has the same crazed intensity that rock music used to have. (117)

Action poetry, we might call it, though surely Duncan is off the mark or even perverse when he insists that the only way to "grasp" this writing is to enter into some imaginative relationship with its author's fantasies. Duncan wants to offer the poetry some depth over and against the play of its surfaces, but that depth is to be found in the history of the language O'Sullivan is acting upon. Our response to that language as readers need not be uniform or necessarily in sync with the author's intentions. But Duncan's emphasis on the privileging of bodily and sensory functions over the intellect and "knowledge" in this poetry does make sense. O'Sullivan's work, like Bunting's and many another poet's, is best experienced in performance; this is part of what it means to call the work bardic. Next to Gunn's poetry, which owes its discipline and finesse to traditions that announce the triumph of the book, this poetry will seem either pre- or postliterary. Part of its force involves its ability to baffle all critical languages or "theories" that would seek to "explain" it or bring it back into the discipline and decorum of historiography and hermeneutics.

Nevertheless, I suggested that reading (and hearing) American writing such as Susan Howe's antinomian forays among the wilderness of historical texts had helped me to "get" O'Sullivan (to the extent that I do). It is worth noting by way of contrast that Duncan elects to frame his discussion of O'Sullivan within the history of recent British poetry:

> The failure of the Apocalyptic or New Romantic poetry of the 1940s was, it seems to me, due to their moderation: their flights of imagination are nailed down by orthodox diction and metrical formalism. Staidness of language stifled the energies yearningly invoked. Even mythographically, they failed to break out of the Christian framework. Twenty years were to pass before an effective solution was found to these problems. The appeal of that group was their passion and the visionary state from which they wrote; their language contradicted these claims at every step. They must have thought that this losing strategy was "passion contained with discipline and skill." In fact such extreme states of mind could only be captured by coordinating all aspects of the linguistic object: metrical, syntactic, logical, lexical. It is in this light that we have to consider O'Sullivan (107–8).

Though Gunn is known partly for his early association with the Movement, those English poets who reacted to what they took to be the stylistic excesses of British neoromantics such as Dylan Thomas, intent on restoring the conventions of neo-Augustan diction and syntax, it is tempting to consider Gunn's "A Sketch of the Great Dejection" beside Duncan's description of British neoromantic poetry of the forties. It does, after all, sound like what Duncan is describing: a passionate—visionary would be too strong—utterance "contained with discipline and skill." But O'Sullivan is not best read beside Gunn, it seems, but rather beside poets such as Henry Treece or Nigel Heseltine, British neoromantics of the thirties and forties. Here is part of a poem by the latter as anthologized by Kenneth Rexroth in 1949:

> I enter and as I enter all is abandoned
> like the apple and like the apple
> in my hand yet naked
> stand and the apple in my hand
> slanting on the desolate shore. O golden bright
> bright here bright O bright here
> the light passes in my skin
> my skin.
>
> (97–98)

When the competition is work like this laboring to break free of syntactic and other conventions only to be caught in a netherland of absurd poeticisms, one sees Duncan's point: O'Sullivan's ecstatic surfaces challenge us in ways that Heseltine's don't. Knowing little about British contexts leaves Americans only to shake their heads: so O'Sullivan succeeds where many failed? But what about dada? What about Artaud or Vallejo? Or is it *British* writing we're talking about?

British poetry includes not just a neo-Georgian or Betjemanian poetry of nostalgia, cheery meters, and fetid pastoralism:

> Oh, gay lapped the waves on the shores of Lough Ennel
> And sweet smelt the breeze 'mid the garlic and fennel,
> But sweeter and gayer than either of these
> Were the songs of the birds in Lord Belvedere's trees.
>
> (76)

It is more, too, than the smug lower-middle-class persona of Philip Larkin extended to the so-called "New Generation" in Simon Armitage's poetry:

> Yes, love, that's why the warning light comes on. Don't
> panic. Fetch some universal brake-fluid

and five-eighths screwdriver from your toolkit
then prop the bonnet open. . . .

(30)

Canadian scholar Patrick Deane thinks that, in North America, "the values
and critical biases of modernism have achieved a hegemony so powerful
that it has become comparatively more difficult in that field to 'see' the
viability of opposing poetic traditions" (13) such as the neo-Augustanism
represented for him by Donald Davie, W. H. Auden, Tony Harrison, and
C. H. Sisson, among others. That might be true or partially true. But
neither Sisson's drily intellectual bleakness

> We have only to live and see what happens
> —Nothing perhaps; for it may be that history,
> As Mairet remarked, is coming to an end
> And we shall wander around without meaning.
> That is what most of us would like. . . .
>
> (1980, 14)

nor Hill's opaque, Eliotic, anxious meditations on the responsibilities and
consequences of poetic utterance

> At Villeroy the copybook lines of men
> rise up and are erased. Péguy's cropped skull
> dribbles its ichor, its poor thimbleful,
> a simple lesion of the complex brain.
>
> (31)

are adequate as a representative sampling of British poetry.

It is probably the case that the best-known British poets of the post–
World War II era in the United States remain W. H. Auden, Philip Larkin,
Ted Hughes, Dylan Thomas, Charles Tomlinson, Geoffrey Hill, Stevie
Smith, and Craig Raine. Even this group is extraordinarily diverse, and
diversely talented, but in what follows I have opted to offer samplings
and readings of less familiar work which constitutes either a list of favorites (Basil Bunting, Mina Loy, Roy Fisher, Tom Raworth, Allen Fisher,
Geraldine Monk, Peter Riley, Gael Turnbull) or examples of neglected
work around which issues of Anglo-American relations can be made to
coalesce—Joseph Gordon Macleod, John Rodker. Would that I had the
space and knowledge to make this a fuller survey, so that I might include detailed readings of poems by David Jones, Charles Madge, David

Gascoyne, Nicholas Moore, Lynette Roberts, Jeremy Prynne, John Riley, Nathaniel Tarn, Bob Cobbing, Thomas A. Clark, Bill Griffiths, Andrew Crozier, Wendy Mulford, Barry MacSweeney, Elaine Feinstein, Denise Riley, Elaine Randell, Cris Cheek, Brian Catling, Gavin Selerie, and many other modernist and postmodernist poets whose work is deserving of careful attention. I have also decided not to discuss Irish poetry directly, for the issues it raises deserve their own book. So too do Scottish and Welsh poetries, two unknown universes in the United States, where even Hugh MacDiarmid, a modernist as prolific as Pound, scarcely gets a hearing.

To begin to establish a context for my discussion of the history of discourses of British-American continuities and discontinuities in the first chapter, I pause here briefly to cite just two passages from some of the "alternative" poetry of the period Eric Mottram has labeled the "British Poetry Revival." First, part of "Sister Midnight," a poem by John James:

> the bell rings but I refuse to answer
> I might have been a painter but there was an accident
> in my life right down the line of a fierce fatigue
> replete with overcoats my cherry which is why it is worst
> when you have forgotten the mayonnaise remember
> I told you there'd be something funny about it she said
> like her potatoes of lead, flash flash, alas a
> cold pallor has overcome my scrotal sac
> in the sharp gusts of autumn in all those places
> I said I'd never go again & then did
> as if I'd never even forgotten
>
> (168)

To an American reader this poem is akin to, and indebted to, the poetry of the New York school of Frank O'Hara, Bernadette Mayer, Ted Berrigan, and others. This is a poetry of the quotidian, of spontaneity and "personism," of campy crossings in diction ("alas") and self-deprecating ironies, of a prosaic and paratactic syntax and lines shifting directions suddenly, as if randomly. Would it be the case that such a debt would factor into its value for us? In England, it would surely—for James's detractors and admirers alike. This would be the case too with a poem engaged with American modernisms but a little more independent of their influence, such as Gael Turnbull's a little "Twenty Words, Twenty Days":

at a certain hour of the morning of a certain day of the
week —
 time, like a bonus, to be expended, not used —
a depth, a largesse —
  and within such magnificence nothing
for it but to dilly-dally, fritter —
     as a BOOMERANG —

thrown overhand to spin vertically will curve up and to
the left, circle, then glide back —

       (26)

As Turnbull has explained, this poem has as part of its compositional process the random selection of a word from a dictionary (here *boomerang* in caps) — one word per section of the poem, each "day." The poem proceeds by both "plan" and "impulse," as David Miller has noted in an essay which mentions the American poetry of Robert Duncan, Jack Spicer, Allen Ginsberg, and Charles Olson but finds Turnbull closest to Louis Zukofsky insofar as Turnbull's poetry, like Zukofsky's, is "informed by a dialectical or dialogic movement *between* impulse and plan, or between heuristic process and projection of structural determinants" (186). Miller is surely correct to identify Turnbull's engagement with a particular (and at the time less influential) American-modernist practice — the work of Jackson Mac Low might also have been mentioned. But the "conversational" tone of Turnbull's poem (which Miller identifies) as well as the meditative turns of its syntax and line, and the use of extended similes sometimes almost Homeric in their proportions, are part of what makes this a poem less overwhelmed by its models (which is not to deny the pleasures and wit of James's buoyant poems).

Reading British poetries, one naturally hopes to find work which seems more than diluted imitations of American models. Among contemporary alternative British poets, nothing might be more silly than imitations of American "language poetry." At the same time, one is disappointed to find work that proceeds in ignorance of much of the poetry of this century. The balance is difficult to strike: works that demonstrate a familiarity with American and other international poetries without losing sight of British contexts and traditions. For me, for instance, *Briggflatts* is Basil Bunting's best work, perhaps the finest English long poem of the century. One reason for this is that in *Briggflatts* Bunting works by wedding Poundian and Eliotic modernist technique with a newly unabashed Wordsworthian sentiment and techniques deriving from Persian and Northumbrian art. A Northumbrian poem, yes, but one cognizant of the most interesting poetry of its day.

After the questions of Anglo-American continuities and discontinuities and the readings of discourse about poetry and nation offered in the first half of the book, and after the readings of Bunting and Loy—that British-born poet the British still refuse to claim—and selected "alternative" contemporary British poets advanced in its second half, I conclude with a discussion of Black British poetry which has at its center a reading of Caribbean poet Kamau Brathwaite's book-length poem *X/Self.* I conclude in this manner because Brathwaite's poem and Black British poetry help me to "decenter" the limited focus in this book on Anglo-American relations in poetry. In Brathwaite's case, the important choices for poets can never be limited to picking among British traditions or American traditions, however these are understood, however they are opposed or located on a continuum. Modernist or postmodernist, experimental or traditional—these terms ring especially hollow from his perspective. Since I too want to cast a skeptical light on these terms and their function in sustaining poetic values among particular communities in both nations, I might seem to have an ally in Brathwaite. And yet his efforts to locate himself as a poet of "nation-language," as the voice of an emergent culture, also throw into relief my efforts to minimize the rhetoric of nation in discussions of modern and contemporary poetry. It is important to Brathwaite, as less and less to American poets and poetry critics in the last twenty years, to think the nation and the shapes of national identities. And that stands as a counterexample and reprimand to those of us, like myself, who are sometimes fearful of more aggressive rhetorics of the nation. However skeptical we may have become of poetic achievement bearing national significance, the linkage between poems and nation is not being abandoned by all poets at the end of the century. As long as this linkage can be made, poets will make it. Critics can analyze the results, but they cannot effectively provide the linkage itself. Chastened by the recent history of the rhetoric of nation in the now calm—dead calm—waters of British-American relations, we do well to hear Brathwaite also.

PART ONE: Histories

1. Anglo-American Relations in Poetry, 1960–1995

Poetry and National Identity

In 1979 American poet Donald Hall, in a tone of some distress, as if stating a fact too obvious to deplore, remarked in the pages of the American journal *Parnassus* that "the poetries of England and America have become discontinuous" (24). Were American readers, most of them poets or critics themselves, surprised by such a statement? Certainly others during the sixties and seventies had sought to account for diminishing interest in British poetry among American readers and writers. Hall's complaint, though, is pitched in a particularly severe rhetoric: "Because prevailing English modes are as distinct from prevailing American modes as haiku from Icelandic saga, American readers must learn to approach English poets *as if* they were reading translations from the Polish" (25). This theatrical analogy, this use of *Polish*—did it mean to persuade Americans that a poetry which presents comparatively few linguistic difficulties is, or has become, truly foreign? In the process of surveying and characterizing contemporary English poetic practice, Hall wanted to argue that attention to current English models might serve as a corrective to "prevailing" American poetic practice. Such arguments might have been expected to appeal to American readers who understand the extent to which an engagement with foreign poetries has enriched American poetry throughout the century. This is how poets read poets from other nations sometimes: Hall is not interested in discovering or detailing affinities among the quite extensive variety of poetry being produced then, as now, in both nations, nor is he especially concerned with any history of cross-fertilization and influence pertaining to particular poets in both nations. He is convinced that he writes from and of a moment when "prevailing modes" in Britain and the United States are homogeneous and distinct enough to warrant talk of two separate national traditions. What there is of the polemical in Hall's essay is directed primarily at Americans, poets and readers; the construction of an English "other" works as a reprimand. Hall takes it for granted that, lately, few Americans have been responsive to British poetry.

Of course, few readers have taken Polish literature to be as important to the development of American literature as British literature. Did cold-war politics briefly make Polish poetry more fascinating than British poetry for some readers? But reading British poetry and its reception in the United States would also have much to show us about a cold-war world. Hall's *Parnassus* essay is not concerned with such matters; he means to identify formal conventions in English poetry which might counter the simple declarative sentences and prosaic rhythms of a free verse orthodoxy he rightly understood as the "prevailing" mode of American poetry in 1979—the work of Robert Bly or W. S. Merwin might have been representative. Here is another English-language syntax one might consider, Hall suggests. But to describe British poetic practice as nearly inscrutable to Americans— that might be said to have very different implications. That affords British poetry a status much diminished from that which it has held for the better part of two centuries. It is this perception of diminished status, which Hall honestly enough expresses, and its consequences for all concerned on both sides of the Atlantic, that is the subject of this chapter.

Hall had been asked to introduce a few recent English poets to American readers. He was known to be familiar with England and some of its poets, having been responsible for the selection of English poets in the influential *New Poets of England and America* (1957), one of the last widely read anthologies of contemporary poetry to publish British and American poets side by side in something like equal numbers. But the discussion of particular poets occurs almost as an afterthought in the *Parnassus* essay, which is also a response to an earlier essay by English poet C. H. Sisson published in the same journal. In the course of a review-essay on an anthology of American poetry, Sisson had begrudgingly admitted that six or seven American poets were important to him, poking at the reputations of Walt Whitman ("What a lout the man is!") and Emily Dickinson (whom he would have us measure against Christina Rosetti). The larger claims of Sisson's essay involved the assertion of Anglo-American continuities. The "widely-assumed" separateness of English and American poetry, Sisson wrote, had nowhere been convincingly argued, and an "unimpeded conversation" between the two poetries had been and would continue to be possible. "A literature is the literature of a language," Sisson continued, not of a nation, and thus the changing circumstances of Britain and America, the "immense international role of the United States, and the diminished and dependent role of the United Kingdom" (524) had little bearing on what was after all still one, English-language literature. It is this idea of an "unimpeded conversation" that Hall challenges with his discussion of "discontinuities," of English syntactic conventions and so forth. For Sisson, something called English-language literature is comfortably whole, a site of some struggle and misunderstanding perhaps but ideally a monad; for Hall the category "nation" is much the same.

Neither poet thinks the material realities of the publication, promotion, and distribution of poetry within and across national boundaries merit consideration. How much British poetry is actually available in the United States, for instance, and what British poetry is it? Was the conversation between poets in the two nations better or worse in, say, the forties, when Dylan Thomas and British neoromantic poets were taken seriously in the United States? Because neither of the categories crucial to this debate between Hall and Sisson—"nation" and "language"—is well-enough defined, the *Parnassus* essays become interesting less for the information they offer than the rhetoric they deploy. In writing on behalf of Anglo-American continuities, of one tradition of English-language poetry transcending national boundaries, Sisson aims his remarks at English contemporaries who had posited the existence of a "'true' English tradition of English" (525); *true* here acquires its scare quotes because Sisson means sardonically to mime the language of English contemporaries—Philip Larkin, John Wain, others—for whom a specifically English tradition distinct from the modernism(s) identified with Americans Ezra Pound and T. S. Eliot was something desirable and in need of articulation. Cultural concerns specific to Britain—a "little-englandism" that has had consequences in politics and culture—enter loudly into his plea for internationalism. Sisson's argument might seem hardly relevant to Americans for whom a real or caricatured English insularity is a matter only of bemusement or curiosity. To an American like Hall, Sisson might only seem belligerent.

One response to Sisson's polemic was authored by his friend and fellow *P.N. Review* editor Donald Davie. In 1981 Davie published in the *London Review of Books* an essay entitled "My Americas." Davie began by noting that "we have all been told about the demographic shift in the United States from the North-East to the Sun Belt of the South-West: and the commentators on politics have been eager to explain that among the consequences of this shift is the Reagan Presidency" (3). He went on to argue that citizens of the United States had become increasingly preoccupied with North-South relations, with the cultures of the Americas, and that therefore by necessity their literature was less and less a concern to British readers. Davie concluded that "American literature, whether in Spanish or in English, is for us [British readers] a *foreign* literature, and a lot of unnecessary anguish could be avoided if we plainly admitted as much" (3). For Hall the problem of Americans ignoring British literature was the missed opportunity to expand the formal resources of American poetry; for Davie there was no problem with the literatures going their separate ways, only the "anguish" created by perspectives like Sisson's which insist on obsolete, idealized versions of "tradition." The "anguish" is a matter of feeling cut out of the picture, of being relegated to the position of a mere onlooker in events mostly beyond one's concern, while remembering a time when things were otherwise, the anguish of a former significant other become a fading memory. Alluding to Sisson's Eliotic arguments, Davie calls them "the merest whistling in the dark. The two halves of the American continent have begun speaking to each other; and in that dialogue the British voice cannot intervene except as a sterilizing distraction" (4).

Perhaps Hall might have responded to Davie by noting that, from an American perspective, the urgency of thinking about the poetics of the Americas does not excuse an ignorance of British poetry. But Hall's essay raises other problems. In seeking to explain what he takes to be the most important differences between "prevailing" modes of English and American poetry, he writes that "national identity is crucial, and nationhood is a mystery" (27). First, he proposes, as others before him also have proposed, that the level of engagement with "tradition" as such differs in England and America:

> American literature differs from English not only because of the difference between the traditions, but in the extent to which tradition informs the work at all. . . . The tradition that matters most, to a nation's literature, is not the style or the content of its great writers. It is the

soil of its history, the bones of its dead ground up in that soil, and the ideas and passions, the battles and revolutions, the glories and defeats of nation and spirit. Our tradition (like it or not) is enlightenment, protestant, and capitalist. In England tradition is inevitably layered (27).

Hall's idea of tradition, stripped of its florid poeticisms, seems close to the anthropological definition of culture as a "way of life," and it offers us the opportunity to see poetry as embedded in social practices (though he will not discuss these). Traditions in England are "layered," one presumes, because of a more visibly complex residual presence of cultural practices no longer dominant. The older the nation, the more complex and powerful the presence and memory of different, even contradictory cultural practices, Hall seems to say, writing from a nation sometimes supposed to have crushed the struggles and contestations of its past into a mindless, modern uniformity. The passivity with which Hall's essay describes, as late as 1979, such a homogenization of diverse American cultural and religious practices within a purportedly dominant WASP "tradition" will make it tempting for some readers to identify him with a particular version of American culture that one associates with a New England and upper East Coast past dominated by anglophile institutions. Just two years later, poet David Antin would talk at a conference in Iowa on the avant-garde and, in the course of celebrating a book by Marjorie Perloff which discussed "the french connection" of specific American poetries, suggested that her book was

> designed to challenge what i have always thought of as the anglophiliac model of american poetry that is so dominant in those literary strongholds east of the mississippi. . . . or maybe more precisely this book is bringing the news to these outposts that the british empire has long since passed away and that the messages from england would no longer be coming and had not been coming for a long time and that there was a french connection as there is a russian connection and a spanish connection and for many a chinese connection and a japanese connection. (45)

Antin would go on to attack Harold Bloom—who here embodies that "anglophiliac" model for him—for the absurdities of his theory of poetic influence; for the narrowness of his canons and idea of tradition ("all that unites us in this country is the present"); for his contempt for most contemporary poetry, and for being provincial enough to imagine that he is part of a "great tradition" centered in English romanticism. It's clear in his frustrated tone that Hall understands the weight of opinion like Antin's that he must struggle against, and it would be unfair simply to associate Hall with the high-minded absurdities of an academic literary culture affecting or inventing a singular descent (albeit one tortured with the oedipal anxieties Bloom describes in terms brought over from Hebrew and Greek) from English poetry. Hall's efforts to diagnose the rupture between American and British poetic practice are provoked by a concern with a range of contemporary practice rarely demonstrated either by Bloom or by academics in elite institutions such as the one Bloom was then identified with. But he goes about making his case for a renewed engagement with British poetry in exactly the wrong way; not by examining exceptions to his rule, examples of a productive engagement between poets in the two nations, or investigating pressures and circumstances pulling the poetries apart, including the material realities of inefficient distribution systems, and other matters of economic and social content, but by appealing to the simplest platitudes about engagement with "tradition" in Britain and the United States and, more distressingly still, "national identity."

If we understand a national "identity" or "spirit" to be primarily discursive, as a rhetoric created again and again and contested in the sites of our aesthetic, social, and political practices, then we must always suspect mystifying claims about national spirit or character. Such claims invariably minimize or ignore cultural conflict to posit cultural coherence and encourage, as Ian Baucom writes, "the reification of a shared glorious past and the deployment of this solidified memory in the present as an object of consent" (148). The point is not that Hall is somehow incorrect to say what he does about "American tradition" as protestant and capitalist; it is his sense that American tradition is "inevitable"—settled, fated— that makes this discourse, unintentionally perhaps, nationalistic. We know from scholars of nationalism and postcolonial theorists how difficult it is for even that literature which would position itself as "extranational" to escape the imprint of the nation;[1] Hall's desire to encourage dialogue between British and American poets is less successful than some "internationalisms" at concealing that imprint exactly because it assumes that British poetry might be defined as a forgotten resource that a nation such as the United States might once again import for specific uses and without all the baggage and distorted nexus of values to which Antin refers, as if all that were involved here were the production of a better microchip made possible by the introduction of foreign technology. It is precisely his inno-cence that is striking. In times past, one might have called it American.

In order to represent what he views as "impeded" conversation between English and American poets—bypassing quickly the realities that may be obstructing such conversation—Hall constructs a great divide between Britain and the United States and then offers to step in to do what he believes cannot be done except with great difficulty—namely, to read con-temporary British poetry as an informed and sympathetic American. He is savvy enough to know that "no generalization about national character will hold" (31), but he is not reluctant to sketch English national character in rough outlines:

> I am struck [in Sisson's own poetry] with his self-accusation and self-distrust. He displays an emotion or an idea, then sees through himself to report on his own dishonesty or vanity or greed or egotism; distrust has the last word. In the best English poet of all, Geoffrey Hill, this self-distrust is almost the basis of the style, of the grammar, clauses balanced so that the final antithesis contains in a precise doubleness both the statement and an acidulous criticism of the statement. I sup-pose this is called irony—but I want a more serious word: an ironic American tends merely to display a consistent tonal sarcasm, saying something and denying its seriousness, wearing protective covering. In Sisson and in Hill this irony is deadly serious, not mask nor armor plate but vision. (31)

This is an admiring description of Hill's poetry, and Sisson's, and it is accurate enough. A comma in Hill's work can make all the difference: "To dispense, with justice; or, to dispense / with justice." [2] Anxieties concern-ing the instabilities and consequences of interpretation and textual pro-duction are regularly thematized in his poems. Where Hill agonizes and despairs, others—including some Americans—have taken indeterminacy into the center of their poetic practice as a mode of acknowledging or even celebrating the ephemeral. Hill's agony of exactitude must seem an archaic high modernism to a poet such as John Ashbery, for instance, for whom writing is "pyrography," as the title of one poem has it, its inefficien-cies and slippages not cause for such an intense near paralysis but rather for possibility. Beside Hill's austerity Ashbery will seem to be discarding and searching again for a language fit to approach "this new yet unap-proachable America"—to use the Emersonian phrase invoked by Stanley

Cavell in his critique of models of "thinking" which represent thought as a "grasping [of] something."[3] But whether we want to promote his poetry or not, one cannot assume that Hill's profound ambivalence or "irony"—his poetry itself—constructs or reflects a persona or sensibility that is exclusive property of the English. Hall's most dangerous gambit is reading the poetry of Hill and Sisson as unmediated expressions of a self which then is conflated with a (settled) nation. Finally, it is British "character" that he is describing, and with no concern for the particulars of gender, race, region, or the idiosyncrasies and struggles of desire, and furthermore without much effort to link the two British poets he admires with specific, evolving cultural practices and traditions.

A broader view of the possibilities of contemporary English and British practice will force us to question this conflation of poetic and national identity that underwrites Hall's reading of Hill and Sisson. This is not just a matter of asking what poetries count as British poetry for Hall, of noting his neglect of alternative British poetries. Even if he is right about the predominance of irony in the recent English poetry that he describes as "prevailing," and I think that it is true that some "mainstream" British poetry reveals a range of ironic discourses, not all of them so "anguished" as these, we need to know what might explain this. Hill's irony is not the reflection or expression of Englishness but rather one response to a complex field of social and cultural discourses in a post–World War II Britain experiencing specific problems such as the shrinking of its sphere of influence in the world (to name but one). If it turns out that we want to argue that Sisson's or Hill's poetry is important because it is somehow representative, we must know what it is representative *of*. Both Hill and Sisson are cultural conservatives; their "irony" bespeaks a late-modernist, Eliotic ideal of organic cultures—bespeaks orderliness, custom. Sisson is a monarchist: the poem by Hill from which I quote is still, via Charles Péguy, quarreling with a technologized modernity. The success of this poetry in certain circles should surprise nobody. But these are not Hall's concerns.

We can't leave the nature of Hall's map of British poetry alone. How would our American ideas of England change if we decided that the Northumbrian poetry of Basil Bunting or Tom Pickard, or the feminist poetry of Denise Riley, or the dub rhythms of Linton Kwesi Johnson, were essential (or even marginal) parts of what is most valuable about British poetry? Our rhetoric would wobble, of course, our talk of British poetry might be, if not "unimpeded," then a little less prone to caricature and generalization. We might remember too that American poetry includes not only the largely unironic work of Walt Whitman but also the Audenesque poems of James Merrill. We *must* remember that British poetry includes not only the books of Sisson, Hill, or Philip Larkin, but also the Blakean poems of Kathleen Raine, the surrealist poems of David Gascoyne, and the evacuations of lyric ego in the poems of J. H. Prynne if we are to understand the complexity of the field we wish to survey.

Abandoning the idea of British and American poetry as unified and coherent, as national poetries opposed in an intellectual tug-of-war across the hypen in Anglo-American, allows one to recognize poets in both nations who have gone their (mostly) separate ways and others who have found parallel practices or significant models via transatlantic communication. Finding such affinities and naming differences is the first and easiest task for anyone who might wish to improve conversation among British and American poetries. But, as Americans, we might also begin to attend to the history and consequences of a subtly shifting balance of power—a direction of influence—among the poetries. Even here, though, as we explore the realities of cultural hegemony, we must remain sufficiently aware of the great variety of poetry being written in Britain and America, and to the ways in which the work of particular poets in both make for exceptions.

I am not altogether prepared to give up on the sort of generalizations that allow one to speak of "prevailing" or "mainstream" or "alternative" British and American poetries. But it seems to me (as not to Hall in 1979) that when we are obliged to speak in generalizations about British and American poetry there are continuities and discontinuities both to consider. Basil Bunting's poetry, especially the earlier poems such as "Villon," are unimaginable without the work of Americans Pound and Eliot. So is the later poem "Briggflatts," but in that poem there is also Northumbrian content and a synthetic Northumbrian idiom. The textured weave of the Lindisfarne gospels meets modernist collage and juxtaposition—continuities and discontinuities both. With J. H. Prynne and Charles Olson too, with Gael Turnbull and Louis Zukofsky, Donald Davie and Yvor Winters, or Charles Tomlinson and Marianne Moore, we see British poets adapting American models. Recently, influence more rarely flows in the other direction, as it did from Auden to Merrill. David Jones's work informs the poems of John Matthias; Bunting's work offers a model for Robert Creeley, August Kleinzahler, and a few others, but American poets who might be said to have learned from Jones or Bunting could be counted on two hands. Since the waning of Auden's influence in the United States, no British poet has mattered here as Charles Olson, Edward

Dorn, Robert Creeley, Jack Spicer, and many others have mattered in Britain.

But this is to talk about poetry. When we talk about national poetries, we are not discussing poems but rather one part of a discourse about poetry, one wherein too often, unfortunately, we have seen constructions of an "other" national poetry, or, alternatively, an idealized and decontextualized rhetoric of one, fluid but recognizable, idealized "international" tradition in which local worlds are ignored. Narratives of tradition and the individual talent, Eliot's or Sisson's, which are inattentive to the material realities of cultural reception and oblivious to contexts are easy to dismiss now. But it is harder to imagine narratives that might replace them which do not restore the provincialism they were meant to attack.

The "Two Poetries" Debate in the Sixties and Seventies

The *Parnassus* essays of Hall and Sisson, as well as the essay by Davie in the *London Review of Books,* belong to a post-World War II critical debate about poetry and national identity and the respective merits of contemporary British and American poetry. Coming at the end of a decade (or, in Davie's case, the beginning of another) that saw the rise and consolidation of Reaganism and Thatcherism, they represent something of a terminal point in that debate, which was most intense in the sixties and early seventies. While the question of American influence on British poetry remains of some lesser interest in Britain today, the current interest in British poetry of any variety in America is minimal, as any survey of literary or scholarly journals or working dissertations will show. It is true that books such as Hugh Kenner's study of twentieth-century British literature, *A Sinking Island* (1987)—the title hints at the book's severe criticism of British literary culture—and Donald Davie's survey of postwar British poetry, *Under Briggflatts* (1989), have extended debates that were most intense two decades ago. Poets on both sides of the Atlantic have continued to pursue contacts, surely. There are signs that poets working in exploratory and innovative forms in both nations have continued working to promote the work of poets of some interest to them in the other, even while it is true that, during the years of the Thatcher government and the cutbacks and urban renewal that had devastating consequences for the publishing and performance of exploratory writing in England, contacts between American and British poetry outside the respective mainstreams in both nations seemed to dwindle. More recently, *New American Writing* in 1991 devoted the bulk of an issue to Richard Caddel's selection of alternative British poetries; in the same year, an anthology of experimental writing from London, *Floating Capital,* was published by a small American press and introduced by an American poet, Bruce Andrews; several of Britain's leading experimentalists continue to be published by small American presses. *Talisman* and *West Coast Line* have also published gatherings of British alternative poets. Poets more invested in other, more traditional poetic modes have pursued contacts and alliances too. Robert Richman's anthology *The Direction of Poetry* (1988), for instance, imports a few British poets whose work seems to support his conservative polemic on behalf of so-called traditional (primarily post-1700 English) meters. This book is praised by British poet Dannie Abse in his introduction to *The Hutchinson Book of Post-War British Poets* (1989), which whines about Americans ignoring British poetry "since the death of Dylan Thomas in 1953" while suggesting that, generally, British poets have paid more attention to "traditional metrical devices" (xiv). So British poetry remains a battleground of sorts, Americans choosing up sides, but by this point most of the shots fired over the water are muffled. In academic literary criticism in America, the work of a few British poets, particularly the late Philip Larkin and Donald Davie, and Hill, Ted Hughes, and Stevie Smith, continues to generate the occasional essay or book. But criticism of contemporary British poetry, like the poetry itself, is hardly thriving in the United States.

There is no reason to believe that the discourse of two poetries going their separate ways in the sixties and seventies has anything singularly to do with a neglect of contemporary British poetry, as there are other, more sweeping developments which have impacted not just the study of contemporary British poetry in America but the study of poetry of all nations and periods. The collapse of New Criticism, with its methodologies of "close reading," its special esteem for lyric poetry, and a generally Anglocentric canon, the rise of several varieties of cultural studies concerned primarily with narrative and the extraliterary and remarkably apathetic to poetry and generically hybrid writing, the interest in postcolonial literature and theory—all of these and other developments have contributed to the decline of academic interest in contemporary British poetry in ways too complex to detail here. A proliferation and fragmentation of poetries—the presence of so many poetries that the mapping of them is almost impossible—might offer another explanation for the decline of interest in contemporary poetry, British and otherwise, in the academic world. One American academic critic who has worked on contemporary British poetry in the past tells me that he's sticking with the modernists these days; it's hard enough to figure out who *they* are. Whatever one thinks about the intense polemics of the sixties and seventies, there was at least an ongoing interest then in contemporary Anglo-American relations in poetry, or so it seems in retrospect. Moreover, many of the questions and issues raised in these debates are unresolved, the problems they point to still real.

One book which did as much as any other to set the terms for discussions of "American" as opposed to "British" poetry is A. Alvarez's poetry anthology, *The New Poetry* (1962). While this book, partly because of its Penguin imprint, has had great influence in America, introducing readers to a portion of contemporary British poetry which eventually came to constitute a British center, within the British context it has had a truly remarkable lifespan—Alvarez's attack on the "gentility" of British poetry especially. The editors of many anthologies of British poetry published since 1962 have acknowledged Alvarez's collection, even while they have sometimes been explicitly opposed to the aesthetic and cultural values expressed in his introduction or implied by his selection of poets and poems. The editors of anthologies published, like Alvarez's book, by Penguin seem especially prone to attacks on the famous introduction. Michael Horovitz's Blakean afterword to his counterculture Penguin anthology *Children of Albion: Poetry of the Underground in Britain* (1969) refers to Alvarez and his readership as "slaves of bad habit, stuck in the stocks" (353). Edward Lucie-Smith's eclectic Penguin *British Poetry Since 1945* (1970) quietly assures readers that the parochialism of the British center attacked by Alvarez no longer obtains (30–31). Blake Morrison and Andrew Motion's *Penguin Book of Contemporary British Poetry* (1982), which might be said to define a more recent or updated version of the center in British poetry for the eighties and early nineties, discusses Alvarez's book at some length and includes lines by James Fenton poking fun at Alvarez's theories of the origins and consequences of "gentility." Even while dismissing it, Morrison and Motion's anthology shares an important tactic with Alvarez's: while Alvarez had led with American poets he hoped would reinvigorate British poetry, they lead with poets and poems from Ireland, like him looking elsewhere, suggesting that Seamus Heaney and Derek Mahon were setting examples to follow. In 1993 Bloodaxe Books, which according to its catalog now publishes more books of poems than any press in England, brought out an anthology with the very same title as Alvarez's anthology, *The New Poetry*, a collection which defines a new, more multicultural center in British poetry. *The New Poetry* features poets mostly under forty years of age at the time; they were promoted as a group with some rather extraordinary publicity stunts undertaken by publishers, bookstores, the Arts Council, and other patrons—a "new generation" lined up outside the Poetry Society for group photographs. Aware of the marketing success of their famous predecessor, the editors make no apologies for using Alvarez's generic title, referring to the earlier volume as a "pioneering" anthology (16).

Alvarez's book seems hard to escape, then, and his terms, particularly *gentility,* have shared its long lifespan. For most readers, one suspects, *gentility* names a set of values located in a particular social class. And class identifications do play a role in Alvarez's introduction as he follows the shifting demographics of poetic production in Britain after 1945. But *gentility* is an epithet that has proved to be transportable across discourses and classes—stuck to British poetry, it has become synonymous with all that anyone might wish to attack in a British "mainstream." In a 1990 essay subtitled "Nigger Talk in England Today," a British poet of Indo-Caribbean descent, David Dabydeen, writes that "the charge that Alvarez leveled against the Movement—the disease of gentility—is still relevant today" (11). Dabydeen's is a discourse of racial politics; his subject is the marginalization of Black British poetry and, more broadly, of poetry diverging from "standard" English. In a 1992 essay in the American journal *Sulfur* entitled "Rimbaud My Virgil," Peter Redgrove, less concerned with race per se than with intellectual honesty, defines gentility as "a convenient way of behaving in ritual forms for superficial and necessary purposes," adding that "if there is only gentility it is as stifling as England is today" (177). Redgrove writes on behalf of a modernist tradition beginning in France and continuing through surrealism and beyond it, but here *gentility* names not just "rituals" identified with a class but an entire national ethos. Probably Redgrove's use of the word is closer to Alvarez's, but whatever the case, *gentility* typically names the flip side of that "irony" Hall writes of in describing the dominant or "prevailing" values in British poetry—it is the rigorous adherence to custom against which a terse, bleak irony poses itself.

We had better try to understand what Alvarez himself meant by the word. In the famous introduction, "The New Poetry; or, Beyond the Gentility Principle," Alvarez defined gentility as the "belief that life is always more or less orderly, people always more or less polite, their emotions and habits more or less decent and more or less controllable" (25). He saw the culture of gentility in Britain reigning across class divisions; the upper middle-class Tory poet John Betjeman, then poet laureate, and the lower middle-class Movement poets of Robert Conquest's important anthology, *New Lines* (1956), were both implicated in the term. The values and culture of gentility, Alvarez argued, reflected a willful denial of the horrors of the modern world, which psychoanalytic theory had shown us were also the horrors of our individual selves. Neither gentility nor the cultivation of an English insularity designed to encourage it were viable options in a time of world wars, mass destruction, and genocide. In the work of several of the poets he was most eager to promote—not especially the Movement, which belonged to Conquest's book, and which was quietly attacked for its cult of common sense—Alvarez thought he found evidence that British poetry was ready to move beyond its recent quietism, parochialism, and modest ambitions to explore the underbelly of the consensus culture that had dominated the 1950s. A new poetry would need to wed the "psychological insight and integrity" of D. H. Lawrence with "the technical skill and formal intelligence" of T. S. Eliot (32). Ted Hughes's poetry seemed promising in this regard, but Alvarez did not hide his belief that the Americans Robert Lowell and John Berryman—a second edition would add Sylvia Plath and Anne Sexton—were showing the way to a practice that would be "without evasion." Theirs was a poetry which showed what Bruno Bettelheim's observations at Dachau and Buchenwald had also shown: that "much of what went on around him expressed what went on inside himself" (27). A poetic discourse of sincerity could counter social conventions ("gentility"). A poet "without evasion" would be able to find an authentic expression able to expose the darker instincts papered over by ornamental rhymes and class guilt.

Alvarez's valuations are accompanied by a condensed, Freudianized literary history which might be subtitled "Americans—the Horror!" Literary history as the history of Great Men, it reads developments in British poetry as neatly linear developments after and reactions following upon the intervention in British poetry of two Americans, Pound and Eliot. In the early thirties, Alvarez remembers, F. R. Leavis had called the work of Eliot and Pound a "significant reorientation of literature," and since then, he thought, English poetry had been "controlled"—Alvarez's word—by the reactions to the modernism these two writers represented or were made to represent (21). Like a pearl built up around the irritant speck of sand, so too the rest of the history of twentieth-century English poetry is secreted as a series of reaction formations. The great bulk of British poetry, the mainstream that never dries up, consists of versions of Georgian and neo-Georgian gentility. Alvarez's literary-historical narrative, however bare, however void of discussion of the complexities of literary influence and minimally attuned to sociopolitical contexts and alternative currents in British poetry, is not without its merits as a blunt attack on the persistence of antimodernism in England: thus its fame, one imagines. First there was the rejection of the difficulty and experimentalism of Pound and Eliot in the thirties, when Auden and others reinvented the "traditional lyric" in order to communicate the urgencies of the political climate. Then there was the reaction to Auden's neo-Augustanism embodied by Dylan Thomas's neoromanticism, the reaction to Thomas embodied by the Movement poets of the fifties, who seemed to fulfill Thomas Hardy's famous prophecy that *vers libre* would come to nothing in England. By 1960, poets were coming around again to see the value of Eliot's work, Alvarez hoped, though it was not the Eliot who had promoted Augustan and neoclassical ideals — an Eliot of some interest to Auden and to Movement critic Donald Davie — but an Eliot whose poem *The Waste Land* "follows, with great precision and delicacy, the movement of a psyche, not just of society, in the process of disintegration" (28). The possibilities of this new Eliot, dressed in Freudian critique, had best been understood by the American Robert Lowell in his book *Life Studies* (1959). British poets were ready to follow "the new direction" evident there.

Alvarez's vision of American leadership in British poetry might have contributed to apprehensions about American poetry and the Americanization of British culture, even if he was not much of a prophet about the future of British poetry (nor fully aware of important influences on *Life Studies* such as the work of William Carlos Williams and Allen Ginsberg). The poetry of Lowell and Berryman have been and remain well known in England — Berryman is the most frequently cited American influence among the poets of the British "New Gen," for instance — but so-called confessional poetry has had few imitators in England.[4] The best work of Ted Hughes is closer to Lawrence than to Lowell. The Movement orthodoxy of the 1950s, as Robert Sheppard has noted, "outlasted the turbulence of the 1960s" and "led to the obscuring and devaluation of much other work, not just of emerging writers, but of older talents like W. S. Graham and Basil Bunting" (161). It survives today, says Sheppard, in Morrison and Motion's *Penguin Book of Contemporary British Poetry*, where the Movement's "anti-modernist poetic of social realist irony" is perpetuated and developed in the "Martian" poetry of Craig Raine and others, a poetry which is "a little flashier in its metaphors, a little laxer in its rhythms, a little more open to a safely historical modernism," a little less interested in the laconic plain style (161). One reason that Alvarez's anthology has had such a remarkable lifespan is that so little has changed since he wrote it.

I will discuss the Movement orthodoxy in more detail in the next chapter, but for now I want merely to state that it was not the Eliot-Lowell "confessional" nexus that emerged as the primary irritant to insular British poetry in the 1960s and 1970s, but rather another group of Americans collected in Donald Allen's anthology *The New American Poetry* (1960). These writers, the most important of whom in the British context were Charles Olson, Robert Creeley, Edward Dorn, Robert Duncan, Denise Levertov, Jack Spicer, Allen Ginsberg, Frank O'Hara, and John Ashbery — joined at times by older or younger poets not part of the anthology, such as Louis Zukofsky, Carl Rakosi, and Jerome Rothenberg — represented a loose gathering of poets united perhaps only by their opposition to the then current prevailing modes in poetry as represented in Donald Hall, Louis Simpson, and Robert Pack's anthology *New Poets of England and America* (1957). Allen's anthology is much discussed lately, so I can use shorthand here in noting the opposition of the poets included therein to the poetic values and canons of the New Criticism.[5] More than to New Criticism or its modernist hero T. S. Eliot, these "New American" poets looked to Pound and William Carlos Williams for models, and sometimes to a middle generation of objectivist poets such as George Oppen and Louis Zukofsky, or to then neglected modernists such as Gertrude Stein and H. D. and to an international historical avant-garde. It was partly the engagement with this "New American" poetry in the work of various British poets and critics and editors such as Tom Raworth, Nathaniel Tarn, Michael Horovitz, Tom Pickard, Eric Mottram, Roy Fisher, J. H. Prynne, Elaine Feinstein, Bob Cobbing, Andrew Crozier, Gael Turnbull, and many others that presented the real challenge to the Movement-inspired orthodoxy in Britain itself. A few of these poets were also editors for trade publishing houses, many of them ran small presses, and most played a major role in the flourishing little magazine culture of the period, in journals such as *Grosseteste Review, Migrant, English Intelligencer,* and *Resuscitator.* As it turns out, Alvarez's neglect of "New American" poetries left him with a vision of American poetry which the British poets listed above, readers of Olson and Lorca, would have recognized as itself rather "genteel" — if one wants to spread the epithet around.

These New American poets gathered by Donald Allen, who Alvarez apparently knew nothing about and who were important to British poets such as those named above, had little use for most British poetry beyond

Blake and Shelley. Edward Dorn's sixties poem "Oxford," for instance, which like its companion poem "North Atlantic Turbine" is partly about travel and life in England, ends with this plea to the English and Europeans:

> We have lived world,
> contrary to what you
> may think, on the refuse
> of what you thought best to send us
> > > to choose.
> (oh my Maryland)   Please
> don't send any
> > more. The Indians (american) I have their word
> for it, are tired of it.
> > > (215–16)

It is unclear whether this worrying about the covering over of the United States has entirely passed, though it has taken new forms in the industries and discourses of diverse specific identity. In our American multiworld we are so complexly mixed and densely covered over it is all the more tempting to imagine a position or a path we might occupy more or less "authentically." One of the virtues of Dorn's poem is that it harbors no such romance about the possibility of finding any particular "American identity" which might be distinguished from all the "used shit" (189). The global reach of its concerns and reference might have been one of the things, together with its expansive and ambitious post-Poundian, post-Olsonian verse technique, which might have made the poem attractive to British poets seeking an alternative to the withered canons of neo-Georgian lyric as they were being extended and ironized by the Movement.

Dorn's poem, which mentions or alludes to his British friends Prynne and Raworth, seems partly addressed to a British audience, but it might equally be construed as skeptical of British intellectuals too eager to import American culture. "America" is what the whole world wants, the poem says, even as it puts it down:

> I get sick myself
> sometimes when the people of the world, who have all
> gone there, make an
> account and the title is America
> and the signatories are

every motherfucker
in the world, only now
they think they
        can have the Idea
without the thing, they think they can
distill the poison out
pour it off
        forget
the oldest danger, that to think
is to be locked inside the thing.
                                    (213–14)

An America that can't be exported, that is particular to places and things: this might be a warning even to British intellectuals partly sympathetic to American culture, even to those like Eric Mottram who would later be savvy enough in *Blood on the Nash Ambassador* (1989) to identify those values and practices which "wreck" (216) American culture while nevertheless demonstrating his interest in a "new morphology of culture" (181). As it expresses Dorn's fascination and exasperation with the Americanization of the world, the poem sets out to do battle with the international triumph of the commodity and consumer capitalism, which makes it possible, he writes, for the Soviet poet Yevtushenko to talk "like a chamber of commerce / in Washington / inside the same general language / it is that bad . . . as if commodity / had turned all sound off, and into / the international times."

While it did not provoke nearly the degree of anti-American hysteria that other transatlantic contacts and affiliations would breed later in the sixties, Alvarez's identification of American leadership in poetry has to be understood within the context of widespread fears about Britain's diminished cultural and political role in the world. John Seed has described in some detail the extent to which "delusions of Britain's status as a 'first-class' power—and with it a sense of the Tory leadership as statesmen on the world stage—persisted within governing circles in the 1950s" (16). Such delusions were "punctured" by the Suez crisis (1956) and by other events surrounding the dismantling of empire. A declining economy in the early sixties, leading up to the Conservative defeat in the general election of 1964, helped accelerate the demoralization of British society:

The impossibility of continuing to finance an independent nuclear capability was finally recognized in 1961. Policy shifted to purchasing directly from the United States, with all the dependence and subordination that implied—a policy disapproved of by seven out of ten people, according to a 1962 Gallup Poll. The Cuban missile crisis in the autumn of 1962 further exposed British impotence; unilateral action on the part of the United States could clearly draw Britain into a nuclear war. The last of a series of humiliations in the international sphere was the rejection of Britain for Common Market membership in 1963. (17)

Anxiety about diminished influence, about American power—Alvarez's references to the profound impact of a century of holocausts and horrors make no mention of the specific national crises outlined here, although nuclear warfare might be imagined as the one ultimate, sublime, and unspoken horror that stands over his catalog of psychic disasters. His placing British poets after Americans, as a symbolic gesture, threatens all nostalgia about empire and cultural glory. As early as 1948, British poet George Barker had written of "a world filled with Americans and hate" (120) and widespread concerns about American power and British helplessness, totemically figured in the hysteria surrounding nuclear weapons, would only increase as the realities of postwar existence settled in, or were exacerbated by political or economic instability. By the early seventies no less a figure than Stephen Spender was proclaiming an "American advantage" in all areas of literature and culture, arguing that "it is only since 1945 that [the British] have begun seriously to wonder whether American civilization has not begun to affect them negatively, limiting them to provincialism in their relation to it, just as the United States were formerly provincial in relation to Europe" (5). In 1972 George Steiner would suggest that "English as it is spoken and written in England today is an enervated, tired version of the language as compared with the almost Elizabethan rapacities and zest of American English and of the breathless literature it is sending into the world" (149). One idiom had crested; the other had zest: it must have been hard to hear this.

Because, in Britain at least, anti-Americanism has never had much impact on official governmental policy—both parties since the war have been pro-American—discussion of it must remain partly anecdotal, a matter of cultural climates among particular groups. In a letter to me, British émigré Peter Quartermain remembered how, in the early fifties, the United States seemed to him simply "remote, exotic, strange." Crossing the Atlantic was a major undertaking. American books were prohibitively expensive and therefore impossible to buy; even jazz records—which were worth their weight "in if not gold then food; anyone who owned such was generally pretty popular"—were difficult to obtain, partly due to musician's union rules. Immediately after the war and for some years thereafter there was jealousy of American prosperity, "envy of their self-assured ways, fear of their self-possessed arrogance." In another letter, British poet and critic Andrew Crozier tells me of friends much more recently amused by the refrain "I'm so bored with the U.S.A." in a song by the Clash, the British punk-rock band of the seventies, and of a poet friend saying to him still more recently, "Right now we're better than the Americans." This is one kind of information the historian is obliged to deal with when discussing British anti-Americanism; it is not inconsequential. Anecdotes in the two letters I mention span the course of four decades.

In the years following the publication of Alvarez's anthology, increased interest in the poetry associated with Donald Allen's "New American" group seemed to some in Britain destined to change the British poetic landscape. The late Eric Mottram wrote on several occasions about some of the events that led to what he called the British Poetry Revival of 1960–75—of an explosion of small-press publishing dedicated to experimental poetry from America, Europe, and Britain, of the birth of American studies programs in several British universities, the increased popularity of poetry in performance, and so forth. He writes with considerable bitterness and anger discussing his activities as a professor at King's College and as editor of the Poetry Society's journal *Poetry Review* between 1972 and 1975:

> Since the 1930s, officially-sanctioned British poetry had favoured minimal invention and information, and maximum ironic finesse, with personal anecdote, covered with a social veneer or location of elements in the country. It favoured the urbanely witty or baroquely emotional rather than the thoroughly informed intelligence willing and eager to risk imaginative forms. Official preference could not tolerate an art that went beyond a leisure-hours consumer inclination to rapid reading; work which might necessitate concentration, trained ability to read, and a willingness to entertain the prospect of new forms and materials. Poetry of the official preference had become a mere adjunct to politics,

business and academic scholarship, in distinct enmity to the inclusive and exhilarating forces in, for example, Lawrence, Pound, William Carlos Williams, MacDiarmid, Jones and Bunting. Those taking part—as poets, publishers and readers—in the British Poetry Revival that took place all over Britain, irrespective of schools', universities' and reviewers' orthodoxies, recognised that poetry was not a consumer product to be easily ingested. The performances of the Liverpool poets . . . at least showed that there could be an audience for poetry outside the study, the university library and the tradition-bound classroom. In the summer of 1965, the Albert Hall reading by poets from a number of countries, including Britain . . . demonstrated that it might not be too late for an exciting growth of live poetry readings such as had become common in the United States during the past decade. *Live New Departures,* organised by Michael Horovitz and Pete Brown, showed that poetry and music in combined performance could open new audiences. (26)

Some of this requires a gloss. The Liverpool poets Mottram speaks of, the foremost of whom was probably Brian Patten, benefited from and participated in the popular music scene in Liverpool which also gave us the Beatles. As Mottram hints, their accessible, often rhymed verse hardly presents a challenge similar to that presented by the work of David Jones, Ezra Pound, Edward Dorn, or J. H. Prynne. The Albert Hall reading now has legendary status, thanks in part to a movie. Allen Ginsberg was its main drawing card, just as he was the hero of the afterword to Michael Horovitz's 1969 anthology *The Children of Albion.* (Ginsberg returned for the thirty-year anniversary reading, accompanied by Paul McCartney on guitar, though the audience, while gigantic by poetry standards, was some thousands less.) Even the title of the movie made about the reading, *Wholly Communion,* reflects Ginsberg's influence as what Horovitz called a poet-priest. Horovitz's anthology of counterculture poetry includes not just early work from Tom Raworth, Lee Harwood, Roy Fisher, and Gael Turnbull, but also poems by the eminently forgettable Ted Milton—"English Intelligencers rubbing shoulders with the Carshalton chapter of the Dharma Bums . . . and a few blokes Horovitz met in the pub," Iain Sinclair has written (xvi). The Albert Hall reading was perhaps the single most public moment of the British Poetry Revival but it was only one among an explosion of poetry readings in the sixties and seventies, in the provinces as well as the cultural centers, and more of lasting value to poetry was produced offstage as it were, in the creation of networks and small communities of poets and readers working, sometimes crudely, with small-press technologies and the scant budgets and the word-of-mouth distribution of most cottage industries. There were readings by Bunting, Hugh MacDiarmid, Robert Creeley, Robert Duncan, and many others at the Morden Tower in Newcastle. There were the Cambridge Poetry Festivals organized by Richard Burns in 1975, 1977, and 1979; at the first of these Charles Tomlinson, Nathaniel Tarn, Ted Hughes, Lee Harwood, David Gascoyne, and Roy Fisher were among the British poets reading with an international group, including Chinua Achebe (Nigeria), Miroslav Holub (Czechoslovakia), Roberto Sanesi (Italy), Takis Sinopoulos (Greece), and American John Ashbery. There were readings organized by Mottram and Bob Cobbing at the Royal Festival Hall. Many small presses and journals were started; some, like Cobbing's Writer's Forum, survive at this late date as what one might call an "alternative institution." All of this I mention might be relegated to a footnote, but I insert it here because, too often, that has been its fate. Iain Sinclair writes of the "secret history" of the British Poetry Revival, noting that it would take a "team of private detectives and a hefty bank balance" to gather together the pamphlets, journals, and chapbooks it generated. Even the Royal Festival Hall's poetry library, about the best one can do today for an archive, is frustratingly incomplete in its collection of important journals.

In mentioning an "officially sanctioned" British poetry of ironic finesse, pastoral settings, metaphorical ingenuity, and urbane tones, Mottram refers to the dominant or—in Hall's phrase—"prevailing" modes of British poetry from Auden, Day Lewis, and Betjeman, up through the Movement poets Donald Davie, Kingsley Amis, Elizabeth Jennings, Thom Gunn, D. J. Enright, and Philip Larkin, and beyond them into the recent past as it is represented in *The Penguin Book of Contemporary British Poetry*. If the rhetoric of the phrase "officially sanctioned" seems harsher than talk of "prevailing modes," Mottram is speaking from his experience not only with the culture of universities and London reviewers but also with government-funded patrons such as the Poetry Society and its parent, the Arts Council. His bitterness is disappointed enthusiasm; his vision of insiders and outsiders, government flunkies and heroic rebels, unsophisticated and now antiquated. It must be admitted, too, that, despite all the activity of the "revival," the "whole episode was strictly off-*piste*, unnoticed."[6] Much of its limited fame is due to the brute force with which it was repressed; its lessons are cautionary tales about the ways in which discourses of national tradition and anti-Americanism can be manipulated as powerful weapons in British culture.

Elsewhere in the same essay from which I have quoted, Mottram writes of the efforts of Charles Osborne, once the literature director of the taxpayer-supported Arts Council (the nearest British equivalent of the U.S. National Endowment for the Arts) to nominate three members to the Poetry Society Council, and of Osborne's desire to counter what he perceived to be too great an interest in poetry reflecting the influence of American and European avant-gardists, some of whom were themselves published in the Poetry Society's long-established journal *Poetry Review*. Osborne's concerns about the Poetry Society and its journal, which Mottram edited in the early seventies, led to an investigation of the Poetry Society by Sir John Witt, vice chairman of the Arts Council, and eventually to the resignation from the Poetry Society of some of Britain's most important "experimental" poets. Mottram viewed the events surrounding his editorship of the *Poetry Review*—which before his tenure was even more ultimately inconsequential than *Poetry* is today in the United States—as a watershed in recent British poetry. The episode remains one of the first object lessons British "alternative" poets refer to when speaking of negotiations with a mainstream.

Some British poets, and not only the guardians of neo-Georgian traditions, contest not only Mottram's sense of the dimensions of the "British Poetry Revival" but the consequences of the scandal that emerged at *Poetry Review*. The wounds created by Mottram's editorship of *Poetry Review* persist into the present in British poetry, dividing not just mainstream poets and avant-gardists but the avant-garde itself. The poetry cultures of London and Cambridge, for instance, have sometimes seemed to be at odds with each other (with crossover figures such as Raworth complicating matters) even while both "groups" have remained more or less open to a range of American and international modernisms. I discuss the Cambridge/London divide in a later chapter, but for now I can briefly note that the London group is often said to be more devoted to performance and to mixed-genre traditions and "intermedia" as well as to the legacies of Dada and Situationism, the Cambridge group to a more specifically literary tradition that adds the Americans Pound, Oppen, Zukofsky, and Olson, and Continental modernists such as Paul Celan to the canonical texts of English poetry. Among the poets associated with the Cambridge group, one still holds the view that the attempt to gain control of the Poetry

Society, although successful, was misguidedly grandiose and "diverted time and effort from activities of a more temporary and ad hoc type," from a "loosely coordinated series of guerilla actions and campaigns" against the British literary establishment—one example being Burns's Cambridge Poetry Festival. In his view the Poetry Society had been "moribund since Harold Monro was axed as editor of the *Poetry Review* in 1911 or so," and the "takeover" of the society and its journal by Mottram and others should be understood either as "entryism" or, in another jargon, a "buy-out of a company with undervalued assets."[7] He remembers that *Poetry Review* had been for decades home to Georgian and neo-Georgian poetry, to fustian versifying and Betjemanian nostalgia. As institutions the *Poetry Review* and its parent body were prizes not worth the capture, since, as events showed, possession could only be short-lived. It should be clear that this view hardly applauds the cultural conservatism that led to letters from subscribers complaining about an assault on canons of taste under way at *Poetry Review;* instead, particular tactics are at issue. Such a view obviously has the benefit of the hindsight that knows that by the time events at the Poetry Society became news the audiences for readings by poets favored by Mottram and his colleagues were in decline as countercultural enthusiasms gave way to the economic and ideological forces that would shortly bring on Thatcherism. Resigned to the more or less inevitable, it risks sanctioning a withdrawal from all efforts to engage a broader public, contentiously or not. An alternative view, associated with some in London, risks not so much resignation as entrapment in a foundational story or myth wherein the avant-garde is cast as the victim whose only solace as it seeks to recover from its wounds is the endless iteration of events fading into the past; this pose also limits possibility. Perhaps the least partisan analysis of these events is Martin Booth's: "That the controversy made the national newspapers was sign enough that poetry was more of a big deal than it had been in the cosier years of the pre-uprising. Whatever harm Mottram might or might not have done to the *Poetry Review,* its parent body or the Society or the art itself is lost now. That he created such a stir was good enough. It added much to the world of literature. One can hardly see the press taking much notice of such a thing nowadays" (70). Booth's more remote perspective refuses to take sides on the principle that any noise in the poetry world is good for poetry. Like his last proposition, this may or may not be true but is in any case meaningless to those writers who were briefly illuminated by scandal before their work was pushed back to the margins and slim budgets of a self-sustaining and nearly invisible avant-garde.

Mottram's polemical history of a twenty-five-year campaign on behalf of particular poetries, of a titanic struggle between inclusive and "exhilarating" British modernists and the rest of the poets who exist as flunkies for consumer culture, does simplify matters. Without denying Mottram's influence or importance, his work on behalf of American and British poetry, his encyclopedic essays on American culture collected in books like *Blood on the Nash Ambassador* (1989), it must be said that polemic was often Mottram's *modus operandi* after the midseventies, and the binary oppositions polemic sometimes creates, rhetorically useful and even provocative as they may be, can obliterate real differences within the camps identified. Movement poets, just to mention one example, might include not only the willfully provincial and antimodernist Philip Larkin, but also Donald Davie, who translated Russian poetry, wrote extensively if ambivalently about Ezra Pound, taught in the United States, and (like Mottram) facilitated contact between American and British poets; and Thom Gunn, who has long played a vital role in the counterculture of San Francisco and written important essays on Basil Bunting, Robert Duncan, and Mina Loy, among others of considerable interest to writers and readers seeking to expand the resources and possibilities of poetry.

Mottram lived long enough to witness the Faber promotions of the mideighties, poets touring in helicopters, bankrolled by ticket sales from *Cats,* and the Madison Avenue–style promotional schemes, photoshoots in costume, and television appearances used to promote the twenty poets of the so-called New Generation in the spring of 1994 — poets "marketed like sportswear," Tom Raworth has written (1995, 316). In retrospect, it might seem that the readings and events of the sixties were comparatively free of the lurid excesses of such commercialization, but in another sense New Generation publicity might be said to have perfected some of the promotional tactics employed by the "alternative" poetry culture Mottram admired. As we have also seen in the United States since the seventies, a counterculture can be bought and sold by various interests for various purposes. This does not mean that alternative or oppositional practices are ineffectual or inconsequential, only that we must resist both pessimism and nostalgia — Mottram's essay evokes both — when considering the past and contemplating present opportunities. Those very Faber promotions of the mideighties, and, especially, the "New Gen" promotions of 1994, suggest the extent to which the countercultural agenda of Mottram and others to move poetry's audience outside the schools and universities can easily be co-opted for a range of poetic practices which he would mostly deplore.

In Mottram's essays concerning the British Poetry Revival, two contradictory forces are often at work—a resentment of a poetry too easily accessible to its audiences, "consumable," and a desire that a more surprising and challenging poetry find and sustain new and larger audiences. Unwilling to rethink the terms of poetry's possible relationship to an audience, Mottram is stuck on the modernist terms *difficulty* and *accessibility,* as if it were possible to divide up poetry and its audiences into two camps by graphing cognitive skills. For all of his work within institutions, too, Mottram seems to have had little faith in their ability to change, and staked most of his hopes on an "outside" where he would pick and choose between manifestations of "popular" culture that he might link with the poetries he valued. Our faith in that "outside"—to say the least—has since diminished, together perhaps with our confidence in any rhetoric naming a regression in listening or a degradation in awareness. Cognitive abilities might be reshaped or redirected but the evidence that they actually diminish seems entirely rhetorical.

For the recent "New Gen," the possibilities of an extra-academic, popular poetry are no less attractive than they sometimes were for Mottram. One hears, for instance, that the following writing wants to imagine itself the new rock 'n' roll:

> A poem is a little church, remember
> you, its congregation, I, its cantor;
>
> so please, no flash, no necking in the pew,
> or snorting just to let your neighbor know
>
> you get the clever stuff. . . .

> (18)

I really can't go on quoting this "Prologue" by Don Paterson, who half-sarcastically introduces himself in a contributor's note as follows: "Hi. My name's Don. I'm a Scorpio. I hate doing this. One day I'd like to be famous enough to just not do it, rather than spend 200 words telling you why I don't want to. The reason I don't want to talk about my poetry is because I don't consider my own remarks to be more relevant or interesting than anyone else's; this isn't so much humility as an abdication of responsibility, but a poem has to generate its own context and its own illumination. If it can't, then hell mend it" (17). This too, for all its campy absurdity, is a rhetoric, like Mottram's, directed at academies and orthodoxies. Antiacademic and populist rhetoric is not the exclusive property of any one group or generation, as the prose of Philip Larkin—one of the bogeymen more contemporary with Mottram—also suggests. In his diary of the events surrounding the New Gen circus, Paterson jokes about his friend and fellow poet Michael Donaghy fantasizing about becoming a kind of rock star, his poetry the new "rock and roll," and then continues to say more seriously, "We can appeal—if that's the word—directly to the reading public, rather than relying on academics to plead our case whilst simultaneously marginalising and misinterpreting us through the need to protect the myth of their own expertise" (25). One can understand the attack on "expertise"—the colonization of the ordinary by disciplines and institutions is a complaint that can serve many, different ends, progressive and reactionary both—but the romance of "directness" here is a little too much. No poetry is ever encountered altogether free of the preparatory and mediating discourses that surround it, whether these emanate from academic literary criticism and theory, avant-garde manifestos, pop books and TV shows on the history of rock 'n' roll, other poetries and art, or some combination of these. And it is nowhere written in stone that academics must value difficulty. Nor do complaints about (or celebration of) difficulty typically make clear exactly what *difficulty* means; poetry some would call difficult today is not difficult in the way that, say, Pound is, requiring knowledge of esoteric traditions and a range of languages and histories. The difficulty in reading Maggie O'Sullivan or Allen Fisher is largely a matter of resisting the habits of interpretation taught by the professors who schooled you and them. For Paterson *difficulty* means cultural elitism, as if the two were synonymous; for Mottram it means that which resists easy consumption. Neither view is much help.

An American reader encountering Mottram's remarks—not just in the essay I have quoted but throughout the essays he has devoted to the British Poetry Revival—cannot help but note that, for him, the practice and culture of poetry has been far healthier in America than in Britain in recent times. He is, after all, arguing that British poetry, or some of it, benefitted by engaging and even modeling itself after American poetry, particularly modernist and postmodernist "experimental" poetry, and an American poetry culture of readings and small presses. While essays such as Mottram's "Dionysus in America" show that his interest in American culture had limits—he writes there of antidemocratic forces which threaten to wreck it—one wonders sometimes about his confidence in his ability to "distill the poison" out of America, to use Dorn's words. He has little if anything to say about the possibilities of the direction of poetic influence being reversed. In that regard, he is typical. Suggesting that "any real dialogue between British and American poets largely disappeared in the Sixties," the American poet-critic John Matthias adds that "influence, where it existed, was that of the Americans on the British" (1992, 209).

Mottram's view of America and American poetry, romanticized as it may be, has been shared by a number of supporters of the New American poetry in Britain. Nathaniel Tarn, now living in New Mexico, is one such poet, and a couple of his essays, the earlier of them published in 1968 amid the ferment of counterculture events and manifestos, will stand here as representative of the kind of polemical discourse about the United States that angered a number of British poets, forcing them to justify what some would call their little-englandism or insularity with dubious claims about an essential English tradition and character. In his *International Times* essay of 1968, "The World Wide Open: The Work Laid Before Us in This Disunited Kingdom," Tarn identified himself, as Alvarez had before him, as an enemy of gentility and of "the miserable timidity" and "smallness of mind and purpose which keeps us almost totally alienated from our true potential." He found the bulk of contemporary English poetry to be "relentlessly superficial," a manifestation of the "immemorial British shyness, a shyness which can, at the drop of the hat, become rabid arrogance when it is suggested we might learn from the outside world." While the remedies for such a state of affairs were various, and included a need to remain open to poetic, religious, and cultural influences from around the world, Tarn insisted that the British needed to pay special attention to the Americans. In a statement which, intentionally or not, rubbed the face of the British in contemporary geopolitical realities, he added, "Fifty-first state or not, now or in the future, our local stance is inevitably conditioned by the kind of yes or no we say to the poetry of the United States." He thought that the work Alvarez had done in introducing Lowell and Plath was fine but only a beginning: "the British 'academy' responds to the American 'academy'" (16–24). Beyond the academy, Donald Allen's New American poetry was pointing the way.

Doris Sommer has written that, for Tarn, "America was and still is the one place that satisfies the desire for national identity while it assumes that absolute, irrational identity is impossible." According to Sommer, it is the "alienated and self-willed quality of America that makes it so attractive and available to Tarn," the fact that Americans "may sense that their culture is made, whereas other societies may more easily mistake culture for nature, human products for natural givens" (14–15). Because many Americans are not so far removed from immigrant beginnings, the argument goes, we recognize national identity as a made thing subject to the contestations of our own wills and cultural practices. In other words, Americans refuse to insist upon an *essential* national identity. This is a thesis, of course, and subject to the scrutiny of all those who have witnessed the use and efficacy of rhetorics of American exceptionalism in recent political campaigns and elsewhere. But there is no doubting Sommer's accuracy in depicting Tarn's beliefs circa 1968. Tarn's self-described "universalism," and his claim that "we have no alternative to taking the whole world as our mother" (58), combine to make him fundamentally skeptical of the relevance of national boundaries, but there also is little doubt that, for him at this time, America, "by its charter," seemed to be the place where such ideas existed most comfortably, especially considering his experience of the little-englandism rampant in influential literary circles in Britain in the late sixties.

One can see the way Tarn's universalism positioned itself against British mainstream poetry in the roughly contemporary book *The Beautiful Contradictions* (1970):

> Himantopodes creeping on all fours   the dwarfish Psylli
> the Blemmyae with sunken eyes and mouths   the Troglodytes
> guzzling in caves and ignorant of speech   the ethnocentric ones
> the Garamantes' mare who fetched the gold of ants
>
> rose out of Carthage to harry Rome once more
> shattered each scallop shell in golden Compostela
> silenced the university of Paris   stopped Flanders looms
> sank Britain in its miasmata   anchored the Hebrides
>
> (n.p.)

No pastoralism here, nor irony, but instead the vatic tonalities of Whitman; no terse, neo-Augustan balance or Tennysonian verse forms but instead the capacious parallelisms of a more self-consciously oral, perhaps breath-based, poetic line. And ethnocentric Britain takes a beating much worse than the one it receives in the campier tones of Tarn's British contemporary John James's "Good Old Harry," a product of much the same cultural climate: "we are the English / easy-going & lazy . . . when Edward goes for a walk / we take off our caps & wave them in the air / England is a mature nation / & is not a bit like America" (157).

Tarn's generalizations about the United States, where they occur, are not without precedent; there is a long tradition in Europe, ranging from Tocqueville to Baudrillard, attributing to Americans a weak historical consciousness and a corresponding utopianism. For Baudrillard, for instance, as for Marcel Duchamp and others before him, America *is* modernity, and an "unbridgeable rift" separates its "achieved utopia" from Europe and its intellectuals mired in the dialectical analysis of history (73). As far as the "two poetries" are concerned, Tarn understood the basic conflict in both nations as a struggle between modernist and anti-modernist practices, the latter of which included Lowell, Berryman, and Plath, whom he reads as "the overwhelmingly model-poets of the Movement and its successors." In a more recent essay, Tarn remembers how it had seemed to him that there was "an America in England and an England in America" (58), a nice phrase and one sensitive to the extensive cross-cultural influences in the two nations. The "America in England" consisted largely of British supporters of Donald Allen's New American poetry, the "England in America" of "academic" formalist poets (such as Richard Wilbur or Howard Nemerov, perhaps, though they are not named), Ivy League institutions, and journals such as the *New York Times Book Review* and the *New York Review of Books,* which represented the "last of her Majesty's Government's possessions in these our states" (57–58). The later essay thus defines England and the United States as something approaching states of mind or types of cultural and poetic practices. The earlier one had proclaimed "the Modern revolution in English language poetry" an American revolution, directed by Eliot and Pound. It had nothing to say about the presence or the significance of Eliot and Pound in England, and after reminding his readers that Eliot and Pound were Americans Tarn nodded in the direction of British modernism only to say that, in his opinion, the only post-Georgian poetry of value "is not English but Celtic: Yeats, Joyce, MacDiarmid, Dylan Thomas." This leaves out Basil Bunting, David Jones, D. H. Lawrence, Edith Sitwell, John Rodker, Joseph Gordon Macleod, F. S. Flint, and David Gascoyne, among many others, though he does mention Bunting in passing: "a fine poet like Bunting scarcely gets a hearing" (16–17).

By the early seventies it was so common to hear English and British poetry attacked as insular, uninteresting, and genteel by Americans and American-identified British writers that it became nearly incumbent upon

American readers of British poetry to defend their very interests. In 1971 John Matthias edited an anthology called *Twenty-three Modern British Poets,* which was designed to prove to Americans that there was indeed "a contemporary British poetry which is modern; for a while that seemed to be in doubt. Perhaps, in America at least, it's still in doubt." In 1974 Calvin Bedient published a book on eight British poets in which he felt obliged to begin by defending British poetry against those who found it genteel or trivial. In 1977 Marjorie Perloff edited a special issue of *Contemporary Literature,* featuring her own and Lawrence Kramer's essays on the discontinuities among the two poetries, which, for Perloff, as for Hall, Davie, and others, involved different understandings of the possibilities of syntax (which can be attached to any other number of subjects, such as the role of speech rhythms in poetry, the construction of a relationship to audience and "meaning," to name but two). There were other books and briefer essays in journals too; I mean only to outline the extent to which the debate about "two poetries" persisted throughout the seventies, often, in the United States at least, without reference to the realities of economic and political power to which I have referred here.

The besieged elements of the British poetry world were not silent, as I have suggested, and they were sometimes more eager than Americans to confront the question of cultural and economic power. In 1972 Donald Davie published his study of the tradition of Thomas Hardy in British poetry; an American edition included a postscript addressed to American readers. Also published in England in 1972 was Michael Schmidt and Grevel Lindop's aggressive anthology of essays on British poetry, *British Poetry Since 1960,* which included an introduction attacking American detractors of British poetry and much American poetry, too. Louis Simpson was singled out for having somewhat incoherently complained that English poets were not sufficiently willing to talk about technique, which was related, Simpson thought, to the lack of substantial avant-garde movements in contemporary poetry in England. If the American rhetoric of experimentalism and innovation had been wielded against the British, these editors were not above calling the Americans themselves insular, and warning that "if two traditions seem to develop, the impetus for the apparent development will be largely American" (4).

Alan Brownjohn's essay in the Schmidt and Lindop anthology is particularly interesting for its harassed tone. Brownjohn, at one time associated with those poets collected in Edward Lucie-Smith and Philip

Hobsbaum's *A Group Anthology* (1963), is the author of a poem once well known to schoolchildren in England, an ironic little poem "after Prévert" about the industrialization of England:

> We are going to see the rabbit,
> We are going to see the rabbit.
> Which rabbit, people say?
> Which rabbit, ask the children?
> Which rabbit?
> The only rabbit,
> The only rabbit in England,
> Sitting behind a barbed-wire fence
> Under the floodlights, neon lights,
> Sodium lights,
> Nibbling grass
> On the only patch of grass
> In England . . .
>
> (19)

One quickly gets the point; the meaning is clear. Or is it? Is the poem critical of the nostalgia it seems to invoke? It is easy—too easy—for academic writers to dismiss poetry with traces of light verse. The author of this famous poem, noting that "English poets at the moment are under increasing pressure to accept a state of demoralised inferiority by comparison with their American colleagues," sets out in his essay to contest the usual characterizations of English poetry, dismissing out of hand the "vulgar" argument which "allies supremacy in the arts to military and economic power." He urges English poets not to capitulate to the "modishness and irrationality" of either American projectivism (the Olson-Creeley-Duncan-Dorn-Levertov wing of Allen's New American poetry) or European postsurrealism, and writes of the former that "no intelligent and coherent critical approach has yet managed to grasp and appraise it." In a rapid-fire barrage of epithets, he cuts down the ranks of the New Americans at the rate of a poet per sentence. Charles Olson's early talent had begun "trickling itself out through the holes in an ever-expanding grid"; Robert Duncan's poetry was talking itself "to death in a tedious welter of derivation and pretentiousness"; Robert Creeley's was "in real danger of dwindling tensely to the point where all that is left to stand for a poem is half a syllable implying an implication" (240–49). To be fair to Brownjohn, these epithets are not without wit, even while unfair and unsympathetic, and they do show some (small) understanding of the work being attacked. Some of these criticisms, together with more familiar ones about the difficulty or obscurity of this work, had been made before by unsympathetic Americans reading these poets.

But in Brownjohn's essay the remarks are made as part of a generalized assault on the British counterculture, and in defense of a national tradition, an Englishness (*in Britain*). Dissent had "come to invade the English campuses and there become something like an inflexible, in-group orthodoxy," he writes. Dissent in this prose "invades" British society, one supposes, much as Americans "invade" Vietnam: the military metaphor simultaneously describes dissent as "alien" and exploits the anger that motivated much of the counterculture. The counterculture, he continues, had "more justice in its cause and less sense and coherence than any previous, comparable movement" (247). Like the work of Olson and Creeley, then, the larger cultural movement that the poetry of the so-called British Poetry Revival found itself embedded in lacked coherence. This was apparently to be deplored—this excess of lifestyle and critique was not to be allowed stuttering contradictions in the assertion of difference and opposition. To resist countercultural enthusiasms, Brownjohn argues, one should remember that "one peculiar and excellent strength of the English creative intellect" is its reliance on "reasonable" and "defensible" utterance. One would also do well to remember that "empirical, critical attitudes *are* the English tradition" (248–49). The emphasis in the last sentence speaks volumes.

The New American poetry and its British counterparts, insofar as they, in their small way, helped energize an English counterculture, represented a threat to English national culture, or, more cynically, to Tory nostalgia. But as the seventies progressed it became increasingly clear that they were only part of a larger threat to what Anthony Easthope has called "the inherited national culture with its ingrained vices of *empiricism, moralism,* and (epistemological) *humanism.*" As structuralist and post-structuralist "theory" gradually made its way into England from France in the late sixties and early seventies, its challenge, Easthope writes, "was typically ignored or, where it was acknowledged, responded to with hysterical denunciation" (61). The "hysteria" reached its peak in what Brian Doyle remembers in his *English and Englishness* (1989) as "five months of unprecedented coverage in the media" (130) surrounding the status of "Cambridge English" and English studies in general. In what became known to some as the MacCabe affair, traditionalists defended their sense of their mission or calling to "teach and uphold the canon of English literature" against the incursions of a range of "theoretical" approaches to the study of literature and culture. Tensions between an Oxbridge center and the newer universities and polytechnics were made visible (even in *Punch*) by the refusal to tenure MacCabe at Cambridge and his 1981 appointment as Britain's youngest professor of English at the University of Strathclyde. Noting that the one "ism" not attacked by traditionalists was criticism—the engine of a Leavisite machinery designed to instill in students and readers the ability to appreciate what they might not (as I. A. Richards had long ago demonstrated) appreciate on their own—Raymond Williams linked the crisis brought on by methodological pluralism to the "more general reflexes and campaigns of the English ruling class as a whole, whose talk and propagation of 'heritage' have increased in proportion with their practical present failures" (195–96). Tracing the idea of a national literature back to the late eighteenth century, Williams says of the attack on "theory": "What is often being defended, it seems, is not just a body of writing but a major projection from this, in which the actually very diverse works of writers in English are composed into a national identity—the more potent because it is largely from the past—in which a mood, a temper, a style, or a set of immediate 'principles' . . . are being celebrated, taught and—where possible—administratively imposed" (195). The role of experimental or alternative American and British poetries in these debates was minimal, no doubt, but one should note alliances where they occurred. MacCabe, for instance, would review the British poet Tom Raworth's book-length poem *Writing* (which had been published in the United States) for the *Times Literary Supplement* in 1983. He began the review with a direct assault: "In an England which has given itself over to the seductions of conservatism Raworth's poetry strikes the wrong tone" (1455).

Discussing the interventions and the institutional practice of the film criticism inaugurated in the British journal *Screen* during the seventies, Easthope offers a brief and necessarily reductive tripartite definition of the discursive formation that represents for him, as surely also but with different consequences for Brownjohn, the "foundational structuring of English national culture since the seventeenth century." I abbreviate his definitions below:

1. *Empiricist.* It assumes that representation—signification—can reproduce the real without any serious material intervention of its own. . . .

2. *Moralistic.* What is thought to matter is a supposedly free individual's choice between the pleasure-seeking demands of fantasy and the necessities imposed by the real.

3. *Humanist.* The ontological priority of some universal human nature is assumed such that to partake of it (it's everywhere) is to be placed in a position of epistemological certainty. (61–62)

If we ponder for a brief moment Brownjohn's riposte to Creeley, we can understand how the act of "implying an implication" might very well upset Brownjohn, for the effect of Creeley's stuttering, recursive verse is hardly epistemological certainty. And it was Olson who wrote, in his manifesto "Projective Verse," of the necessity of "getting rid of the lyrical interference of the individual as ego, of the 'subject' and his soul, that peculiar presumption by which western man has interposed himself between what he is as a creature of nature (with certain instructions to carry out) and those other creatures of nature we may, with no derogation, call objects" (24). There are significant differences as well as important similarities between the claims of French structuralist and post-structuralist theorists and the precepts underlying or enabling New American poetic practices—and there are of course differences among the French theorists and New American poets themselves—but there is little question that both groups represent a challenge to "English national culture" as it is defined here—in their understanding of basic issues of epistemology and language, of the "individual" and her relationship to cultural practices.

Not all English efforts to celebrate a distinctive English tradition, to set it apart from an American tradition, were as hysterical as Brownjohn's. Donald Davie's 1972 study *Thomas Hardy and British Poetry* seems genuinely motivated by a desire to improve the conversation between the "two poetries." But Davie's rhetoric periodically constructs America and England as monolithic entities virtually opposite in their natures:

The Englishman supposes he is trying to operate in some highly specific historical situation, conditioned by manifold contingencies (hence his qualifications, his hesitations, his damaging concessions), whereas the American poet, conditioned since the Pilgrim Fathers to think in utopian terms, is sure that he is enacting a drama of which the issues are basically simple and permanent, and will be seen to be so once we have penetrated through their accidental, historical overlay. (186)

Even if one agrees that there is (sometimes) a correlation between awareness of historical contingencies and skepticism, or between utopianism and vatic posturing in poetry, one might want to insist that neither skepticism nor utopianism is the exclusive property of one or another nation or people. Empiricism, moralism, and humanism have, after all, not been without considerable influence in America, and in England there is the legacy of Blake and Shelley to consider, important to British poets such as Kathleen Raine and George Barker as well as the so-called Neo-Apocalyptic poets the Movement established itself against. These are complications Davie must neglect as he sets out to critique the likes of Yeats and Lawrence, with their mythopoeic and bardic sensibilities, imagining them odd aberrations or real dangers in the British poetic landscape—the attack on Lawrence coming by way of criticism of Kenneth Rexroth, whose influence on various of the New American poets was well understood by Davie.

In taking up the case of Thomas Hardy and those poets he identifies as part of a tradition of Hardy—Philip Larkin, Charles Tomlinson, Roy Fisher, the early J. H. Prynne—Davie reverses the valuations of Alvarez's introduction. What is gentility, he asks, but civic sense and political responsibility? If a Hardyesque tone and manner has come to dominate English poetry, this is the result of social and political developments, of the triumph of "scientific humanism" and "social democracy" in modern England. Robert Sheppard has noted that *Thomas Hardy and British Poetry* gave "short shrift" to the more "extremist" poetics of Ted Hughes and Sylvia Plath (1992), and indeed some of Davie's most resonant remarks are directed at the politics of antidemocratic modernists such as Pound, Yeats, Lawrence, and Eliot. He is especially scornful of the academic critic who "toys with" the political opinions of these men only to be transformed into a social democrat "as soon as he attends his university senate, voting there" (5). Ultimately, Davie's book was a passionate, centrist plea for a consensual politics that had largely broken down by the end of the sixties. Trying to participate in the debate about the "two poetries," a debate which, as I hope I have shown, was misguided in its insistence on representing both poetries as monolithic entities, Davie ends up uttering phrases such as the following: "the distinctive quality and the distinctive task of poetry in Britain were defined, and are still to be defined, by the fact that Britain as a whole is the most industrialized landscape in the world" (72). Tell that to the poets of New Jersey—to William Carlos Williams or Amiri Baraka.

Modernism and the Common Reader

To this point I have said only a little that begins to explain what still strikes some American readers as remarkable or "different" about the history of British poetry in this century, especially in the last forty years—the sustained resistance to modernism, particularly to the more avant-garde or "experimental" manifestations of modernist poetry, the persistent success of poetic modes introduced by the Movement and perpetuated in the poetry of many younger writers. In an essay on Tom Raworth's poetry, British critic John Barrell has discussed the difficulties of modernism in England:

> Epistemology, subjectivity, and language, are everywhere the concern of English poetry from William Wordsworth, say, to Arthur Hugh Clough, where they are understood as central to the issue, among others, of the authority of poetry and of the poet. They are the concerns also of the early twentieth-century modernism that hardly happened to poetry in Britain, or that happened only in the work of writers who, precisely because their concerns were the concerns of modernism, have been represented as marginal and as isolated figures—isolated in the same sense as the Continent is isolated by channel fogs. Issues like these are nowhere to be found in what many of the most influential institutions of British literary culture represent as the most important poetry now being written. They are kept out by a series of arguments— that they are undecidable and therefore not worth discussing, that they empty poetry of its human content, that they are properly the province of philosophers and not of poets, that they are elitist preoccupations which can never engage a wider public. All these arguments do something to explain why poetry in Britain has become such a trivial affair. (388)

Barrell's main focus in the essay from which I take this passage is syntax in Raworth's work. Much of Raworth's poetry is syntactically disjunct; "narrative" and "meaning" in this poetry are obliged to confront the constructedness of the text, entertained and regularly defeated by the temporality of reading: "the obsolete ammunition depot / unmissed and unreported / put it in categories / still glistened with dampness / suits seemed to be identical / through the window behind him / a battered cardboard box / won somewhere gambling / dim bell in his memory / was making a duplicate / to see if that needed explanation / sharply, and then, more gently / the door opened" (Raworth, *Clean and Well Lit,* 11). We're visited by syntactic and narrative frames that hold for a line, or possibly two or three, as if every still in a motion picture were to be isolated for a second and then pushed back into the motion the machine projects as an illusion (to use an analogy Barrell favors). What we seek of coherence and continuities we must seek elsewhere than in standard narration or discursiveness—in tonalities, in idioms, in rhythms. Modernist defamiliarization techniques and disruptions of syntax—the exploration of the possibilities of paratactic and asyntactical poetic discourse—have (as I have noted) often emerged as a national dividing line in polemics about modern and contemporary poetry, not least in Davie's *Articulate Energy* (1955), a defense of the expressive energies of "traditional" syntax and a critique of the symbolist-inspired practices of numerous modernists. Barrell's fine essay on Raworth links Raworth with the modernists and postmodernists, against models of an expressivist self, and—within the unfortunate history of this discourse—also implicitly with the Americans.

But, reading the passage above, one might wish to ask Barrell which is the case: did modernism "hardly happen" to poetry in Britain or has its reception made it seem more of a marginal phenomenon? The same questions might be asked of the British critic Andrew Lawson, who writes more angrily that "the problem for any putatively postmodern poetry in Britain is that Britain has yet to go through a modernist period and, thanks to the efforts of Betjeman and Larkin and their current disciples, never will" (413). The presence of Pound and Eliot in England, the work of Mina Loy (most of it written and published outside of England), Basil Bunting, Hugh MacDiarmid, David Jones, David Gascoyne, Joseph Gordon MacLeod, and any number of other, more contemporary poets would suggest that it is not modernisms that Britain has lacked but rather an apparatus for their promotion. Our job then is to explain what it is that has hampered the reception of modernist poetry in England, what has made it marginal, along the lines of the reasons sketched by Barrell.

The previous discussion has touched upon some of the instances in which poetic modernism in Britain has been read as an American-influenced product, and one might develop the brief remarks on French theory to show how the American and the Continental have sometimes been conflated and posed against an English national culture. But in what follows I want to limit myself mostly to the last of the objections that Barrell mentions—the claim that the experimentalism of modernist poetry reflects "elitist preoccupations which can never engage a wider public"—to ponder why it may have been the case that experimental writing in America, if it has not always been met with open arms, has sometimes seemed to have met with less resistance than similar writing in Britain.

Efforts to link the notoriously "difficult" poetry of modernists such as Pound, Eliot, and Stein to "elitist" agendas are pervasive in the literary criticism and journalism of our century, and with good reason. Pound and Eliot, for instance, regularly appealed to the need for and the utility of elites, though, as Bob Perelman has recently argued, this does not mean that the works of Pound and Eliot and others were written in such a manner that "the public was never considered." The fact that these works now find their principal audience among specialists in the professionalized setting of the university does not disallow the possibility that "the referential, formal, and syntactic singularities of this writing that now seem riddles so provocatively addressed to specialists can also be read as the conflicted vehicles of polemics, appeals, and pronouncements aimed at, if not exactly addressed to, the writers' contemporaries." These works have become "monads," Perelman writes, as much "through the effects of history" as by the writers' own choice (*Genius,* 5). This means that to discuss the reception of modernist poetry in Britain, or to compare it with the reception of modernist poetry in the United States, one must be attentive to the development of a range of institutions that help shape that reception. One must be attentive to subtle differences in the institutions of literary study, literary production, and literary criticism in the United States and England, as well as to the bigger if more precariously defined effects of shifting economic and political relations in the international context.

It may very well be the case, as Alan Brownjohn suggests, that linking economic and political power with superiority in art is "vulgar." There is no reason to believe that powerful nations produce art that matters very much to others; the Carthaginians are the classic example. But powerful nations have the resources, should they choose to employ them, to support and indeed promote the art that they have. Moreover, a more complex, diversified, growing economy has room to allow niches for an experimental art that may have a more difficult time penetrating the institutions of more centralized, or contracting, economies. If one tallies up the academic critical prose directed at the likes of Creeley, Olson, Duncan, and, more recently, the American language poets, and compares it to the academic critical prose written on behalf of or explicating the poetry of J. H. Prynne, Roy Fisher, Gael Turnbull, Denise Riley, or Geraldine Monk, one will begin to see that the size and diversity of American culture, and particularly American academic culture, does matter. Think of a journal like *Boundary 2* in the 1970s and the work its abundant pages did in bringing postmodern art and theory into dialogue with theory produced for American academics, or think of the various journals published at the University of Maine by the National Poetry Foundation.

One of the things that allowed for what Eric Mottram calls the British Poetry Revival of the sixties and early seventies was the growth of funding for regional arts, which occurred roughly simultaneously with the expansion of the British university system and the growing influence of universities other than Cambridge and Oxford. Similar developments occurred in the United States, of course, with New York and the Ivy League's status as cultural centers being challenged by developments taking place elsewhere, particularly in San Francisco. Such decentralization made for vitality in the arts, for openness to the innovative and the challenging, in Britain as in the United States. But the power of the dominant institutions of publishing and culture in England seems to have been harder to dislodge—as a matter of degree—than similar institutions in the United States. As recently as 1994, an editor of the new *Poetry Review* wrote that "the central channels of literary culture, the BBC, Oxbridge, Penguin books, Faber & Faber, the *New Statesman* and *Listener,* all had to adapt [in the eighties] to being just one player among several. . . . Ten years ago [1984], new poets had strong links both with each other and with a tradition, as had always been the case in England. Craig Raine, Andrew Motion, James Fenton, Blake Morrison, Christopher Reid, for all their differences, had a programme—basically, the Movement plus visual fireworks—and eagerly set about promulgating it by editing magazines, reviewing strenuously, editing anthologies, and running the major publishers' poetry lists."[8] There is some irony in this statement appearing where it does, in an establishment journal promoting the work of twenty poets who were chosen by judges including Melvyn Bragg, a broadcaster for BBC Radio 4; Michael Longley, a Penguin author; and James Wood, "chief literary critic" of the *Guardian.* But let us assume—and there is some reason to do so—that the editor is correct in saying that those of Britain's younger poets represented in this journal reflect a more decentralized, pluralistic and multicultural poetry world, that the coteries which now exist are, as he says, "a loose network dispersed about the regions." Even so that would date the beginnings of a more decentralized poetry culture and the diminishing influence of London and Oxbridge coteries to as late as the mideighties. This is one way, sadly, of measuring the lasting influence of the British Poetry Revival. One hears nothing of its poets in this account, of dispersive and decentralizing efforts twenty years previously. That is obliterated history—history in the wake of the Witt report and the Osborne affair, in the wake of Thatcherism.

The editors of the recent Bloodaxe volume, *The New Poetry* (Hulse 1993), which includes many of the twenty poets who were in 1994 part of the New Gen promotion in *Poetry Review* and on radio, television, and in bookstores throughout England, write in their introduction of a "new poetry [that] emphasises accessibility, democracy, and responsiveness, humour, and seriousness, [a poetry which] reaffirms the art's significance as public utterance" (16). There is nothing wrong with such a statement in and of itself—who could be against these things? And yet "accessibility" is a word that cannot help but summon the spectre of that word often opposed to it—that "difficulty" so notoriously associated with modernism and experimental poetry. And reading the responses to a survey of the New Gen poets, we note that the poets listed by them as influences include Elizabeth Bishop, John Berryman, Robert Lowell, Ted Hughes, W. H. Auden, Louis MacNeice, among others; there is virtually no reference to a modernist poetry other than the safely historical Rilke, Montale, and one or two others. No Stein, no Pound, no Bunting, none of the objectivist poets, none of the New American poets beyond one mention of Frank O'Hara. Several Scots poets—the New Gen group is indeed diverse in terms of region and gender—mention MacDiarmid. One Scots poet, W. N. Herbert, is said to admire American language poetry. A reading of the poetry of the New Gen itself shows that, while it is not Movement poetry, it is fairly conservative in its syntactic practices and other formal conventions. There are poems in a manner not far removed from America's New Formalist and New Narrative poets, others closer to the poetry of older formalists such as Richard Wilbur and James Merrill, still others in a range of modes such as one might encounter among the performance poets at New York's Nuyorican Café. Many of the poems seem to be aimed at what the American New Formalist polemicist Dana Gioia has called a general audience, which he defines as "an audience of prose readers—intelligent, educated, and sophisticated individuals who, while no longer reading poetry, enjoyed serious novels, film, drama, jazz, dance, classical music, painting, and the other modern arts," readers who unself-consciously enjoy "rhyme, meter, and storytelling as natural elements of the popular arts like rock, musical theater, and motion pictures" (18). Like the New Formalists, many of the New Gen poets seem to be part of an attempt to create an idealized general or common reader.

Now, the common reader has never existed in flesh and blood but only as the figure in a rhetoric. The English common reader as "he" was understood by Samuel Johnson, and also later by F. R. Leavis and his circle, was never a member of a mass audience. As Frank Kermode notes, the English common reader was in Johnson's day and throughout much of the nineteenth century a member of "an elite minority, clearly differentiated from the uneducated on the one hand and the specialists on the other" (49). After the advent of television and radio, it has become much harder to define such a reader (or audience) or to locate him or her, as Johnson did, in a socioeconomic class. The contemporary common reader—some call her the student—is the reader identified most strictly with the prevailing conventions of literacy. Even so, among Movement poets, there are important differences when it comes to the imagining of an audience. Davie, in *Articulate Energy,* argued that it was preferable that poets wrote as if there were a "contract" (sustained by grammatical syntax) between poet and reader (xiii). These readers were to be imagined, in Davie's words, as "civilized" people, and there has never been the sense in Davie's criticism that "specialists" or "professionals" or academics were to be excluded. But other appeals to a common reader have certainly demonstrated more hostility to "specialists" and professional literary critics. I have already quoted New Gen poet Dan Paterson describing the desirability of speaking directly to an audience, without the mediation of the academy or its criticism. Among the Movement poets, Philip Larkin is the poet who seems most prone to appealing to an audience for which the phrase "common reader" is something of a misnomer.

For Larkin, the common reader is not student nor literate man aware of the conventions of English verse so much as he is a caricatured lower middle-class individual suspicious of being duped and intent on speaking back to an academic elite. The common reader is Larkin himself, or the persona he appeals to, the reader "in the know" enough to understand what forms of literature mean to exclude or sucker him. Here is Larkin on modernism:

> All I am saying is that the term "modern," when applied to art, has a more than chronological meaning: it denotes a quality of irresponsibility peculiar to this century, known sometimes as modernism. . . . I

am sure that there are books in which the genesis of modernism is set out in full. My own theory is that it is related to an imbalance between the two tensions from which art springs: these are the tension between the artist and his material, and between the artist and his audience, and that in the last seventy-five years or so the second of these has slackened or even perished. In consequence the artist has become over-concerned with his material (hence an age of technical experiment) and, in isolation, has busied himself with the two principal themes of modernism, mystification and outrage. . . . [Larkin provides several colorful examples.] There has grown up a kind of critical journalism designed to put it over. The terms of the argument vary with the circumstances, but basically the message is: Don't trust your eyes, or ears, or understanding. They'll tell you this is ridiculous, or ugly, or meaningless. Don't believe them. You've got to work at this: after all, you don't expect to understand anything as important as art straight off, do you? I mean, this is pretty complex stuff: if you want to know how complex, I'm giving a course of ninety-six lectures at the local college, starting next week, and you'd be more than welcome. The whole thing's on the rates, you won't have to pay. (293)

It is sometimes difficult to know how much affectation is involved in Larkin's vulgar persona, as many have noted. The barbs here, though, the most savage of them directed at academic critics and teachers, make perfect sense. Or, rather, they make sense from within a consumerist logic holding that the audience, whatever audience, knows what it wants and is prepared to accept it. The supposed cult of technique among modernists would perhaps refer to imitators, readers and supporters of, say, Ezra Pound, who, as a polemicist for modernism, spoke most forcefully of artistic technique as a test of the seriousness and even "morality" of the artist. Like any other, Pound's seriousness, whether it be a devotion to the traditions of the art or a willingness to extend its possibilities in "experiment," can risk delusions of grandeur and solipsistic excess. But Larkin's suggestion that a modernist concern with experiment is being perpetuated as an academic conspiracy is altogether too simplistic. The lack of respect for the abilities of the British "everyman" is remarkable. However, populist complaint is effective, as Larkin's sales suggest.

In an essay on Pound, Donald Davie writes that "in our [British] national tradition, in the arts as until recently in sports, it is the amateur who is most admired." Davie was not altogether prepared to abandon such a tradition of amateurism, which depends upon the idea that "the practice of our art should *ideally* be an avocation rather than a vocation" (1979, 158–61). He traces the lineage of amateurism back through the bourgeois idea of "the gentleman" to the Italian aristocratic idea of the "courtier"— we must remember Alvarez's gentility here. As Christopher Ricks noted in a sometimes scathing review of the book in which Davie's essay appears, Davie's contrasting of amateurs and professionals is not especially grounded in examples. Speaking of Davie's own values, Ricks writes that "the idea of thesholds is crucial to Davie here, and he argues persuasively that below a certain threshold of competence a dedication to the artist as amateur may issue only in the slovenly and amateurish, and above such a threshold a dedication to the artist as professional may issue only in the facile and professional" (19). But here the words *amateur* and *professional* function more as codes for cultural values than as descriptions of the location of artists in institutions and practices. *Amateur* means the opposite of Pound's *serious* or *accomplished* more than it means the opposite of *professional.* In Auden's essay on American poetry, Davie's compatriot claimed that the British poet inevitably thinks of himself or herself as a "clerk," a member of a "professional brotherhood," whereas the American poet belongs to a "country of amateurs where the professional, that is to say, the man who claims authority as a member of an elite which knows the law in some field or other, is an object of distrust and resentment" (365–66). The American poet, Auden continues, will not be caught dead writing light verse, not unless he wants to give up the idea of seriousness, whereas the British poet, asked why he writes, will answer, "For fun." Auden's terms are a little more precise, though the level of generalization about national traditions is similar, and there is a hint of agreement on the question of whether the real opposition isn't between the serious and the unserious. More important, the characterization of the two nations is exactly reversed—Auden's Americans are in love with amateurs, Davie's Americans in love with experts and professionals. Auden's American poetry flows through and from Emerson, Thoreau, and Whitman in a nation mysterious to those trapped within the perspectives and values of a more settled Europe. Davie's American poetry flows from and through Pound and Olson in a nation whose cult of technique and professionalism functions as a reprimand to some of the British. But then Auden's view of the differences between the two poetries is more attuned to a pre–World War II moment; Davie's, to postwar institutional histories.

In order to determine why, comparatively speaking, the United States has been more receptive to innovative and self-consciously "experimental" poetries than Britain, one has to look at the shape of particular professions and institutions. As one British poet writes, there has been in Britain "a profession of letters since the late 17th century, with on the job training at various levels. The problem for poets is that there's been no market for poetry as a fresh commodity since the 1820s, but this just puts poetry at the point of contradiction between the writer as small producer and the writer as professional."[9] Responding to Davie's argument, he writes that Davie omits to mention that "the professions were always historically the safety valve for the gentry—younger sons." British poets will inevitably reject Davie's contrasting of professionals and amateurs—which was intended for an American audience anyway—because what Davie is talking about as a professionalized poetry is really poets and poetry accepted by and into the university. British poets cannot very often be "professionals" in this sense. Even if they are professors they have not been (until very recently) hired as poets, nor even (until recently, and even then in a limited way) as scholars or critics of contemporary poetry, and so they angrily hear Davie's distinction as one between (again) the real poet and the dilettante.

So the contrast worth making would be between markets for poetry. But here the university enters the picture again, as one institution among many (governmental grants agencies would be another) which must be discussed beside the question of the market for poetry. The size and diverse functions of the American university have allowed Americans to create and sustain an important and sizable audience for contemporary poetry and, significantly, for the criticism of contemporary poetry—"difficult" poetry of whatever variety typically prompting more explanation and exegesis than other poetry. Partly because of the economic prosperity of the United States since 1945, and partly because of the distinctive mission of universities in the United States (more of this in the next chapter), the United States has had universities capacious enough to allow creative writing programs (almost unheard of in Britain before the nineties) which teach "technique" and encourage a focus on recent writing to exist beside literature programs teaching literature and theory. While the relationship among subdisciplines has never been cozy, it has seen acknowledged contestants struggling for turf—and these struggles have regularly brought new alliances and relationships into being. In the American academy, there has been room enough, as Perelman writes, for an experimental writing to find a niche among theory, creative writing, literature, cultural studies, and composition studies. Poetry's study in universities is far from being solely responsible for the comparative success of "experimental" writing in the United States; I am not speaking so much of the production as the reception of such writing. But there's little question that the academy has historically been of more assistance to such writing here, easing its reception, than has been the case in Britain, where the power of other institutions governed by different kinds of elites and "specialists," by nonacademic professionals—BBC journalists, London's literary journalists—must also be a little more directly felt by practicing poets, for better or for worse. Necessarily, BBC commentators and literary journalists must remain a little more vulnerable to the immediate demands of the marketplace than university professionals—or at least this was the case until recently.

It is hardly an accident that, in a cold-war era, American literature, and with it American poetry, did a booming business in the academy. One aesthetic sanction is as good as another for some people, we might argue, thinking of modernist poetry and more recent academic regimes. But with the end of that era and the emergence of another one, it's anybody's guess what literature departments will look like. Will we see a postnational future articulated in an American curriculum? If so, what role will poetry have in such a curriculum? And British poetry—will we be able to read it again? Even in the most hopeful scenarios there is little reason to expect that poetry, much less British poetry, will occupy more than a small corner of academic study. It seems likely that, before long, American poets will be left to their own resources for audience building much in the way that British poets have been for some years now. It will be crucial for American poets to begin thinking about ways of building community— or else we will be left with the tired rhetoric of "common readers" and the reactionary agendas that often accompany it.[10] It was a revelation for this critic to see some of the first publications from American small presses in the wake of NEA cutbacks in the arts—they were thinner, more cheaply produced. They looked a lot like many of the books of British avant-garde poets. We're all in much the same boat now, it seems, British and American poets, avant-gardists and much of the so-called mainstream too, for that matter, fighting the brutal indifference of a world where technology and capital move at speeds that make the paltry theorizing of poets, scholars, and critics almost laughable in its belatedness. For those still listening to poetry, it seems only a small thing to try once again to begin to hear one another across increasingly irrelevant national boundaries. Only a perpetuation of the twin evils of boorishness and provincialism will keep British poetry what it has too often been in recent times in the United States—something between a joke and a nonentity.

2. England in America, America in England

Rereading *New Poets of England
and America* and British and
American Fifties Poetry

The American Half

No anthology of contemporary poetry published since World War II
has been as much vilified as Donald Hall, Robert Pack, and Louis Simpson's *New Poets of England and America* (1957). Especially as it is regularly
contrasted with Donald Allen's *The New American Poetry* (1960) in what
Jed Rasula has called the "repetition compulsion" (244) of recent literary history, *New Poets* has been made to seem representative of the poetic
values characteristic of the "mainstream" or "academic" poetry of the
1950s. Most readers of contemporary poetry are familiar with the charges
made against the anthology as it has come to stand for a whole realm of
poetic production in the fifties. Here was poetry, it is said, that timidly
retreated from the ambitions of modernist poetry. Here is poetry shaped
by a hegemonic New Criticism, responsive to the directives of its canon—
seven and not eight types of ambiguity; the wit, irony, and paradox of
English metaphysical poetry; Eliot without Pound; Auden's urbanity; the
polished forms of the well-wrought urn. Narrow turf, this canon, from
a time when in David Antin's words "the blight of Auden lay heavy on
the land" ("Modernism," 221). Here is a poetry, too, of a liberal political consensus, in the age of conformity, the age of criticism, the age of

the Organization Man, the age of Lonely Crowds and sociology, the age of anxieties which would be managed by an army of therapies calculated to help one adjust an upwardly mobile self to the age of "the age of."[1] Here is the poetry that poets wrote in universities and colleges as they sat comfortably in their suburban bungalows feeling neglected by something called a general public and watching with considerable trepidation the banal and distracting success of American mass culture at home and abroad, proud if pathetic in their resistance to what some viewed as a protototalitarian monolith. Here is poetry of travel, an enfeebled tradition of griffins and gargoyles, of Eurocentrism—a word not much in currency then—and especially Anglocentrism. In the fairly representative view of James Breslin, the "final impression" many took away from their reading of *New Poets of England and America* was a feeling that they had encountered "a sedate generation of poets . . . comfortable with each other, with their predecessors, with their audience, with their wives, their children, their professorships, their grants" (51).

I don't want so much to contest these characterizations as to complicate them a little. Probably the easiest way to do this would be to turn a particularist's exactions toward a close reading of individual poems in the anthology. But this is not the path that I want to pursue, not only because I think that there is some value in discussing generational tendencies and group aesthetics but also because this would defeat the purpose of exploring the subject that I want to comment upon here—the interface of British and American poetries in this anthology. Too much respect for differences among the poems in the anthology will altogether erode the concept of "nation," and as the deployment of that concept is one of the more intriguing aspects of *New Poets of England and America,* I want to be able to sustain the categories of British and American poetry. It is worth considering the way that "nation" figures in the book, in its construction as an anthology of poetry. The anthology was an American product which had its real impact in the United States, and its organization—the way the poets were displayed—implied a significant continuity between the British (or in this case, "English") and American poetry included in it, more continuity than may have actually been visible in the poems.

The first edition of *New Poets of England and America* organized its poets alphabetically without regard to nation of origin or residence. Robert Frost, who would read at the next presidential inauguration and whose first book had been published in England, wrote the book's introduction. By contrast, the second edition, published five years later in 1962 and equally an American product, grouped its British and American poets in separate sections, thereby implying that some distance had opened up between them. Or perhaps it is rather that the organization sought to *insert* some distance between them, or at least that it was worth considering the poets first within the nation, beside their compatriots. The second edition also had two introductions—Donald Hall introducing the British poets with a brief mock dialogue which softly and comically reprimanded Oxbridge publishing culture and the general lack of interest in modern poetry in England; some of Hall's complaints echo familiar charges against British poetry such as those made in the same year by A. Alvarez in his introduction to the British Penguin anthology *The New Poetry* (1962). Both introductions are nervous, defensive. Pack introduced the Americans and defended academic poetry and a recently expanded academic poetry audience against the attack on these we associate with the poets of Donald Allen's *The New American Poetry* (1960).

In pondering the space opened up between the poetry of the two nations as it is suggested by the organization of the second anthology, one would have to consider the different poets and poems included in the two editions—there are eighteen new British and eighteen new American poets in the second edition; seven British and nineteen American poets appearing in the first edition are dropped from the second, ostensibly because they no longer were under forty years of age. Developments in the poetry of both nations over the course of five years changed the second edition as well. The British section of the second edition includes Peter Redgrove and Edward Lucie-Smith, for instance, both of whom would have then been associated with Philip Hobsbaum's Group poets and their anthology, as well as Charles Tomlinson, who had early on attacked the Movement poets featured prominently in the first edition; the American section newly includes the confessional poets Sylvia Plath and Anne Sexton.[2] But even in the first edition the poetries of both nations are not so homogeneous as is sometimes assumed. The British poetry in the first edition was certainly dominated by Robert Conquest's *New Lines* poets, the Movement, but Jon Silkin was also included; he would have been associated with an anthology called *Mavericks* (1957), which had a neoromantic agenda distinctly opposed to the Movement. So was W. S. Graham, a Scottish poet typically associated with the forties neoromanticism the Movement had set out to vanquish. (It must be noted that both editions were vastly disproportionate in their representation of male to female poets, and oblivious of the presence of African-American and other minority poetries.)

To refer to Graham and Silkin, however, is to use the language of nuance, and the rhetoric of nation has little to do with nuance. Characterizing the fifties academic poetry *New Poets of England and America* is associated with, Jed Rasula has written that "the spectre of English verse, from the metaphysicals to Yeats and Auden, animates postwar poetry in a spectacularly ghoulish way, as if the American poet were little more than a wax mannequin outfitted with British couture" (9). But I'm not sure that Rasula's point is altogether supportable—that it is useful or productive to say that American academic or mainstream poetry in the fifties was "haunted by" British poetry. There were more important spectres. To ponder the interface of the two poetries one might do well to look beyond surface similarities in metrical forms and consider the cultural work the two poetries were performing, with attention first to the American side of things. I think that it can be shown that, whereas American "mainstream" poetry in the fifties participated in nation and empire building, the relationship of the British "mainstream" poetry in the anthology to British "national culture" is considerably more critical and complex. The difference between the organization of the two anthologies also allows us to see the extent to which an American "mainstream" was in motion in the late fifties and early sixties. If one edition mixed poets and the other sought to separate them by nation, what does that show us? Is it possible that it is not just Robert Pack's defensive introduction (in the second edition) that demonstrates the impact of Allen's *The New American Poetry* and its scorn for academies and Anglocentric canons, but also the very organization of the book?

I'd like to begin with the American half of the anthology, summarizing the account of Fifties mainstream poetry offered in two of the best histories of the period—Rasula's own *The American Poetry Wax Museum* (1996) and Robert von Hallberg's *American Poetry and Culture 1945–1980* (1985). These two studies are fundamentally opposed in their valuations of the American fifties poetry I am speaking of and in many other ways too, though they also share a good deal in their description of the geopolitical imperatives of the period. Oddly enough, they both also depend in small and different ways on the prose of Karl Shapiro, who offers von Hallberg his term *culture poetry,* poetry taking up questions of cultural identity beyond the self—von Hallberg seeks to rescue the term from Shapiro's scorn. Rasula makes Shapiro a mandarin voice underwriting his Baudrillardian thesis about the futility of speaking of "tradition" or "official culture" in the United States. Like Baudrillard, Shapiro believed that high culture in the European model has never been successfully transplanted to the United States: at best we have copies or simulacra, Rasula's wax museum. I'm not sure that von Hallberg would altogether dispute this claim, but it's clear that he does find much to admire in fifties academic poetry as well as in fifties academic culture itself, while Rasula has no use for this same poetry and is suspicious of the "administered" and administering nature of American academic culture as it assumed its place within American culture at large. Rasula's preference is for the New American poetry of Donald Allen's anthology, though more for the high seriousness of Robert Duncan and Charles Olson than for the "flamboyant hedonism" of the Beats, who seem to him like the confessional poets insofar as the models of subjectivity instantiated in their work represent for him a "late . . . efflorescence of the Puritan ego" (38).[3]

Let me begin with von Hallberg, and his defense of fifties academic poetry and an Arnoldian "tone of the center." Discussing the Marshall Plan and the new and increased military and economic power resulting from World War II, von Hallberg writes:

> Traditionally, Europeans had figured in American thought as guardians of the past; after the war America took over the military guardianship of Europe, and with it came a challenge: could Americans measure up culturally as well as they had militarily? We answered this challenge by assuming the outward signs of European tradition, the way one might undertake the administration of a museum—vigorously, ambitiously. Americans suddenly recognized a new relationship not just to their past but to the entire history of the West. (3)

There's not a whole lot Rasula would disagree with in this description of the goals and rhetoric of the American center in the fifties; we also hear in his book of "an evident need to consolidate a sense of tradition—which in American cultural life meant a justification of the new political superiority of the United States in world affairs" (148). But the term *vigorously*—one of von Hallberg's favorites—Rasula would surely reject, as in his view the strategies and goals of the would-be guardians are little more than ineffectual pantomime in a consumerist culture. "Culture brokers," he writes, "artificially tone up the tradition by exposing literature to the critical equivalent of ultraviolet sun lamps" (2). There is perhaps a milder form of Rasula's skepticism about the ability of Americans to assume European models in von Hallberg's phrase "outward signs." That fifties academic poetry in the United States "assumed the outward signs" of European tradition does not mean that it prostrated itself before Europe or assumed European values, or even that it was, in the now fashionable term, *Eurocentric*. A better term for this American poetry and its culture is *Atlanticist*, as I will shortly explain.

Partly because von Hallberg is concerned primarily with subject matter and tone, and with the politics *in* rather than the politics *of* fifties academic poetry, he finds the poetry of John Hollander, Charles Gullans, Turner Cassity, Richard Wilbur, and others of value for its work in nation building, and for its self-consciously sophisticated and urbane mode of address as it took up, in his words, "the most consequential ideas of the time" —the responsibilities of imperium among others. Against the charge that the fifties poetry he admires is "narrowly academic," von Hallberg writes, "to the extent that poets looked to universities for an audience, they were addressing an audience with an explicit commitment to the most consequential ideas of the time. Another way of putting this is to say that such poets . . . were in the honorable tradition of addressing the audience that felt greatest responsibility for the refinement of taste and the preservation of national culture" (34). This framework not only commits von Hallberg to a focus on subject matter and tone; it also requires him to defend contemporaneity as an evaluative standard, and he does that early in the book. And to the degree that American universities and colleges did become increasingly central to American life in the three decades following World War II—some would argue that this is less and less the case today—von Hallberg's sense that these poets were engaged with *consequential* ideas is entirely defensible. Moreover, his suggestion that these poets were concerned with the "refinement of taste"—and here he is remembering widespread concern among intellectuals about the encroachments of mass culture as well as longstanding European complaints about the vulgarity and gadget-mindedness of Americans—also seems accurate. But it is precisely here—on this matter of taste as well as, to a lesser extent, with this idea that "preserving" a national culture is important—that Rasula attempts to speak to the limits of fifties academic poetry and academic culture.

What Rasula finds particularly damaging about the liberal consensus of the fifties is its "concession of priority to administrative protocols" (125). Sounding here more like Adorno than Baudrillard, he writes that "the deeper issue behind the academization of poets was the dramatically escalated administration of everyday life—or of 'culture' in several senses, high, low, and middlebrow" (125). For him fifties academic poets were "the boy in the bubble," expected to do little more than "produce raw data for the managerial class assigned to look after" poetry—namely, academic critics (137). Writing of the American poets of *New Poets of England and America,* he notes that these writers, unlike their New Critical poet-critic predecessors and their New American poetry contemporaries, were abstemious "in the matter of poetics: the New Poets appealed, instead, to *taste*" (241–42). Robert Duncan is cited to suggest that the business of poetry must involve something more than the refinement of sensibilities, the sophistication of the nation (if I may be allowed the jingle): "Taste can be imposed, but love and knowledge are conditions that life imposes upon us if we would come into her melodies" (242). Rasula has other complaints about this poetry too—that it assumed that poetry was "emphatically and resolutely . . . an art of reference and representation," that "what was asserted in the poem was the articulated intentionality of 'the speaker,' a figure of sensibility, perceptual resourcefulness, and determinate contours," that this poetry's return to formal structures primarily associated with English or European poetry was fatuously represented as "experiment." He won't accept von Hallberg's unstated assumption that poems should be "*about* a demonstrable subject matter," and he is more insistent in raising issues of form and the politics of form (203).

But I want to linger for a moment on Rasula's claim that "mainstream formalists mistakenly presumed that the classroom"—as opposed to the manifesto, mock manifesto, journal or article—"was a suitable place for elucidating their poetics" (245). He's certainly right about the comparative paucity of critical prose among these poets, something which distinguishes them, by the way, from English counterparts such as Donald Davie. Some first edition "new poets," like John Hollander, were also scholars, others like Reed Whittemore critics and editors of poetry journals such as *Furioso,* but the absence of prose (except for the introduction) in the anthology itself, as well as the nature of the prose published by these poets, does distinguish them from the poets of Donald Allen's anthology.[4] But then poets writing in more conventional forms might very well feel less need to write prose to educate their audience; new to the academy and precariously situated there the point was less to challenge current practice than to prove one's competence within it. I hope that Rasula doesn't mean to ridicule pedagogy itself, which can be an important part of the cultural work done by poets on behalf of poetry, as Ezra Pound would attest. The New American contemporaries of these poets, like Olson and Creeley, might have started outside of universities, but universities—or individuals working in them—have been instrumental in promoting and publicizing their work and have employed some of them who have, at times, initiated programs and counterdiscourses the academy constantly requires as it attempts to make use of a purported avant-garde as oil in the machine. Fifties "mainstream" poets might be evaluated not for choosing to do much of their work in the classroom but for the nature of the pedagogy they participated in.

When von Hallberg discusses fifties academic poetry like that published in *New Poets of England and America* he sometimes uses the phrase "minor poetry." He takes it from Pound, just as he takes the idea that poetry can offer an "aesthetic sanction" for national policy from T. S. Eliot. Minor poetry, he writes, is "one of the more reliable indices of the cultural level of a nation," instantiating "minimal standards of taste" (23). For von Hallberg, the university is properly concerned with such standards. As long as we insist that we are talking about "minor" poetry—he is a little slippery here—von Hallberg has no less an avant-garde bohemian experimentalist than Kenneth Rexroth on his side when he speaks of the value of fifties academic poetry and culture. Here's Rexroth:

> There is nothing objectionable about a bureaucratic literature, given a bureaucratic society. It was good that to get a job as a minor executive in the postal service of imperial China you had to turn out a respectable essay on a passage in the Classics and a conventional poem. Some of the best poets of China in the great ages of its literature were generals and statesmen, and almost all were what we would call civil-service employees. America would be a better place if every army officer, postmaster, sanitary engineer, or industrialist, could turn out a nice poem when he took his wife and kiddies for a picnic by the reservoir. This is the long-term objective of academic poetry, of the thousands of courses of creative writing. I have never understood why my colleagues resent it when I point this out. (131)

Despite his sarcasm, Rexroth is serious here, and he is also right that one of the early if not often admitted rationales for creative writing courses—you can see it in some of Reed Whittemore's fifties prose, for instance—was the cultivation of sensibility, which went hand in hand with the New Critics' desire to create an audience for modernist poetry practically *ex nihilo.*[5] Given his skepticism about such agendas, it is not especially surprising that Rasula's objection to the academic poetry of the fifties merges rather easily with his critiques of therapeutic self-expression in the growing workshop culture of the seventies and eighties and with the logics and programs of so-called universal education itself.[6]

The accumulated force of Rasula's critique in *The American Poetry Wax Museum* is surely meant to serve the interests of Robert Duncan, Charles Olson, language poetry, and other avant-garde poetries, but in the end it reminds me most of Wyndham Lewis—rather than imagining alternative modes of incorporating creative writing and contemporary poetry into American institutional life, he lets loose with a guffaw designed to dismiss not just the particular incarnations of academic poetry culture we have known but also the possibility that any "administered" curricula might represent positive change. The practice of Duncan and others, as Rasula notes, does not represent merely another "taste" in poetry but a rejection of taste itself as some understood it—as in "good taste" or "refined taste." However, if the ends of poetry are understood to involve knowledge, or mystery, or meaning, or critique, or Duncan's "life," there is no reason that the teaching of poetry and poetry writing in the university cannot be adjusted to accommodate these ends.

Before the master of fine arts degree really took off, contemporary American poetry and working poets entered American colleges and universities as part of undergraduate and general education. Seamus Heaney once told me that, at Harvard, the powers-that-be still work pretty hard to keep him away from graduate students; prestigious universities still are the most reluctant to mix "creative writing" with scholarship. Closer to the period we are discussing, Reed Whittemore suggested that "Mostly the writers . . . appear to be teachers. Having a writer in the barn is one way for a college to drum up trade. Aside from his merits or demerits as an educator a writer is a useful person to photograph and describe as a 'creative influence' in the college's brochures; and when and if he gets published anyplace he also spreads the college's name around on his own in a small way. Colleges have become increasingly aware over the last couple of decades that they *are* business organizations" (255). Whittemore's position is accommodationist—he reluctantly accepts the existing hierarchies within the English department and the university—but it is also critical of these same hierarchies. As Whittemore knew, there was considerable anxiety in being viewed as an ornament rather than as a knowledge producer. Such anxiety surely accounts for the hyperspecialization and relentlessly narrow focus on (established) "poetic technique" that has bedeviled writing programs as poets in universities have sought professional credentials centered in their ability to transmit knowledge about "craft"—which, in practice, often means little more than socializing one into the "good taste" required to proffer spurious judgments of student work. Too rarely have poets challenged the hierarchies of knowledge on display within the university and the blunt and subtle functionalisms that survive to this day.

Discussing postwar American educational paradigms and the weaknesses as well as the possibilities of a multiculturalist paradigm that is now taking its place, the historian Michael Geyer reminds us that

> the rise of the American university system is obviously a complex process that cannot be folded neatly into one educational project. But crucial to the success of the American university as institution—its very foundation—is the merger between general and higher education. The consequences of this merger go a long way toward explaining the near-unique place universities and colleges have achieved in the modern era. In contrast to continental European universities, their autonomy is not the result of an unequivocal mission, the production of knowledge. Rather, it is a result of their "border" position in society. As knowledge producers the universities and colleges began [after 1945] to reach into the higher echelons of the federal executive as well as large corporations, educating the professionals and serving the growing institutional appetite for expertise. . . . Simultaneously, they reached deep into society as educators, providing the avenue of upward mobility for a broadening middle class. (504–5)

In the widespread agreement on the importance of general education in the postwar era Geyer locates a national ideal that is both actively engineered—Rasula would say "administered"—and Atlanticist. But the subtler points of his essay involve the "border" position of American universities—their functions apart from "the production of knowledge." Not too much has changed in this regard since the fifties, he seems to say, even as a multiculturalist paradigm has (mostly) replaced Atlanticism, and some of the other missions of the university have been taken over by different institutions and media. The blindnesses of Atlanticist education—its neglect of questions of race, class, and gender, among others—have been replaced by other, parallel ones. For instance, too often, he writes, contemporary multiculturalism "imagine[s] a spatial or social autonomy of cultural zones," inventing " 'whole' and often wholesome communities" (516) with which to critique existing social conditions in the United States, exactly as a distorted and overly homogenized picture of the glories of European culture was earlier created to reform American life, to prepare crass Americans for world citizenship. Some forms of multicultural education are every bit as guilty as their Atlanticist predecessors of studying "the past in order to offer it as an antidote to the present" rather than taking the "destruction, dissolution, and radical transformation" of cultures as "the actual subject of history" (516).

Geyer admires not the character but the accomplishments—the power —of Atlanticist education, its ability to create a picture of Europe which might transform America while not forgetting that such transformation (not just of America but also of the world) was after all its raison d'être. It actually enabled, he argues, what radicals dreamt of in the sixties, an "Atlanticist consensus, which in holding together a democracy pulled into its orbit the 'Western' world." Rather than reinscribing European models, he suggests, this was an education of "transatlantic synthesis" (509–10). Even as it "linked American norms and values back to a European past," it projected these onto a "global stage with a Solon, like FDR, or an atomic Pericles, like JFK, as their embodiments." The "subject" of this education, Geyer writes, was the nation, its "object" the world (506–7). This is a different view of academic culture than the one we get in Rasula's book, where the term *academic* is nearly synonymous with "ineffectual"—Geyer is more respectful, if only of the power of the monster. (We will hear later of awe-inspiring monsters.) Fifties academic poets, I think it's plain to see, are implicated in this Atlanticist educational paradigm, with all of its successes and failures. This was a distinctly American paradigm, the "product of a tense and highly problematic modernist fusion of technological progressivism and neoclassicism"—to quote Geyer yet again.

By now it will seem that I have left far behind the British poetry included in *New Poets of England and America*. In speaking of it, one would do well to consider its place within the United Kingdom itself, a very different matter than the role it might be said to have played within an American poetry anthology. In considering the interface of British and American poetry in the anthology, Rasula's suggestion that the American academic poetry of the fifties was somehow haunted by, or laboring under the influence of British poetry, is not helpful. It is true, W. H. Auden was an immense presence; half a generation imitated the mannerisms of his poetry; his work as editor of anthologies and judge for the Yale younger poets series in the early and midfifties made his influence pervasive. But Auden was in the United States, as previously Eliot had been in England, and the symbolism of this cannot be ignored. My quarrel with Rasula is a matter of emphasis: what might an *American* Auden have meant? Rasula writes that "the American modernists had all notoriously sought to found an American art on a European basis, exporting themselves and their art in the process; but it was Auden who was prepared to reverse the trend, demonstrating to Americans how to import a poetry culture, much as horticulturalists imported French vine stock to get the California wine industry going. The sense of tradition he elucidated turned out to be British" (148). But just as California wines are not exactly French wines, the tradition that emerged in the wake of Auden was not a British tradition exactly but an *Americanized* British tradition. British tradition was no longer the master tradition: Auden would be made *one of us*. It would be closer to the truth to say that, temporarily perhaps, it seemed—in the first edition of *New Poets* especially—that British poetry had been altogether absorbed into American poetry. Frost's introduction, "Maturity No Object," is all about boys and girls in American colleges; he promises them that "maturity will come" (11) and hopes for their sake that they'll find a Landor among them, an "old age writing" which would "grace our history" (11). One came after the British like a child after its father—replacing him.

But there was little oedipal anxiety involved, I think. Rather, the anxiety, as Whittemore suggests, involved the poet's role within an institution whose ideological ends had become transparent to all. Fifties mainstream poets weren't dupes, and they weren't "haunted" by British poetry. After 1957 it was possible just to *assume* British poetry, rather as a footnote in the history of American poetry. No longer struggling to emerge from its shadow, taking British poetry for granted, we could afford to ignore it, as all evidence suggests we pretty much have since. If then, in 1962, we set it apart again, it was only to condescend to it, to display it as a curio. No doubt the editors of these anthologies had no conscious intent in this regard, despite the organization of the first edition. But it's helpful to remember that this first edition appeared the year after Britain's Suez fiasco, when the United States publicly upbraided and embarrassed Britain after its pathetic, late-colonial aggression in Egypt. There, in the geopolitical arena, as in the anthology itself, it was clear who was calling the shots, and whose version of "tradition" mattered. Frost's introduction did not so much as mention the British.

If the notorious little englandism of the Movement poets was present in *New Poets,* as it surely was in Philip Larkin's famous "At Grass" and Donald Davie's "Homage to William Cowper"—"For Horror starts, like Charity, at home" (53)—it is also the case that such poetry suited an American

Atlanticist culture perfectly. The very first poem in the anthology was Kingsley Amis's "Masters." This was a poem that meant somewhat ambivalently to celebrate a small, submissive self as it might be distinguished from the stoic authority of a British public sphere, where to a large extent discourse still reflected and perpetuated aristocratic values, especially in matters of "culture." Amis's poem was very much responsive to shifting class demographics in England. And yet it's tempting to read it as a poem about the new realities of global power:

> By yielding mastery the will is freed,
> For it is by surrender that we live,
> And we are taken if we wish to give,
> Are needed if we need.

One can imagine a boorish and confident American reader thinking, "It's nice to have a humble and polite pet to show around the mall."

Unlike von Hallberg, and like Rasula, I don't take a great deal of pleasure in reading fifties academic poetry, especially the American variety. Nevertheless, I don't think that we can afford to ignore or caricature it, exactly because it helped set the terms for the most powerful poetic and educational orthodoxy we have yet seen in the postwar world. Moreover, with regard to the relationship of American and British poetry, this fifties academic poetry has had profound consequences. In absorbing British poetry into its particular orbit, *New Poets of England and America,* the first edition especially, has too often afforded some of us an excuse to ignore British poetry altogether, or at least to limit our engagement with it to the poetry of the Movement and its most obvious successors, and to read even that poetry unself-consciously through American lenses. It will always be difficult, of course, *not* to do this. But one way that we can begin to have a better perspective on British poetry is to restore to it some of its full complexity and diversity. Other British poetries ignored or marginalized by *New Poets*—not only those which might have affinities with the poetry of Allen's *The New American Poetry* (Gael Turnbull, Roy Fisher, Elaine Feinstein, Christopher Middleton), but also work which has its origins in the romanticism of the forties—has remained comparatively invisible in the United States. The effectiveness of Donald Allen's *The New American Poetry* in undressing the emperor of Atlanticism and fifties academic poetry is apparent in the second edition of *New Poets of England and America,* with its condescending introduction by Donald Hall and its separation of the two poetries. But one of the most unfortunate aspects of the anthology wars of the period was the way that they contributed to the common opinion in America that nothing of great consequence was happening in British poetry, nor was likely to soon.

The British Half

World War II transformed Britain overnight from a military, political, and economic power to a nearly bankrupt nation. There was the destruction of four million houses and much of the industrial base and a massive war debt which would be repaid only years later; there was the loss of export markets to the United States and Canada. Britain's economy had been in decline throughout the century, and hanging on to empire—even with the independence of India, Pakistan, and Burma in 1947—diverted funds for recovery and reconstruction until the final withdrawal from East of Suez in the early seventies. Nevertheless, Britain was not altogether lacking in the prosperity we associate with the United States in the fifties; after immediate postwar austerity Britain's gross domestic product rose by 2.6 percent per annum throughout the decade.

The war had other consequences that many, intellectuals in particular, would have found positive too. The nearly total war effort—except for Russia, no belligerent put more man- and womanpower into the struggle —restored a patriotism if not altogether missing then latent in intellectual culture for thirty years. In wartime industries and the army, social classes came into greater contact, helping to prepare the way for what Harold Perkin calls a society "more equal and caring" than Britain had previously known. The war saw civil service jobs nearly double as well as the creation of the Committee for the Encouragement of Music and Arts, parent of the Arts Council. The 1944 Butler Education Act expanded access to higher education. There was, in general, a "revolution of expectations" (409) that helped pave the way for the welfare state and greater fluidity among the classes, so much so that, by 1958—the year of the Notting Hill riots—race rather than class seemed to some to be the most pressing problem confronting British political and civic life.[7]

One of the more provocative essays of the period concerning dominant trends among British intellectuals was authored by sociologist Edward Shils, who had an appointment at the London School of Economics after 1946. Shils notes that one of the effects of the loss of empire was an enhanced sense of national identity among intellectuals, a feeling that "the nation seemed to be cleaner and more worthy of being embraced when it was divested of its immoral imperial appurtenances" (141–42). But the shrinking of oppositional politics and the growth of consensus values in the early years of the welfare state was accompanied, writes Shils, by

> the vindication of the culture associated with the aristocracy and gentry, and its restoration, in the decade following World War II, to preeminence among the guiding stars of the intellectuals. All English society had undergone this process of submission to the moral and cultural— but not the political or economic—ascendancy of the aristocracy and gentry. (144)

What is "provocative" about this statement is its separation of cultural authority from economic and political systems. British intellectuals of the fifties, he argues, typically found neither the thirties Left of Auden nor the thirties Right of Wyndham Lewis viable options, nor "the business-man's Dissenting culture of the nineteenth and early twentieth century— the culture which founded the modern universities, the musical and literary institutions of the provinces." For evidence of a "surrender of the British bourgeoisie to its upper-class antagonists," Shils offers an account of "sons sent to Oxford or Cambridge, or into the army as professional officers, themselves removed southward and Londonward, the Chapel renounced for the Church" (144). Such an analysis has all of the schematic virtues of the decade's ascendant intellectual discipline—sociology. But it also is blunt and unsubtle. For our purposes it might explain the Tory nostalgia of John Betjeman and its popularity, but it hardly offers us an adequate picture of the cultural forces at work in the dominant British poetry of the fifties—the Movement poetry which gathered the weight of group identity in Robert Conquest's anthology *New Lines*.

Much has been written about the Movement by its detractors and supporters, by onlookers and participants. In 1959 Donald Davie, who together with Amis, Philip Larkin, Elizabeth Jennings, John Wain, and (briefly) Thom Gunn, was among the group's poets and surely its most influential critic, was able to publish an article entitled "Remembering the Movement." More fascinating than Davie's echoing of by then familiar complaints about the Movement's philistinism and insular little englandism and his identification of stylistic conventions that amounted to "craven defensiveness" and "inert gestures of social adaptiveness" was his apparent need to write such an essay to begin with. He was then thirty-seven years old; *New Lines* had been out just three years; and here was

Davie beginning his brief essay by writing that "I've been thinking for some time that I ought to set down my recollections and impressions of the last few years, so far as they may amount to a chapter of literary history" (72). Some would say that there is no end to the hubris of poets, but I would argue that Davie's article shows how completely Movement poetry was saturated with the values of academic culture. Only literary scholars, after all, are especially interested in "chapters" of literary history. That a professionalized, industrious study of contemporary literature was perhaps a little slower in making its way into British universities than into their American counterparts is not the fault of the Movement poets, some of them dons themselves, and many of them capable of equating F. R. Leavis's "minority culture" or common reader with the culture of dons. Indeed, Davie's article shows him thinking about poetry as dons of his generation did: poetic production becomes meaningful as it enters into narratives of literary "history," into periods which thereby contain it. This is an overt concession to what Randall Jarrell once called "The Age of Criticism," where criticism and scholarship trumps poetry and begins not so much to follow as to lead it. It must also be read, however, as a deeply ironized "concession," for the very title of the essay alludes to Davie's much-anthologized poem "Remembering the Thirties," which had been included in the Hall-Pack-Simpson anthology and had as its opening stanza lines directly pertinent to both the culture of dons and the premature memorializing of Movement activities: "Hearing one saga, we enact the next. / We please our elders when we sit enthralled; / But then they're puzzled; and at last they're vexed / To have their youth so avidly recalled." The poem is both brash in insisting on generational difference and the irrelevance of a would-be heroic past, and finally a little craven too—self-hating perhaps—in stating that "A neutral tone is nowadays preferred. / And yet it may be better, if we must, / To find the stance impressive and absurd / Than not to see the hero for the dust" (51–52).

What Davie's ability to *publish* such an article also shows us is the *success* of the Movement, which was, as Blake Morrison has demonstrated, not at first due to academic culture but rather to the ability of Movement poets to circumvent small literary quarterlies and gain access to the larger audiences of the BBC's Third Programme, the *Spectator,* and the *Times Literary Supplement.* Secondary and higher education would follow later, solidifying a canon of contemporary poetry in Britain that has remained far more stable than its counterpart in the United States. In 1980 Frank

Kermode wrote of the Movement that "their anti-modernist position is still strongly held, their resistance to innovation in the novel and poetry may even have increased, and a native tradition is not so much something one argues for as what is taken for granted, like a fact of nature" (1980, 6).

In his book on the Movement, Blake Morrison writes that "the identification of the Movement with a wider class-struggle was one reason why the group established itself so quickly in the years 1953–55: it gave them the advantage of seeming to represent a newly empowered class, and it helped them to define themselves in opposition to the 'haut-bourgeois' 1930s generation" (58). Many Movement poets had lower middle-class backgrounds, and memory of their class origins as well as regional identities are important parts of their poetry. It would be wrong, though, Morrison argues, to think that class consciousness in their work is undivided or unambivalent, just as it would be wrong to take their Leavis-like complaints about the corruption of the old boy network of the London metropolis at face value. Morrison continues:

> What emerges in the work of the Movement, then, is an uneasy combination of class-consciousness and acceptance of class division; an acute awareness of privilege, but an eventual submission to the structure which makes it possible. On the one hand, the Movement writers were identified with a view-point hostile to the "old order." They resented social inequality, and were not so credulous as to suppose that it had been eliminated as a result of wartime Coalition and post-war Labour government reform. Oxford and Cambridge—as Amis explains—still seemed to them to be riddled with class prejudice: "A few provincials might have got in because of the vulgar recency of their subjects, or as egalitarian window-dressing, but the main outline fitted with my early picture—of British culture as the property of some sort of exclusive club." On the other hand, the "club" which the Movement writers resented was one in which they had succeeded in joining. . . . As spokesmen for the new self-proclaimed lower-middle-class intelligentsia, the Movement was forced into an ambivalent position: on the one hand opposed to the "old order"; on the other hand, indebted to, and respectful towards, its institutions. (74–75)

In postwar British academic culture we begin to see a little movement towards what Michael Geyer identifies as the border position of American colleges and universities, but this movement was slow and halting, a matter of the newer and provincial universities still dwarfed by Oxford and Cambridge, where, as Amis knew, class consciousness still powerfully organized life. Edward Shils would point to what's in the "other hand" in this passage of Morrison's as an indication of the ultimate triumph of British aristocratic-gentry "culture" (if not "politics") in the fifties.

Sociology is not a discipline skillful at mapping the conflicts and boundaries of an ambivalent self, and indeed—as I will argue momentarily with reference to a critique of Movement poetry authored by Andrew Crozier—the ability to instantiate such a self as the center of poetic value is one of the lasting accomplishments (for better or worse) of Movement poetry as it countered the legacies of modernism and forties neoromanticism both. If we are content to examine the way that this poetry presented and operated within empirical models of the relationship of self and world, one can find real affinities between Movement poetry and fifties American "academic" poetry, similarities which defy differences between class structures in the United States and Britain or between a newly confident global power and a nation deprived of its empire and struggling to imagine the moral force of a native tradition. That is, the British and American poets in *New Poets* work with much the same model of poetic expression, though idioms will vary and within the predominance of "traditional" meters used to carry and support this expression one will find varieties of more or less metaphorical and plain-style writing. But it can be argued that the similarity among models disguises a difference in content, tone, and motivation. One would not want to confuse the soft ecstasies of Richard Wilbur's baroque pastoralism—"tell them there's something new / To see in Rome . . . What is praise or pride / But to imagine excellence, and try to make it?" (336)—with Larkin's bitterness: "Yet still they leave us holding wretched stalks / of disappointment" (170).

But I am getting ahead of myself here. Having subjected Kingsley Amis's "Masters" to a willful decontextualization, it is time that I quoted the entirety of the poem in an effort to restore something of the British context which it emerged from:

> That horse whose rider fears to jump will fall,
> Riflemen miss if orders sound unsure;
> They only are secure who seem secure;
>   Who lose their voice, lose all.
>
> Those whom heredity or guns have made
> Masters, must show it by a common speech;

Expected words in the same tone from each
  Will always be obeyed.

Likewise with stance, with gestures, and with face;
No more than mouth need move when words are said,
No more than hand to strike, or point ahead;
  Like slaves, limbs learn their place.

In triumph as in mutiny unmoved,
These make their public act their private good,
Their words in lounge or courtroom understood,
  But themselves never loved.

The eyes that will not look, the twitching cheek,
The hands that sketch what mouth would fear to own,
These only make us known, and we are known
  Only as we are weak:

By yielding mastery the will is freed,
For it is by surrender that we live,
And we are taken if we wish to give,
  Are needed if we need.

(13)

"Masters" is aphoristic, a series of moralizing propositions articulated in a plain style heavy with parallel constructions. Neo-Augustan "common speech" is here ceremonial, formal, dominated by the collective pronoun. But, in its content at least, if not its form, the poem will later seem to identify the limits of this mode of public utterance. The poem's opening figures—horse and rider, riflemen—express familiar wisdom about equestrian and military discipline, but they also function as emblems for an aristocratic culture whose authority is the product of "heredity" or "guns." Whatever subtlety this poem has to offer in its early stanzas will be, as it were, snuck in the back door, hinted at matter-of-factly within the pounding iambs and stately syntax. "Guns" suggests something other than "heredity" both in its reference to violence and its location in a more colloquial idiom, though this is hardly to be noticed, a mere chipping away at the sound of sense. By the end of the third stanza an irony which begins to undermine the balanced sentences and the orderly quatrains will become more overt, but "slaves" too is smuggled in via simile. Careful, semantically loaded rhymes set up neat opposites or highlight key elements in the propositional discourse—secure/unsure, all/fall, made/obeyed, speech/each. Until the off-rhyme at the close of the fourth stanza, and despite the two more or less buried ironic moments mentioned above, the poem seems a veritable apology for the stoic and impersonal culture of the gentry, a handbook in aristocratic mannerliness. "Expected words" are ritualized words, "common" because they do not bear the imprint of idiosyncratic desire. Public and private worlds are collapsed into one; civic duty must always already match the "private good" of the individual. This can be the case, of course, only for those who in some sense occupy and define the public sphere, and not for those at odds with it. The public sphere is the site of power, of "mastery," where "twitching cheeks" and downcast eyes only reveal weakness, needfulness.

All of this changes, though, after the colon, in the last stanza about yielding mastery; this stanza is the most opaque of the poem. The moral is visible enough: expressing need allows us to be needed; "surrender" creates possibilities for an intimacy and love which discipline and ritual will not allow. But who is it exactly who is to yield mastery? Is it the "we" who are "weak" and "known" in the previous stanza or is it the culture of "heredity" identified in the second stanza? The final stanza can be read as suggesting that a ceding of the public sphere to aristocratic values frees those outside of the governing and otherwise culturally powerful classes to pursue their private concerns within a stable, orderly society. Pity those who must shoulder the responsibilities of the collective good, this reading seems to say, for they cannot be loved as others can be loved. But of course it can be said that the weak have never known "mastery" and thus have nothing to "yield"—that they yield *to* mastery but have no mastery to yield. The alternative reading, where those who have inherited mastery will yield it, makes the poem a sentimental hymn to an egalitarian society, to a welfare state of mutual helpfulness and greater intimacy between the classes. That the poem cannot easily be read one way or another, that its earlier clarity collapses into such opacity might or might not have been intended, like the small ironies mentioned above, to keep the poem from becoming altogether platitudinous. It's close to that already, though, and if the difficulty of the last stanza almost saves the poem it is probably the result of the uncertainty of the social changes the poem means, indirectly, to address, more than of Amis's finesse. If, as Blake Morrison argues, Amis was fairly ambivalent about British political developments in the fifties (later, like other Movement poets, he would drift to the Right), the ending of this poem manifests that ambivalence in an ambiguity that creeps into its neo-Augustan syntax like a dangling modifier stuck on the end of your best student's paper.

In Andrew Crozier's critique of the Movement and its shaping of the British canon up through the present, he writes that "the high regard for regular rhyme and stanza displayed throughout *New Lines* does not engage notions of finish, of the polished object; the poems are not discrete events in the sense that they correspond as such to their discrete occasions. They are discrete, rather, in the way they wrap around their author-subject." The language of "discrete polished objects" here must allude to objectivist poetry, such as George Oppen's *Discrete Series,* even while within a specifically British context Crozier is concerned to show how models of subjectivity instantiated in Movement poetry were effective not only in warding off American modernists like Oppen but also in displacing modernist and romantic values present in the forties poetry of W. S. Graham, David Gascoyne, J. F. Hendry, and Dylan Thomas. Concluding his essay, Crozier writes:

> In the poetic tradition now dominant the authoritative self, discoursing in a world of banal, empirically derived objects and relations, depends on its employment of metaphor and simile for poetic vitality. These figures are conceptually subordinate to the empirical reality of self and objects, yet they constitute the nature of the poem. Poets are now praised above all else as inventors of figures—as rhetoricians, in fact—with a consequent narrowing of our range of appropriate response. Poetry has been turned into a reserve for small verbal thrills, a daring little frill round the hem of normal discourse; objects and relations in the natural and social worlds have an unresistant, token presence; at its most extreme, they serve as pretexts for bravura display. It does not wish to influence the reader's perceptions and feelings in the lived world: its intersection with that world is attenuated and discourages reading back; transformation is confined within the surprises and routines of rhetoric. (229–30)

Crozier's critique of the "authoritative self" is in keeping with Jed Rasula's suggestion that fifties academic poetry in the United States articulated the "intentionality of 'the speaker,' a figure of sensibility, perceptual resourcefulness, and determinate contours" (203). Moreover, just as in Rasula's case this model of subjectivity in poetry obtains across a continuum, with the baroque, Empsonian figures of Richard Wilbur on one end and the vatic howls of Allen Ginsberg on the other, it hardly matters to Crozier that what he says here of Movement poetry equally applies to Ted Hughes, Seamus Heaney, Craig Raine, or other "mainstream" British poets who have won some success more recently. Donald Davie has criticized Ted Hughes's poetry for holding up the poet's ingenuity for celebration, but for Crozier, apparently, it is simply not an issue whether the self at the center of the poem is flamboyant, ascetic, moralizing, uncertain, or anguished, so long as it is *some* convention of a bounded, determinate, authentic "self" on which the poem depends for its authority.[8]

It is hard to disagree with this analysis insofar as it describes much postwar "mainstream" poetry (on both sides of the Atlantic) and distinguishes it from various modernist and postmodernist poetries. The "guiding and controlling presence of a speaking subject constructing the poem's framework of interpretation around its personal authority" (228) — to cite another of Crozier's descriptions of Movement poetry — is surely a characteristic of the Amis poem discussed above, even as it finally is most interesting for its possibly inept loss of control. And the description of period conventions relating to poetic subjectivity has both heuristic and polemical value. But such global maps of poetry do not allow us to discriminate among poems in terms of their treatment of particular subject matters, or in terms of their effectiveness within the set of conventions described. As John Koethe has argued with reference to American language poetry of the seventies and eighties, a poetry which explicitly rejects Crozier's "controlling presence of a speaking subject," the act of "Rejecting naturalistic conceptions of expression and Cartesian accounts of the self in favor of views that argue for the social constitution of these notions may involve a reorientation of one's attitude toward them, but should not prevent one from exploring and exploiting all the expressive possibilities afforded by language, however socially constituted these may be" (71). If the question is the Movement aesthetic's success in blotting out poetic practices prior to or contemporary with it, then we are talking about something to regret, I think. But if the question is conventions of subjectivity in poetry, then I think that we must at least endeavor to determine which poetry written within the (now very tired) conventions associated with the empirical self is most successful. To his credit, Crozier does not begrudge Larkin his fame (as one might, for instance, Amis, on the basis of "Masters," anyway.)

When we ponder the interface of British and American poetries in the fifties, as evident in *New Poets of England and America,* the terms Crozier advances against the Movement aesthetic can apply equally well to the poetry of Americans such as Anthony Hecht, Richard Wilbur, James

Merrill, and Edgar Bowers. You will find the same models of subjectivity and the same use of canonical metrical forms in these poets as in Movement poets. You will find, perhaps, more range of opinion with regard to the virtues of the plain style—Bowers being an advocate of such a style (thanks to his apprenticeship with Yvor Winters), Wilbur and Merrill, not. You will find urbanity and von Hallberg's "tone of the center" in poets of both nations. But you will not find in many of the Americans that particular mode of irony I have called *ambivalence* isolated in my reading of Amis's "Masters." The ambivalent or uncertain self (however controlling of poetic utterance) in Movement poetry is the product of both geopolitical realities and cultural tensions specific to Britain. What could a poet like Bowers, writing of the destruction of World War II, have to do with these?

> How quietly in ruined state
> The effigy of Charles the Great
> Wastes in the rain! Baton and orb,
> The rigid figure and the crown,
> Tarnished by air and wet, absorb
> His change, impassive in renown.
>
> Northward along the Rhine, towns lie
> Shattered by vague artillery:
> Julich, Düren, whose Rathaus doors
> The molten eagles seal, effaced,
> Like Gladbach's partial walls and floors,
> By snow impersonal as waste.
>
> The South's white cities, terrible
> With sensuous calm and beauty, fall
> Through darkness to their fragrant streets.
> France's smooth armor seeps her blood.
> The European plain repeats
> Its ageless night of ice and mud.
>
> Despair shall rise. The dragon's gore
> From off the torn cathedral floor
> Forces his mind's dark cavity:
> His sleep has been his innocence,
> And his malignant growth shall be
> Monstered by lucid violence.

(35–36)

Here we have "the Roman feeling," to use another of von Hallberg's phrases. The poet looks on the destruction of postwar Europe as an outsider, slightly bemused by the monuments to past European glories. The possibilities of the resurrection of the "dragon" — of an old, prewar Europe — are dismissed with the promise of "lucid violence." Americans are their own monster now, as the poem's most inventive verb suggests. But the poem is cold and confident. No Betjemanian nostalgia here for the old regime, no Movement ambivalence or uncertainty about changes underway. Bowers knows the future, and knows that it is American. Is it any wonder, then, as Edward Shils noticed, that for the British intellectual it was sometimes the case that "patriotism in this atmosphere was nurtured by anti-Americanism" (142)? Official governmental policy and the active alliances in NATO and elsewhere were one thing. "Culture" was another.

3. Uncovering, Recovering
British Modernisms in Poetry

British Americans

In 1925 British-born modernist poet Mina Loy, then living in Paris, published in the American magazine *Charm* a brief article entitled "Modern Poetry." Linking poetry with music, and more especially modern poetry with jazz, Loy begins with a definition: "Poetry is prose bewitched, a music made of visual thoughts, the sound of an idea." If we are to understand modern poetry, she writes, if the "infinitesimal" public of modern poetry might become the more "universal" public of jazz, readers must "obliterate the cold barrier of print" and learn to read not just with the eye but also with the ear: "More than to read poetry we must listen to poetry." Poetry is "the movement that an active individuality makes in expressing itself," its rhythms the "chart of a temperament," and modern poetry has "more than vindicated the rebellion against tradition" in adjusting itself to a new "way of life": "Would not his [the modern poet's] meter depend on his way of life, would it not form itself, without having recourse to traditional, remembered, or accepted forms?" A new poetry, then, in its "evocation of speech," depends upon a new world, in this case a modern "way of life" more "spontaneous" in its "movement." It is no surprise, Loy thinks, that a "renaissance of poetry should proceed out of America, where latterly a thousand languages have been born, and each one, for purposes of communication at least, English—English enriched and variegated with the grammatical structure and voice-inflection of many races, in novel alloy with the fundamental time-is-money idiom of the United States, discovered by the newspaper cartoonists." Two agendas in the article collapse into one — justifying modernist poetry as the most adequate response to the new rhythms of everyday life, and insisting that the only truly "modern" everyday life is in some way essentially American. The article proceeds to sketch the outlines and major figures of modern American poetry. "To speak of the modern movement" is to speak of Ezra Pound, for without this "masterly impresario" the modern movement "would still be rather a nebula than the constellation it has become." E. E. Cummings, H. D., Maxwell Bodenheim, Marianne Moore, Lawrence Vail, and William Carlos Williams are mentioned and briefly discussed. No matter where the American poet may wander, Loy writes, there occurs no "Europeanization" of the American's "New World consciousness" (1996, 157–61).

My concern here is not parsing among Loy's comments to identify a poetic — speech-based, expressivist, performative — or in tracing the origins of her synaesthetic discourse. Instead, I mean merely to note that Loy's brief article belongs to a centuries-old and still powerful European discourse identifying the United States as the site of true modernity. Sometimes with condescension, sometimes with honest admiration, and almost always with a critical eye on their own national cultures, Europeans from Tocqueville through Marinetti, Duchamp, and Baudrillard have made claims like Baudrillard's in *America*: "The confrontation between America and Europe reveals not so much a *rapprochement* as a distortion, an unbridgeable rift. There isn't just a gap between us, but a whole chasm of modernity. You are born modern, you do not become so" (73). No doubt many Europeans would take exception — would make themselves exceptions — to such a sweeping, rhetorical claim; certainly Loy thought of herself as "modern" before she thought of herself (or became) "American." From our positions this late in the century, suspicious not just of the revolutionary but of the future itself, it is difficult to understand such enthusiasm about a renaissance in American culture, but that enthusiasm is deeply embedded in modernisms that predate a nativist turn in American literature and the post–World War II international marketing of an American Century. Ezra Pound's *Patria Mia* (1913) eagerly advanced Pound's belief in and program for such a renaissance, reading America's immigrant "mongrel" population — he understands "one stock" as neutralizing "the forces of the other" and argues that climate has "as much to do with the characteristics of a people as their ethnology"—as a productive (though also fearful) turbulence, a chaos which might be resolved in a new and truly modern cultural donation (102–3).[1]

Not that European enthusiasm concerning the United States was without considerable ambivalence. Americans are no longer the caricatured infants Wyndham Lewis wrote of in *The Enemy* in 1928 in a vituperative attack on D. H. Lawrence and the "widely-held notion in Europe that the American is a kind of baby-man" (24). Such condescension is the flipside of European enthusiasm. With reference to H. L. Mencken's *Americana* and the fiction of Sherwood Anderson, Lewis diagnosed a range of American ills from inferiority complexes to sexual impotence, fantastically naming them as the source of a post-Poundian nativism emerging in American literature as well as of the European "neo-barbarism" (9) of Lawrence's *Mornings in Mexico,* which seemed to embrace the Americas.[2] Lewis was to exhibit some greater degree of optimism about American culture in the later book *America and Cosmic Man* (1948), where he admits to being surprised that many different races and peoples manage to exist side by side in the United States without (for the most part) killing one another as they had been wont to do in Europe for centuries. But that book, published in 1948, is, like Baudrillard's more recent book, intended as a critique of the irrelevance and weakness of European culture under a Pax Americana, and like Baudrillard it is more attuned to geopolitical economic realities. Between the earliest years of the century and the Second World War European intellectuals have had to move from celebrating (or bemoaning) United States culture as a fashion to accepting it as inevitable and dominant.

Like many other British poets in this century, Mina Loy had good, practical reasons to believe in the United States as the preeminent site of modern poetry, and of modernism itself. Her work was championed early by Alfred Kreymborg's *Others* and Allan and Louise Norton's *Rogue.* Her first book, *Lunar Baedecker* [sic], was published by the Contact Publishing Company, run by Americans; she would not publish another until in 1957 Jonathan Williams's North Carolina-based Jargon Books brought out *Lunar Baedeker and Time-Tables.* Her foremost critics and supporters over the decades—including Pound, Williams, Kenneth Rexroth, Gertrude Stein, Yvor Winters, Djuna Barnes—were mostly Americans. In this way she helped inaugurate what has become almost a "tradition" wherein British "innovative" poets in this century have looked to the United States for publishers and readers as well as for poetic models. Basil Bunting's second book—a small, first book was printed privately in Milan—was published in America in 1950; he would not have a British publisher until 1965. Until late in his life Bunting's most important friends and contacts in poetry were the Americans Pound, Zukofsky, and Williams. Moving into the generation which began publishing after World War II, we find poets such as Charles Tomlinson, who has professed his debt to Americans and American poetry in *Some Americans* (1981); Jonathan Griffin, whose *Collected Poems* (1989) were published in Maine by the National Poetry Foundation; and Tom Raworth, whose long poem *Writing* (1982) was published in Berkeley by the Figures. There are others like Gael Turnbull who have not depended quite so heavily on American presses and Americans but who have found inspiration in American poetry and some of their most enthusiastic readers among Americans. And there are those like Loy who, originally British citizens, have eventually come to live more or less permanently in the United States—Denise Levertov, Nathaniel Tarn, Christopher Middleton, Thom Gunn, and David Bromige. Loy is often read as an American poet, as the title of the first book-length study of her work indicates. Even W. H. Auden, together with Thomas Hardy, perhaps the most influential English poet of the century, came to America, where he compared the experience of reading American poetry to the "unforgettable experience" of a "plane journey by night across the United States" (358). In return the British have had T. S. Eliot to claim, or at least the T. S. Eliot of *The Use of Poetry and the Use of Criticism* (1933) and other later poems and essays.

The cumulative force of these and other examples of the attractiveness of the United States for innovative British poets is considerable. There can be little doubt that as we have neared the end of the century the hyphen in "Anglo-American" has come to seem increasingly strained in discussions of much modernist and postmodernist poetry. Indeed, the phrase *Anglo-American tradition*, when it is used at all, now seems to be used more often than not in the United States to indicate a conservative reaction to the most challenging modern poetry, an anglophiliac, academic culture, mostly centered in New England and affecting a sophistication and gentility easily parodied. We might call Eliot "Anglo-American"—but not often Pound or Williams or Stein. Since the New Criticism began to lose its hold on academic literary study in the 1960s, fewer anthologies have continued what used to be a fairly regular practice of printing modern and contemporary poetry by British and American poets side by side. In criticism and scholarship as well as in the minds of some of the most exciting younger poets, a version of modernist poetry dominated by Pound and Eliot has been replaced by another dominated by Pound and Williams; more recently an explosion of alternative modernisms focused on Gertrude Stein, Laura Riding, Mina Loy, H. D., Langston Hughes, and others neither American nor British by birth has made "modernism" an intensely contested word and concept. Few poets or critics today would feel moved to speak as Eliot did in 1953, when he stated that "English and American poetry can help each other, and contribute towards the endless renovation of both." Americans might agree with Eliot that "the pioneers of twentieth century poetry were more conspicuously the Americans than the English" (1991, 59) and some Americans might agree that "a satisfactory statement of what constitutes the difference between an American and English 'tradition'" will be impossible to produce (60). But Eliot's claim that American and British poetry might equally nourish one another will now seem to many a quaint product of an Atlanticist cold-war consensus culture with those embarrassing anglophiliac excesses alluded to above.

In this same talk, Eliot hinted that the direction of influence in modern poetry might be subject to change. Eliot thought that Auden and others of his circle had, in the thirties, become every bit as important to poets on both sides of the Atlantic as he and Pound had been earlier. And there is little doubt that Auden's work did indeed assert a considerable influence on many poets who followed him, on both sides of the Atlantic—on James Merrill, Richard Howard, and John Hollander as much as Donald Davie. But for many post–World War II British and American poets, particularly those either a part of or sympathetic to the poetry of Donald Allen's *The New American Poetry* anthology, and also to succeeding generations of self-consciously "experimental" poets, Auden's poetry seems perched on a fault line that emerged in the thirties. On the one hand, the thirties saw the emergence of a number of poets, dominated by but not limited to the Auden circle, who have come to represent a retreat from modernist poetry —poets such as the New Critics John Crowe Ransom and Allen Tate, the British neo-metaphysical poet William Empson, proletarian poets in both nations, and others. In greater or lesser degree, not only the British Movement poets of the fifties but also Americans such as Richard Wilbur and many others can be associated with a range of influences that began to emerge in the thirties, in the neo-Augustanism of Auden, in the more willfully Thomistic and antimodernist prose of Yvor Winters, in the prescriptions of the New Critics. On the other hand, the thirties also saw the considerably less heralded emergence of other poets, more intent on extending and revising the modernist practice of Pound, Williams, Eliot, Stevens, and Moore, as well as of Europeans such as Apollinaire; these poets include not just the Objectivist poets Louis Zukofsky, Charles Reznikoff, George Oppen, and Carl Rakosi but also others harder to categorize such as Charles Henri Ford and Muriel Rukeyser. Among the British we might think of as extending various modernist poetries in directions other than those established by Auden, names from the thirties are less familiar: Bunting, perhaps Charles Madge, others now mostly forgotten. It cannot be surprising that, among British poets who would resist the dominant tendencies of British poetry in recent years, uncovering or recovering some of the poetries obliterated by the success of Auden and his circle should be a project of some importance — and one to which I hope to contribute here.

For many readers the opposition between poets pushing on and others satisfied to retreat from a Poundian or Eliotic modernism is not only familiar but crude. Crude or not, though, the distinctions that seemed to emerge in the thirties have had considerable impact on the poetry that has followed. I will offer just one example for the moment. In his introduction to a recent anthology of British poetry, *A Various Art* (1987), Andrew Crozier writes that "one of the means by which many of the poets in this anthology were identifiable to one another was an interest in a particular aspect of post-war American poetry, and the tradition that lay behind it — not that of Pound and Eliot but that of Pound and Williams" (12). Pound and Williams rather than Pound and Eliot — given the now legendary tensions among these three men this is an odd distinction that only begins to gather whatever coherence it may have if we ponder the emergence of Objectivist poetry in the thirties, a subject long of interest to Crozier, who has been instrumental in collecting and promoting the work of one of the Objectivists, Carl Rakosi. (Eliot was included in Zukofsky's *An "Objectivists" Anthology,* but he was not a part of the special number of *Poetry* which gave a name to the group of poets we today associate with Objectivist poetry, and he seems to have had comparatively little use for poets such as Zukofsky and Oppen.) The notion of a Pound-Williams tradition distinct from a Pound-Eliot tradition alludes to or understands the latter, perhaps, as a product of F. R. Leavis's *New Bearings in English Poetry* (1932), a revolutionary book for its time but deeply limited by its identification of a Poundian modernism with *Hugh Selwyn Mauberley* rather than the *Cantos* and its bizarre faith in Ronald Bottrall's poetry as embodying the future of modernism. The distinction between Pound-Eliot and Pound-Williams becomes more credible with the interest taken in Objectivist poetry by New American poets such as Robert Creeley, Robert Duncan, Charles Olson, and others in the fifties, and still more credible with the second flowering of Objectivist writing itself in the sixties. It is typically thought of—this Pound-Williams tradition which becomes clarified in Objectivism—as specifically American (despite Zukofsky's interest in Apollinaire, the cosmopolitanism of Pound, and other matters that complicate such a designation) in ways that a Pound-Eliot tradition is not, with its debt to symbolist poetry on the one hand and its neo-Augustan progeny like Auden on the other. Of course this Pound-Williams, Pound-Eliot distinction, however meaningful to poets, obviously simplifies matters a great deal, splitting Pound down the middle and suggesting in not so subtle ways that, from the thirties on, the bulk of innovative poetry has been written in America.

In what follows I mean to introduce to American readers some neglected poets who belong to various British modernisms, but I want to begin by exploring a little that moment when the distinction between a Pound-Eliot and a Pound-Williams tradition first came into being—the moment of the emergence of Objectivist poetry. As I have been hinting above, it seems to me that the struggle in the 1930s to construct a viable tradition of modernist poetry, and the concurrent efforts to write a literary history of first-generation modernist poetry which might support then current practices, had profound consequences on the poetry of the next thirty years, even if the success of Auden and later the Movement in Britain and Robert Lowell, Richard Wilbur, Randall Jarrell, and others in the United States temporarily obscured these consequences. I want to focus not so much on Objectivism itself as the British poetry contemporary with it, paying particular attention to the reception that British poetry received in *Poetry,* by then very much an established magazine, and also the magazine which first brought significant attention to American Objectivist poetry. By reviewing *Poetry'*s encounters with British poetry in the early and middle thirties, we can follow an early, modernist effort to bring a post-Poundian British poetry to the attention of American readers.

American Critics and British Poets

It was not always the case that Americans (or Britons!) could write confidently of the United States having assumed the leadership in twentieth-century poetry. Loy's comments in 1925 or Eliot's in 1953 need to be read beside others demonstrating less confidence about the status of American poetry on the world stage, lest we take an American rhetoric about the separation of the "two poetries" at face value (as we too commonly do). One might consider Conrad Aiken's collection of essays and reviews *Scepticisms* (1919), which was written at least in part as a gentle response to the nativist "Americanism" of a survey of American poetry authored by the influential academic critic and anthologist Louis Untermeyer. Aiken's tastes are broad and eclectic. He is capable of writing on behalf of the modernism of Pound, Eliot, Moore, and others when he sees Untermeyer denigrating it in the name of the "American content" of Edgar Lee Masters, Robert Frost, Amy Lowell, Carl Sandburg, or Lola Ridge. Against Untermeyer he will take up what he understands to be an "aesthetic" position: "I do mean that Mr. Untermeyer allows nationalistic and sociological considerations to play an equal part with the aesthetic. To put it curtly, he likes poetry with a message—poetry which is politically, from his viewpoint, on the right side. Surely he must perceive the shortsightedness and essential viciousness of this?" (264). We get what is in effect an attack on then contemporary "political correctness" from a promodernist critic. For Aiken, modernism is understood as "international." But while he is a sympathetic reader, Aiken is not altogether convinced by the poetry of the modernists, and his book self-consciously resists the bellicose posturing of Pound just as it resists the critical evaluations of Untermeyer and Amy Lowell. One essay attacks Pound's prose as full of "sterling platitudes and the most brazen quackeries," calling it "ugliness and awkwardness incarnate" (139), and throughout the book Aiken is at best cautiously approving of the accomplishments of American modernist poets up through 1919.

> Experiment is the order of the day. Desperation to say the last word, to go farthest, to dissolve [British] tradition and principle in the most brilliant self-consciousness, has led to literary pranks and freaks without number. Occasionally this has borne good results, more often it has merely startled. . . . [There follows an attack on the imagists.] Our poets have not quite found themselves. They are casting about for something, they do not know what, and have not found it. And more than anything else it is this fact that gives their work that unfinished, hurried quality, impatient and restless, rapidly unselective, which makes it appear, beside English work, lacking in distinction. (63)

Some of the key terms in a modernist lexicon are already established here—*experiment* is neatly opposed to *tradition*—and yet Aiken seems to fear that modernism may collapse into the programmatic pursuit of shock for shock's sake, without producing work of lasting value, of "distinction." It is, rather, the English who represent "distinction."

Throughout *Scepticisms* the English are used by Aiken as a more traditional other against which American modernism might be defined, and Aiken obviously respects a number of British poets who are not much valued anymore—the narrative poet John Masefield, onetime poet laureate, the lyric poets Frederic Manning and Robert Nichols. Walter de la Mare is praised, and *Georgian* is not a term of opprobrium. In a discussion of the poetry of Harold Monro, Aiken expands on his sense of the differences between contemporary American and British poetry:

> Despite the fact that Mr. Monro manifests a slight orientation in a new direction, we may say that these poets [Ralph Hodgson, Walter de la Mare, and Monro], like most contemporary English poets, hold more or less surely to the main poetic tradition, in particular as concerns the theory that lyric poetry is a decorative rather than an interpretive art, and that its affair should be, primarily, the search for the modulation of beauty, with or without regard to its nearness to human experience. The result is that from a purely literary viewpoint English poetry of the present day is much more perfectly finished, much maturer, than American poetry. On the other hand, it loses proportionately by this very fact. By comparison with contemporary American poetry,—which is more empirical, drawing more boldly on the material of a wider consciousness, without so sharp a literary distinction between the poetic and the non-poetic, and more richly experimental as concerns questions of form,—English poetry appears at once thinner and more "literary." (215)

Ezra Pound's attack on ornament in "A Retrospect" (included in the volume whose prose Aiken attacks in *Scepticisms*) and on decorative rather than heuristic uses of metaphor, Mina Loy's insistence that poetry respond to contemporary life, the rejection of clear divisions between poetry and prose, or poetic and nonpoetic materials, the abandonment of an idea of poetic form as requiring "perfect finish" and the "modulation of beauty" —these and other familiar modernist articles of faith are articulated by Aiken in a series of binary oppositions that can be reduced to the opposition American/English. Against the experimental—think of Pound's and Eliot's fascination with the languages of science—we have the merely "literary," or, more often, the "traditional." Against the bold and the inclusive, we have something that is "thin," an unambitious poetry, mere verse.

This modernist attack was solidified in the thirties by the New Criticism, in books such as Cleanth Brooks's *Modern Poetry and the Tradition* (1939). But if the contrast between interpretive and decorative metaphor should be very familiar to us by this point, Aiken's suggestion that "some sort of fusion of the two methods" is required—fusion between American and English—is less so. Who today would speak out for Masefield and Hodgson against Pound, Eliot, Williams, and Moore?

But *Scepticisms* was written before the publication of such modernist poems as *Hugh Selwyn Mauberley* (1920), *The Waste Land* (1922), and *Spring and All* (1923), the first two of these being especially important to a modernist canon emerging in both Britain and America in the late twenties and early thirties. No less important, it was written before the criticism of I. A. Richards, F. R. Leavis, and William Empson had begun to upset "a country in love with amateurs . . . where the incompetent have such beautiful manners, and the personalities are so fragile and charming, that one cannot bear to injure their feelings by the introduction of competent criticism," as Pound had written in introducing Ford Madox Ford's "prose tradition in verse" in 1914. By the early thirties Ford's poetry was still thought revolutionary, unappreciated, or relevant enough to the future of modernist poetry that Basil Bunting could lead with it in an issue of *Poetry* designed to stand beside the Objectivists' issue of the same journal. Pound, like Leavis and others, was busy writing his version of the literary history of the early part of the century. While still playing the impresario from afar, Pound was busy memorializing a past. For him, the thirties was also a decade of obituaries—of A. R. Orage, Harold Monro, Ford himself—and of revisiting the work of companions from the past such as Wyndham Lewis. Even polemics aimed at the present, such as *Guide to Kulchur* (1938), sometimes slip into a self-celebrating nostalgia.

Some of Pound's memorializing prose was published in Eliot's *Criterion*, even though Eliot himself was regularly subjected to Pound's attacks on his by then considerable reputation. In the preface to his *Active Anthology* (1933), designed to introduce Zukofsky, Williams, Moore, Oppen, Bunting, and others to the British, and in *Polite Essays* (1937), Pound chipped away at the reputation of Eliot, which was in part the result of praise from Richards, Leavis, and others. Reading both the obituaries and the gentle if persistent attacks on Eliot one hears how Harold Monro came round to know something "five years after he had been told" (40), how Monro's "more-esteemed [English] contemporaries have gone on for twenty years in unconsciousness and will die ultimately in their darkness" (4). One hears of literary "gangs" (7) and of "the methods of post-Victorian British literary politics," including Edmund Gosse's efforts to prevent *La Revue des Deux Mondes* from reviewing James Joyce's *Ulysses* (5). In short, we begin to have constructed for us a literary history in which Pound, Lewis, Joyce, Ford, and other, lesser figures—Orage, Monro, and others—are heroic innovators confronting the vast and powerful miasma of British ignorance.

Today this version of that era is preserved for us most influentially in Hugh Kenner's books, such as *The Pound Era* (1971) and *A Sinking Island* (1987). The story of the initial success and ultimate failure of Pound and Lewis's Vorticism has become a kind of paradigmatic example of the hostility to modernism in England, and it is much better known to American scholars and poets than other important stories—for instance the efforts of Edith Sitwell to promote a Steinian modernism just a few years later, or the career of the British publisher, poet, and novelist John Rodker. Kenner has always been brilliant at impersonating Pound, the origin of many of his stories and of what one might call a Pound-centric modernism. Among the many consequences of this monumentalized version of literary modernism is a tendency to perpetuate a view of not just some but nearly all British writers as hopelessly benighted. Oracular pronouncements such as the following from the preface to the *Active Anthology* are abundant in Pound's prose in the thirties: "I believe that Britain, in rejecting certain facts (facts, not opinions) in 1912–1915 entered a stale decade" (149). Such pronouncements have become something like gospel, and my point is not only that they are merely "opinion" but also that we should not let Pound's anti-British rhetoric obscure the extent to which he was still very much interested in and engaged with the British literary scene as late as the thirties, still hopeful for change there.

That is, the rhetoric of his fragmentary efforts at literary history cannot be separated from the performative function it surely intended. The *Active Anthology* itself was meant to introduce poems "Britain has not accepted" (135) and to counteract "Mr. Eliot's condescensions to the demands of British serial publications" (144). If he could be critical of Eliot's activities, Pound could be much more enthusiastic about other developments in England. In the same year that the *Active Anthology* appeared, Pound wrote in an open letter to *Poetry* that "in so far as *Cambridge Left* is the most promising young magazine that has reached me from England (since I should think 1909 or 1914) or from anywhere for some time, I am disposed to repeat another warning: America *had* a chance to take over leadership in publication of writings in our common tongue, and to lose her colonial-mindedness, and I am inclined to think she is about to surrender it" (354). Pound's admiration for this journal is mixed up with his disappointment in the United States, with his sense that it had not lived up to his early utopian hopes for it—but it surely jars when set beside the chauvinism of his other contemporaneous pronouncements on British culture.

In looking for a second generation of writers who might extend the modernist initiative as he understood it, Pound was prepared to make the rounds of the nations again, and other Americans, including one of the editors at *Poetry*, Morton Dauwen Zabel, were ready to join him. We know less about this intervention or interventions of its kind—which typically involve individuals and personal contacts—than we do about the more global celebrations or dismissals of American or British poetry, by Pound or by others. And yet literary influence and literary movements are made in the modern world as much person by person, via direct contact and active encouragement, as they are made by the effective dissemination of some aesthetic or political platform in hortatory prose. To put it another way: productive dialogue between British and American poets in this century has been the work of individual friendships—Bunting and Zukofsky; Dorn and Davie, Raworth, and Prynne; Burroughs and Mottram; Tomlinson and Moore—even if these must always be read against larger cultural and economic forces at work in both nations.

By the early thirties, *Poetry* was among Pound's diminishing number of publishers in the United States. At *Poetry* Pound had more influence than Eliot, who would return to the United States in 1932 to deliver at Harvard what was to become *The Use of Poetry and the Use of Criticism* (1933), lectures proceeding as if Anglo-American relations were wholly unproblematical, as if there were but one tradition dominated by the English canon he was promoting. Pound's renewed interest in British poetry in the thirties has little to do with evaluations of Coleridge or Dryden or arguments with I. A. Richards—Eliot's concerns—and everything to do with his desire to *push* the British in a direction he could follow. Pound was in dialogue with a few men in Britain whose work he valued, but he was not (as Eliot was) part of "the scene." His periodic enthusiasm might very well have been read as the bothersome commentary of an interloper, and so too the remarks of *Poetry*'s subeditor Morton Dauwen Zabel, who in 1931 proclaimed a "new dawn" in British poetry to an American audience. (There is no evidence that Zabel's remarks were so much as noticed in Britain.)

Zabel's belief in a poetic renaissance in Britain was based upon three things: the emergence of a criticism he respected, the birth of several magazines with strong editors competing with one another and with the powerful influence of Eliot's *Criterion,* and three poets, two of whom it is possible to call "Poundian"—Basil Bunting and Joseph Gordon Macleod. (W. H. Auden was the third.) With the exception of I. A. Richards, the British critics Zabel admired—Empson, Leavis, Geoffrey Grigson, and Michael Roberts—each contributed in one form or another to *Poetry* between 1930 and 1937, largely thanks to Zabel. These critics are a disparate group, not uniformly devoted to modernism and even less so to a Poundian modernism. The magazines Zabel admired included Empson and J. Bronowski's short-lived *Experiment,* Leavis's *Scrutiny,* and Grigson's *New Verse.* He also found *The Twentieth Century, Cambridge Left,* and *Seed* worthy of mention (1933, 350). He thought enough of recent British poetry to give over two issues of the magazine to introducing British poets, the first in 1932 including poets gathered by Bunting and Roberts, the second in 1937 edited by Auden and Roberts. The "new dawn" itself was first proclaimed in a review of Joseph Gordon Macleod's *The Ecliptic* (1930), in which Zabel argued that "authentic poetry is present, in several degrees, in the recent work of three Englishmen—Macleod, Auden, and Bunting—who not only reproach, by their courage, most English literary endeavor of the past thirty years, but possibly give the direction by which English poets of the coming decade may be guided (1931, 37). Here was an American editor prepared to tell the British how to go about their business. He still imagined that their business mattered to Americans.

British Poetic Modernism in *Poetry*: Zabel, Pound, Leavis, Empson, and Bunting

Before I look more closely at some of the evidence upon which Zabel's enthusiasm concerning recent events in Britain was based—at Macleod's poetry—I want to outline his view of the history of British poetry between 1910 and 1930. Never much impressed with modern British poetry, Zabel nevertheless begins in 1931 with some small measure of respect for English tradition, and for several poets outside of the Pound-Lewis-Ford Vorticist group:

> The English tradition needs no apology; few histories equal it in continuity and vigor. But few sights are more dismal than the subjugation,

by self-appointed dictators, of original talent to that tradition. Clamped down like a lid, it has been for all but four or five Georgians since the dawn of 1911 a tradition massive, untested, and defeating. . . . It has humored into somnolence the early vigor of Masefield, barely tolerated Miss Sitwell's brighter side, canonized Blunden and Abercrombie, and threatened with court-action or deportation the few poets and novelists who raised a challenge. (1931, 36)

Save for its admiration for the earlier poetry of John Masefield and Edith Sitwell—important exceptions, I think—this passage might have been written by Pound or Basil Bunting, though Georgian poetry is referred to in tones remarkably neutral. Those "threatened with court-action or deportation" are Pound and the Vorticists probably, but the respect accorded Edith Sitwell seems to remember that her work as poet and editor of the journal *Wheels* was a "manifestation in England of a reaction against the Georgian hegemony, the first at least that originated with English poets and caught the attention of the literary public" (428), to quote the historian David Perkins. This view of modern British poetry is a little less Pound-centric than one Zabel would subscribe to just a few years later.

Pound's British friend and associate Basil Bunting never had much use for Masefield, and in the early thirties he drafted (but could not publish) a poem probably attacking Edith Sitwell as the Stein-influenced, free-verse poet of *Façade:*

Gertie Gitana's hymn to waltzing,
come to think of it, that's the goods.
You, thirdrate muse, Polymnia-alias-Echo,
who'll foster our offspring,
begotten in Waterloo Road three-and-sixpenny bed-and-breakfast
between indifference and bad habit
established by Erasmus and other idiots
nuts on the classics?[3]

"Who'll foster our offspring" might be translated as "What will become of poetry given its current state?" Since *Façade* contains poems designed for performance, poems in the rhythms of polkas, fox trots, waltzes, and other popular music and meant for accompaniment, Bunting's "hymn to waltzing" seems to point to Sitwell. Keeping a masculine and heroic distance from such theatricalism, Bunting's poem moves through remedies for the despair that such poetry produces in him—and for the cultural malaise that he thinks gives birth to it. (For all of their bouncy rhythms, Sitwell's poems do not hide what David Perkins calls a "fundamental despair" [431].) Bunting's poem concludes with a nasty remark about "Gertie's" head being stuck in the gas oven. Clearly, he did not relish the idea that the popular mode of Sitwell seemed at the time the only viable alternative to a cult of traditionalism; neither the "idiots" nor Sitwell were likely to counter widespread indifference to poetry. Many would find this unfair both to Sitwell herself—if my attribution is correct—and to the possibilities of mixed-genre performance with which Sitwell was experimenting.[4] I mention the poem here to show the force of opinion Zabel would contend with as he began more seriously to engage British poetry.

Two years after writing the above passage with its small measure of respect for Masefield and Sitwell, Zabel published another that lumped everyone outside the Vorticist circle together—the notorious J. C. Squire, consummate amateur, pillar of the literary establishment and vociferous critic of *The Waste Land; Hugh Selwyn Mauberley*'s token English middle-brow Arnold Bennett; and one or both of the Sitwells—in a "gangdom":

> The past two years have witnessed in England a revival of activity in both creative and critical fields that begins to threaten the proportions of another twentieth-century Renaissance. This revival doubtless profits by contrast with the aimless optimism and cheery ineptitude into which recent English letters have been guided by post-war Georgian patriarchs. Yet it should be remembered that England, in the days of Imagism, *The Egoist, Blast,* and *The New Age,* was a battleground for many of the ideas and projects that lie at the center of the creative problem in modern Anglo-Saxon culture, even though the Georgian dynasty succeeded in running them out of the country once *The London Mercury* and the Squire-Bennett-Sitwell gangdom gained the ascendant. (1933, 346)

This is the kind of polemic one utters when the object is to beat the drum for something. In this case Zabel means to stir up the memory of old hatreds on behalf of a new avant-garde. When he wants to suggest that England might be prepared to rerun the movie of Pound's modernist revolution twenty years after its first screening, England and the United States join in a totality called "modern Anglo-Saxon culture." When he wants to bemoan the failure of that first revolution to sustain itself— an ominous precedent, one would think—he speaks as an enlightened American ridiculing the benighted English. A changed opinion of Sitwell might be explained as the result of Bunting or Pound, though one must consider that Zabel had also read Leavis's *New Bearings in English Poetry*, which had viciously attacked the Sitwells as "belonging to the history of publicity rather than poetry" (73).

When Pound persuaded Zabel and Harriet Monroe that a British number would complement Zukofsky's Objectivists number (though he privately suspected that the British number would be inferior), it was Bunting who was first asked to edit it.[5] Bunting's pessimism cannot have bolstered Zabel's confidence in his British renaissance. "There is no poetry in England, none with any relation to the life of the country," his essay in the special number began. Whereas "the rulers of the United States" might be indifferent to literature, in England the powerful "have been actively hostile": "They have even set up and encouraged the frivolous imbecilities of cat-poetry, bird-poetry, flower-poetry; country-house Jorrocks-cum-clippership poetry (as Mr. Masefield does it); country-family cleverness (the Sitwells); and innumerable other devices for obscuring any work that smells of that objectionable quality, truth" (264). When Bunting contrasts "active hostility" in Britain with indifference to poetry in the United States, he must be referring to the effects of an official culture, to the power of institutions such as the poet laureateship, then held by Masefield. Two years later, in 1934, F. R. Leavis reported in an open letter to *Poetry* that "His majesty the King has decided to award a Gold and Silver medal yearly for poetry written by British citizens" (98). A committee had been formed to find the best first or second books by poets under thirty-five. This kind of ceremonial interest in poetry—poetry exploited for its symbolic value to the nation—Bunting thought promoted mediocrity. Clipper-ship poems and late Georgian pastoral verse are easily exploited in the politics of nostalgia. Whatever the cause, the result, for Bunting, was that "men of good but not specifically literary intelligence conceive a contempt for poetry" (264).

If there is one motif that dominates the letters and notes of *Poetry*'s British correspondents between 1932 and 1937, it is concern about modern poetry's audience, and the British correspondents without exception believe that the situation of poetry in the United States is much more hopeful than the situation of poetry in Britain. Writing polemics very much like those he would publish in *Scrutiny*, Leavis complained about the lack of a "serious" public for poetry beyond one that knew the names of a few poets, read the BBC's cultural organ *The Listener*, and believed that contemporary poetry "would be a creditable thing to have" (98).

He thought that England had no journal as good as *The New Republic*. William Empson, a few years later, made the point about differences between British and American audiences speak directly to "modern poetry":

> The difference in the *public* for poetry in England and America seems to me very real, though I know little about it. For instance [Archibald] MacLeish's *Conquistador* struck me as an able and agreeable verse book which would have no point without a fairly large public for verse books, a thing you don't find in England. This is not the grousing of a verse-writer; publishers are generous to verse, apparently because it looks well in the catalogue, and it gets a good deal of space in reviews, apparently because people who don't read poetry still like to talk about poetry, and there are always corners needing to be filled in the magazines. But of the people I come across and like, I doubt if anyone reads much modern verse who doesn't write it. You could pick out in *Conquistador* a series of authors who had been borrowed from and used, and I felt rather critical about this at first, but of course if you have a public to write for it is an excellent thing to use the existing tools. (221–22)

Conquistador (1932) is a poem very much indebted to the modernist modes of Pound and Eliot—though these modes are made considerably more "accessible" and flaccid in MacLeish's use of them. Empson seems completely puzzled by the fact that modernist idioms had now become available for the use that MacLeish makes of them, and can only account for it by making his dubious point about poetry audiences in Britain and America. Somehow, the implication is, the American public must have absorbed modernism well enough, learned its gestures, to permit this middlebrow adaptation, this long didactic history-poem. He goes on to think about British poets of comparable sales and success and ponders the cases of Auden and Spender, both of whom he also thought of as modernist poets and both of whom had also violated all expectations by attracting a reading public of comparatively large proportions. He convinces himself that Auden and Spender sell well because the "bulk of that new public of buyers . . . was mainly interested in the political feelings expressed" in the poetry (219). Modernists with books published in editions larger than three hundred—the typical print run of the time, according to D. S. Savage (278)—thus need to have their success explained. But it does not occur to Empson that MacLeish's success might be due to factors other than his poetry itself—to his visibility as a journalist and man of public affairs, for instance.

Poetry in the thirties gathered together a number of British and American poets and critics all similarly devoted to modernist poetry (if not always the same modernist poetry), and unsurprisingly it is the Americans among them—like Pound and Zabel—who seem most hopeful about the possibilities of encouraging such poetry in Britain. Leavis's hope for the future, after all, was Ronald Bottrall, and he scoffed at Pound's *Active Anthology* as "too ridiculous in its irresponsibility to be seriously discussed" (98). William Carlos Williams, included in that anthology, read those remarks and wrote back to the journal as follows:

> It is interesting to note from your correspondent F. R. Leavis' *English Letter* that though Englishmen may quarrel among themselves the walls about Old England are still intact. At the same time it seems to me unfortunate that the English, who often have a special critical aptitude far more scholarly in temper than that of most Americans, should allow themselves to be lamed by what is, I suppose, a national prejudice in favor of respectability and conservatism. (217)

It is true, as Williams goes on to say, that Leavis had offered no reason for his dismissal of the anthology, had indeed offered no evidence that he had read its poems. Williams is not much fairer when he appeals to platitudes about British conservatism while pretending to flatter. But the British correspondents had, one might argue, given him some cause—even the most pro-modernist among them hardly represented the sort of openness to the innovative and experimental that would be required for, say, Williams himself to find an audience in England. And just a few years later Geoffrey Grigson would ridicule almost the whole of London literary culture—the efforts of Roger Roughton, Herbert Read, and David Gascoyne on behalf of surrealism, Eliot's *Criterion,* "experts in Persian on leave from Rapallo" (that would be Basil Bunting), just about everyone except Grigson's hero Wyndham Lewis. Everybody who might have mattered had left London, he wrote (101). With this kind of pessimism it is hard to fathom the optimism of Morton Dauwen Zabel.

Zabel, Macleod, and Auden

What Zabel noted in Bunting, Auden, and Macleod was as much promise as anything else. This was especially the case with Auden's *Poems* (1930), where he admired the "progressive consonance in rhymes and phrases, the dove-tailing of images, the sometimes solemn and sometimes ironic juxtaposition of sober words with comic and of traditional with 'new'—all these combine to evoke a music wholly beyond reason, extraordinarily penetrating and creative in its search of the significance behind fact." That last phrase—the "significance beyond fact"—shows the influence of Richards's *Science and Poetry* (1926) on Zabel, and indeed in the same review not just Auden but also Macleod are mentioned specifically as poets who might prove Richards wrong in his "depressing conjecture of the death of poetry through 'the neutralization of science'" (1931, 101). Writing of the long, sprawling line and the "symbology" of Macleod's *The Ecliptic* (1930), Zabel argues that, in Macleod's work,

> imagery was liberated from "specific" employment in order to evoke ideas and discover meaning not already established. Similarly the line lent its quantitative flexibility to the poet's emotion in order to stimulate the sensibility in its search for "the force in or behind things." The poetic "suggestion" does not exist for its own sake; it translates "things" back to that condition of magic which Richards holds to be the primary stimulus of creation. It builds out of scientific reality the material of future poetry (102).

A poetics of "discovery" (more recently poets and critics have tended to speak of "process") as opposed to a poetics of statement and proposition, interpretive rather than ornamental imagery and metaphor—these have long been staples of a modernist practice. And of course the idea that a "quantitative flexibility of line" is more supple and flexible and expressive than traditional English metrical patterns is familiar from many advocates of *vers libre*. From Richards Zabel also takes the opposition between science and poetry and the desire for a new poetry which might represent a synthesis of the two and recover for poetry some of the cultural prestige and influence lost to science and technology. (Behind Richards stands Matthew Arnold and others.) To push beyond "things" in search of deeper structural principles or metamorphic energies, to make of the discoveries of modern science a new sublime—these too have characterized the work of modernists such as Pound and MacDiarmid (in different ways). These are ambitious agendas for poetry, and perhaps especially in the British context.

It is a little difficult to understand Zabel's fondness for *both* Macleod and Auden, poets who seem finally very different. Auden's work has little to do with "discovery," and more to do with rhetoric. Master of many verse forms, Auden's selection of particular forms for individual poems often seems willfully arbitrary, as if there were no necessary relationship between form and function, as if he were intent on proving that *this* rhetoric or *that* proposition might be made to conform to *this* stanza. I should admit, however, that others have felt differently about Auden's use of so-called traditional forms, and also that any generalization such as this inevitably simplifies what is an expansive body of poetry: the neo-Augustan poetry of the later thirties should not be confused with the more terse and syntactically adventurous poetry of *Poems,* which has had more admirers among promodernist critics such as C. H. Sisson and Basil Bunting. But even many of the earlier poems, including some of the most famous among them, often seem the expression of settled opinions rather than a coming-into-knowledge: "Go home, now, stranger, proud of your young stock, / Stranger, turn back again, frustrate and vexed: / This land, cut off, will not communicate, / Be no accessory content to one / Aimless for faces rather there than here." "Stacatto imperatives," Seamus Heaney has called these lines, remembering that his teachers used to speak of Auden's "tele-graphese"—so modern, so technological (119). But for all that Auden is working, more or less, in the pentameter, and, a few lines later, we find the inversion, "Where sap unbaffled rises."

The poetry of Macleod's *The Ecliptic* is not always free of inversions either, and it has at moments a distinctly neo-Augustan rhythm and tonality, as a British poet has recently remarked in a note discussing important but neglected British poets and poems.[6] But, in its more exciting sections, *The Ecliptic* is much more recognizably indebted to a Poundian poetics of juxtaposition and collage than any of Auden's work, and this might explain why ultimately Macleod gets the better of Auden in Zabel's reviews. For Zabel was a devoted Poundian. In introducing Macleod he argued that "Rimbaud outdistances Mallarmé, Hopkins Arnold, and Pound Eliot, because in each case the lesser poet fails to support invention or subtlety of mechanism by a consistent necessitating revitalization of ideas" (1931, 36). Pound was superior to Eliot because his experiments in poetic form had been based upon a more thoroughgoing—we might even say "theoretical"—understanding of the implications and consequences of form and practice. Unlike Auden's first book, Macleod's book-length poem is prefaced by a short essay outlining not just the goals of the poem but also a (mostly incoherent) theory of symbolism, and such a gesture might very well have been attractive to Zabel in and of itself, an indication of a seriousness akin to the professionalized discourse of I. A. Richards. Together with "a grasp of his immediate existence and of the world in which it takes place, a power to reshape inherited forms and language to fit that existence and to express the sensibility whereby it is comprehended," Zabel says that the best poets also have "something to say," an "important subject matter." Against Macleod's book-length poem reading the development of the psyche within a series of archetypes represented by the zodiac, Auden's lyrics in *Poems* might very well have seemed a little thin. But then, as British poets following Auden might argue, Americans have too rarely been suspicious of grandiose ambitions even when they risk absurdity. Certainly in England, it has not often been the case that cosmopolitan poets of the center have written a thematically and formally ambitious poetry—whether or not it risks pomposity—but rather outsiders like Hugh MacDiarmid, David Jones, and Macleod.

Macleod, Pound, and *The Ecliptic*

Like Zabel, Joseph Gordon Macleod was a Poundian. He is one of the least known of British writers indebted to American modernism, though, so a brief introduction might be helpful here. In his own note to his entry in the encyclopedic *Contemporary Poets* (1980), Macleod wrote:

> Though Auden and I were greeted in the U.S.A. as a "Dawn in Britain," I never belonged to his school, nor any other I'm aware of. Like most of my poetic generation I was liberated from the word-joys of classical verse (greek melic) by the actuality-accuracies of Ezra Pound. Seeking accuracy has avoided some of the dangers of having a responsive technique and a wide vocabulary. It results in words sometimes outré or obsolete, or can break through the inadequacies of formal grammar. (962)

Macleod corresponded with Pound irregularly throughout the thirties, and Pound remembered him well enough—and one exchange about "ownership" in particular—to mention him in canto CXIV: "Ownership! Ownership! / There was a thoughtful man named Macleod: / To mitigate ownership" (790). He was an acquaintance of Adrian Stokes and of Basil Bunting, who not only included two poems from Macleod's "Foray of Centaurs" sequence in the special British number of *Poetry* that he helped edit but also wrote in his essay there that Macleod's *The Ecliptic*, or sections of it anyway, represented the most exciting poetry he had encountered since *The Waste Land*. Until he and it went broke, Macleod ran the Festival Theatre in Cambridge, where he pleased Pound by putting on a performance of Pound's translation of the Noh play "Nishikigi" in 1933 (and talked also of wanting to do Pound's "Villon"). He edited and published "a sort of review-magazine-journal-programme" which sold in the theater and at bookstores. After Faber published *The Ecliptic* in 1930, he had no more luck there—Eliot turned down the manuscript of *Foray of Centaurs* because "Herbert Broken-Read thought it was too Greek." He seems to have pretty well detested Cambridge culture, and wrote and produced a play called "Overture to Cambridge" (later also a novel) about "a live and sensitive man in Cambridge" whose "tragic weakness was in not clearing out of that center of Culture." The difficulty of finding a publisher for *Foray of Centaurs* made him, like Bunting, extremely pessimistic about the possibilities of poetry in England. He told Pound that, since W. H. Daunder-Lewis had made poetry "paying and popular" there was little to do but write an essay on the influence of Rupert Brooke; elsewhere, he extends more genuine plans to write something for money so as to be able to return to poetry.[7]

If few readers in the United States (or Britain) have heard of Macleod it is because, in many ways, his career is mostly headed downhill after *The Ecliptic*—or his career as a poet named Macleod at least. The last time, to my knowledge, that he was mentioned by an American modernist poet (not including Pound) was in 1949, when Kenneth Rexroth included a section of *The Ecliptic* in an important and now neglected New Directions anthology of British poetry. Rexroth mistakenly thought Macleod had given up poetry after having been pushed aside by "the highly organized claque [*sic*] of the Thirties" (xxxiv). Actually, Macleod had begun publishing a very different poetry under the pseudonym "Adam Drinan," short lyrics partly modeled after Hebridean folk songs and influenced as much by his experience of living in the Hebrides as by his idea of what a Marxist politics might make of sentimental folk traditions. Indeed, Drinan is also in Rexroth's anthology. Macleod continued to write prose under his given name, thereby existing, like Hugh MacDiarmid/Christopher Grieve, in a dual identity. At least once, in a fascinating essay called "Poet and People," which traces the origins of poetry in a community god and Dionysian ritual and the invocation of folk spirit and "muse" from classical Greece up through contemporary Scotland, he discussed Drinan's poetry, flattering himself by saying of Drinan that "he is also a Marxist, and his awareness of today never allows him any indulgence in Celtic twilights" (122). The *Contemporary Poets* note also mentions that "most of my adult life has been spent in the performing arts (theatre, politics, broadcasting): and the habit of thinking into other people's ears has probably given my verse spoken rhythms and reactions" (968). A Marxist with a sense of humor — as that remark about politics as a performing art indicates — he was secretary of the Huntingdonshire Divisional Labour party, 1937–38, and Parliamentary candidate, and worked between 1938 and 1945 as a newsreader and commentator for the BBC. His last poetry as Macleod is a book published in Edinburgh in 1971, *An Old Olive Tree*, which contains poems set in Florence, where he lived out most of his last years. Like *Foray of Centaurs* and the Drinan poems, this book is not without interest, but I want to limit my attention here to *The Ecliptic*, the volume that made an impression on Morton Dauwen Zabel, Bunting, Rexroth, and Pound.

In that 1949 essay where Macleod wrote about Drinan and discussed the origins of poetry in a "community god" and Dionysian rite, he would also discuss the problems of the modern poet in an era in which the "clans are gone and the people is split in classes" and "the classic shorthand, the glory of the commonplace, the radiancy of accuracy, mean nothing." There is pathos and maybe a little of the self-revealing in another remark concerning the "chaos" of the history of what most of us would call modernist poetry as it moved through various "classicist, aestheticist, formalist, nationalist, [and] internationalist" moments, a "dozen rival schools" flourishing at the same time. Macleod writes of those poets forced by historical circumstances into "assertion of originality" that they "often contradict themselves, lacking the stability of public function" (116–22). But few poets have more thoroughly contradicted themselves than Macleod did in becoming Drinan, moving from *The Ecliptic* to the socialist-realist verse of *Men of the Rocks* (1942). As it turns out, Drinan has had more long-term success to date than Macleod, making it once into *The Faber Book of Scottish Verse*.

Pound's correspondence with Macleod, preserved as undated carbons in a Beinecke Library file, touch specifically upon one section of *The Ecliptic* entitled "Libra, or, The Scales." In this section of the poem, Macleod's verse owes something to Pound's *Mauberley*. The ostensible subject is the emperor Hadrian and the discursive ambiguities and paradoxical absurdities of the codification of Roman law as concepts of "ownership" and "possession" conflict within it. Hadrian's presence also likely signals the kind of rhyming and juxtaposing of British and Roman imperialism endeavored in Pound's *Propertius:*

Publius Aemilius Hadrianus
Publius Aemilius Hadrianus Graeculus
Is in the evenings to be seen in a first class carriage
In the mornings deals with branch office correspondence in
    all parts of the world.

His policy slogan is Pax Romana
Employed to revive Greek Culture—
The shrine of Poseidôn Hippias is locked with wool
Our age respects the god by locking it with a Roman wall.

Were the Greeks better men than we?
He believes in the Roman Empire, bareheaded
In the rights of property he believes, according to Ratio.
In some ways the Greeks were better men than we.

He owns a collection of antiquities
A collection of antiquities he also possesses:
His possession not praetorian, but legal,
His ownership Roman.

More correctly, he owns the right to these
The right to these he also possesses:
But he owns the right of possession
And possesses the right of ownership.

If so, possession is governed by ownership
And ownership can be possessed:
Which is absurd.
Ask any praetor.

Inasmuch as he enunciates Pax Romana
He must hold himself slave to Lex Romana.

(46–47)

Hadrian's notoriously grecophile ways are figured in the poem in his regard for a statue of Antinous, which is ironic if we remember that Antinous was the first of Penelope's suitors to be killed, someone on the spot who had no meaningful "possession."

The poem moves on to ponder Hadrian's imperial relation to Athens as absentee landlord and otherwise:

Athens he owned: but did he possess it?
Absent, he had animus: but its governor had corpus.
Present, he had corpus also: but its governor also had animus.
The governor, though responsible, did not represent him.

(47)

It's the animus/corpus, body/spirit distinctions that finally interest Macleod as he wrestles with the Lex Romana and "Reason" and "Ratio"—that last word indicating the Blakean sign dominating the poem as a whole. He floats the possibility that Athens is owned by the past but then decides that the past is incorporeal and thus in no real sense an "owner." The past of Athens is its present people, who in turn "own" Athens. As we follow Hadrian's thoughts working through absurdities in the discourses of Law and Ratio we hear him recognize that he is confusing human and divine law, fungible Athens with what it might represent, the former being the everyday life of the city, the upkeep of monuments, the latter having more to do with the advertising value of monuments. Everyday Athens was not his but the governor's. Hadrian can only faintly apprehend a divine law which is figured by a "bent moon" and instead opts for the walled world of fact and reason and the "impersonal cosmos" of "ideas" lording it over "supernumerary emotions":

Emotions may have preserved Poseidôn Hippios
But emotions snap wool.
A wall is rational and reliable
To preserve Poseidôn Hippios.

Reason is a weight apparatus
Induction and exhaust
Influences come up for judgment
Two minutes apart like trains in a tube.

(50)

In Blake's quarrel with Locke and Descartes, as Northrop Frye noted long ago, inductive reasoning is "circular because it traces the circumference of the universe as it appears to a mediocre and lazy mind" (22). The cloven fictions of Cartesian dualisms are mocked in Macleod's poem which nevertheless finds them inevitable or inescapable given the shift from the customary to the contractual in modernity, given the purchase of Enlightenment thought. As his own note to the poem explained, Macleod meant to use the signs of the zodiac to trace the development of a "single consciousness" which would experience disintegration, eventually finding itself in a position where "intellectual appreciation is a mere diaresis over the letter of things." A "divorced spirit, its seed still ungerminated" is left to wander "through mystical and valueless faiths" (9). While "death ensues without conscious integration" in this representative consciousness, the poem in its end asserts rather desperately that the individual's endeavors contribute to a "primal meaning and relation" which is continuing. The end of the section under scrutiny, "Libra," hymns an escaping, ungraspable soul in the staggered lines of another lyric mode:

> little soul, little flirting,
>> little perverse one,
>>> guest and companion of the body,
>>> where are you off to now?
>
> little wan one, firm one,
>> little exposed one,
>
>> . . . . .
>>> and never make fun of me again?

The ellipsis creates a fake ruin, a Sapphoesque fragment, generating the sudden transition which undermines the seriousness and sentiment of the foregoing in a gesture fairly typical of Macleod.

In terms of the influence of Pound, we note a Poundian *condensare* in lines like "Up and down elastic gnats jerk," though maybe this is finally closer to some of what Bunting would later attempt in *Briggflatts* and elsewhere. Whole sections of the poem, like "Libra" at its end, employ a collage-based intercutting, as we shall see momentarily in quoting at length from one section of the poem. "Taurus, or, The Bull" moves from its opening, a translation of Greek folksong—" 'Goodly bull, come, Hero Dionysus, / To Eleans shrine, a pure shrine, pounding / Oxhoof graced" (17)—on through undergraduate dialogue concerning the Greek name and meaning of Dionysian ritual sacrifice, through several lyric fragments and a concluding first-person monologue. The book's first section, "Aries, or, The Ram," seems to be taken in part from Sir James Frazer's meditations on sacrifice, and also takes up the Abraham, Sarah, Isaac Old Testament story to announce "the principle of sacrifice upon which the child is offered: what matters to the child is sacrificed to what matters to others" (8). The phrase "Winter abideth king" (12) in that same opening poem names with glum pessimism the primal and the recurrent, allowing Macleod later to assert that "man is a strategem / Used by subsisting forces. We are wholly / Unable to discriminate twixt anathem and catathem" (70). Meanwhile the zodiacal frame within which hope for miracles and the passing of paradigms of knowledge and culture occur is also introduced. High-modernist and remote settings are periodically interrupted to locate the poem again in a contemporary world or a recent past of homespun folk song and domestic ritual, or by Macleod's habit of smuggling in a discourse concerning industrialism via metaphor and simile.

Pound thought that the unravelling of political and legal discourses in "Libra" demonstrated an intelligence needed in England. Ownership, control of the means of production, was not a problem so much as the use and circulation of goods. He wrote to Macleod: "Ownership // vs. use. Communize the product and quit foozlin re / ownership of plant. [P]roperty / capital. [A]ll these dissociations NEED making and remaking and translating into a speech that at least the few who can receive thought can handle." Or, in a related passage, "damn it I don't want to BUY or OWN every hotel I stop in. Ownership is often a damned nuisance, and anchor. It was my parent's OWNIN a hose [*sic*] that put me wise, and I struggled for years to OWN nothing that I can't pack in a suit case / never really got it down to less than TWO cases. which is a NUISANCE and really a stigma of poverty. Given adequate purchasing power one cd. OWN less." [8] This is, of course, Pound's social credit line.

But this was the early thirties and a number of things were happening to Macleod: he was having difficulty finding a publisher for *Foray of Centaurs;* he was becoming increasingly aware of the limited audience for varieties of what we call modernist poetry; he was having difficulties with landlords and personal finances. He was drifting not toward social credit but toward a more orthodox form of Marxism. He wrote to Pound fearful of losing him as a correspondent: "My upfall started with Social Credit. Indeed the dramatic version of Overture to Cambridge ended with a super-Douglas world with no money at all. But as time and thought went on, I saw my landlords still behaving like themselves and English Gentlemen, and all their like continuing to do the same to all my like: you cant save a soul or clean up the remnants of a civilisation with Discount and Dividend: and in any case, what's the benefit if you can only value a man by the money he can spend? So in the fiction form, that world appeared as a return to the fascism of the Hottentot, with Scientist-Doctors as priests, keeping the intelligence down. All this must be making you spit." Even without the circumstances he was meeting, Macleod said, he probably would have "gone left."[9]

Within a decade, Macleod would be Drinan and writing poems like this from *Men of the Rocks:*

> The falls sound: and the sound is a shape
> The falls shape: and the shape is a changing sound:
> The falls changing ever the same
>
> Clever men stand to be stunned by the fall of them
> Blind see laughter in the pounding voice of them
> Dead stones rise from their grip in the force of them
>
> the force of the people
> the voice of the people
>
> where water breeds no slavery of fish
> where earth jumps beyond service of writs
> where gravity wrests itself from the rich
>
> In the song of its freedom I heard the oppressed could sing
> in the roar of its power the friendship of the machines
> in its orchestration a joy that will never finish.
>
> (56–57)

This is, as Andrew Duncan notes, socialist realist verse about the Highlands, a celebration of "the hydro-electric scheme started by Tom Johnston as Secretary of State for Scotland" (58). The field of reference is a long way from Greek mythology and Roman history and Blakean idioms, the verse itself a long way from a Pound-inflected modernism. What continuities there are with *The Ecliptic* involve the invocation of communal spirit, this time in more optimistic registers.

The Ecliptic

Each of the twelve sections of the poem takes its title from a sign of the zodiac. Here is the opening of the section Rexroth selected for his anthology, called "Cancer, or, The Crab," one of this uneven book's strongest:

> Moonpoison, mullock of sacrifice,
> Suffuses the veins of the eyes

Till the retina, mooncoloured,
Sees the sideways motion of the cretin crab
Hued thus like a tortoise askew in the glaucous moonscape
A flat hot boulder it
Lividly in the midst of the Doldrums
Sidles
The lunatic unable to bear the silent course of constellations
Mad and stark naked
Sidles
The obol on an eyeball of a man dead from elephantitis
Sidles
All three across heaven with a rocking motion.
The Doldrums: "region of calms and light baffling winds near
    equator."

(29)

The slight dislocations of syntax, the wrenching that allows a line to end
with *it,* the syncopated, alternating line lengths, the tone-leading in vowel
chains moving from "it" to "lividly" to "sidles" and elsewhere—this strikes
one as both expert and quite "radical" for a poem published in 1930. In
astrological lore the sign of Cancer is said to govern subjects who are
predisposed to mediocrity and generally presumptuous, impressionable,
romantic, paradoxical. As Macleod explains in his preface, neither this nor
any other sign in the poem is meant to reflect an "autobiographical indulgence" (7) but instead to "contribute to a single consciousness" neither
typical nor unique but with "significance for my time" (9). Both the idea
of "autobiographical" poetry and lyric poetry itself are rejected in favor of
a more impersonal and archetypal poetry. "Cancer" is a poem exploring
adolescent sexual confusion, love crossed by hate, desire fractured in a divided consciousness. Its "theme"—anomie, crisis of the will—is not so far
from the recurrent concerns of Auden's first poems, but there the resem-
blance ends.

Pausing at the end of this passage to insert a definition is a technique
Macleod might have learned from Pound, but one can only begin to appreciate the full extent of the debt to Pound by quoting the poem in large
portions, as I must now do, considering that few readers will know it.
Skipping ahead a little we find:

Agesias said: "Nero was an artist because he murdered his
    mother

Sensibility (subliminal) is of more importance than moral
　　obligation (prandial)."
But Agesias paints cottages in watercolours and fears his
　　own mother
Barbaraieus said: "I am passionately in love with Gito who
　　spurns me now for Prainoê"
But until he saw them together he was merely disturbed by
　　Gito's eyelashes
Galônus said: "The subsequent shrivelling of an orchid doesn't
　　alter the value of its beauty."
Decanus said: "Joy in nothing. Either dies joy or what
　　produced it."

But Galônus is attractive to women, Decanus obese, poor,
　　obtuse.
Epinondus said: "I have been a liar, now no longer so."
Zeuxias said: "What I have always been, I shall remain, a fool."
. . .
Each letter is somebody
But the Crab is nobody
Nobody
Nobody
A ganglion of neurotic imitations
Composed of each letter in turn
Jointed by conflicts he does not want
A word that never existed with a sense nobody can understand.
Suffering for the sins his father refused to commit
He sits and thinks about the twiddling toes of Gunerita
A boy-girl or girl-boy of an average pulchritude
Haunted by phantoms of his female self
. . .
This he desires, but despises:
Bhah!
Always sideways, crab walk.

Either he is not fit for this world
Or this world not fit for him. But which?

(30–32)

"Pulchritude," "ganglions"—this is the outré vocabulary to which Macleod referred in his *Contemporary Poets* note. As is the case with Mina

Loy's and Hugh MacDiarmid's poetry, there is simply no word that this poetry cannot be made to contain; by way of contrast one might remember that twenty or so years later Donald Davie would begin his assault on modernism by speaking of "purity" in diction, of the "chastity and propriety" of Goldsmith's exemplary methods. Elsewhere—primarily in passages omitted here—Macleod's parataxis shows him attempting to "break through the inadequacies of formal grammar." The pseudo-classical names are probably fabricated, and their cryptic utterances suggest a comic appropriation of Pound's "Canto XIII," where Kung's disciples one after another offer their vision of happiness and orderliness. The crab is nobody, one supposes, because it is fantasy itself, or consciousness given to fluid fantasy. No "controlling self" here. The crab walks sideways because it lacks direction, will. Even Macleod's moral drama is vaguely Poundian, though the Catullan wit—which sometimes borders on the sophomoric— is rarely sustained by Pound at anything like this length. The conversation skewered here could very well be the sort of talk Macleod heard among hypersensitive would-be artists and poets in Cambridge.

As the poem continues, Macleod suddenly modulates into a translation of Catullus, rendered in short lines, inserted as part of this "collage." The translated passage is included, one supposes, because Catullus, like Rimbaud, is one of the presiding spirits of the explosive, emotional, adolescent sensibility Macleod is exploring. We pick up the poem after the Catullus:

> How can I be hardened when the whole world is fluid?
> O Aphrodite Pandêmos, your badgers rolling in the moonlit corn
>
> Corn blue-bloom-covered carpeting the wind
> Wind humming like distant rooks
> Distant rooks busy like a factory whirring metal
> Whirring metallic starlings bizarre like cogwheels missing teeth
> These last grinning like the backs of old motor cars
> Old motor cars smelling of tragomaschality
> Tragomaschality denoting the triumph of self over civilization
> Civilization being relative ours to Greek
> > Greek to Persian
> > Persian to Chinese
> Chinese politely making borborygms to show satisfaction
> Satisfaction a matter of capacity
> Capacity not significance: otherwise with an epigram
> Epigrams—poems with strabismus

Strabismus being as common spiritually as optically the moon
The moon trampling regular steps like a policeman past the house
   of the Zodiac
And the Zodiac itself, whirling and flaming sideways
Circling from no point returning through no point
Endless skidding as long as man skids, though never moving,
Wavers, topples, dissolves like a sandcastle into acidity.

Is there nothing more soluble, more gaseous, more imperceptible?
Nothing.

(33–34)

Macleod has learned from Pound, but he is no mere imitator; there is
an exuberance and playfulness in his poem that is not Poundian. And it
is hard to imagine Pound, or anyone else for that matter, apostrophizing
Aphrodite with a celebration of badgers in the corn. The chain of similes
here—rooks are like factory metal which is like toothless cogwheels and
so on—unfolds at such a relentless speed as to destabilize the individual
terms and images linked by the similes, lumping the rural and the urban,
the technological and the mythological, in a seething, fluid mass of discourses run amok beyond their boundaries. (Jeremy Prynne is one recent
British poet who might have learned from this.) One assumes that the
language is precisely enacting the way that our terms, our speech-acts, and
our "civilizations" gesture frantically at stability, identity, and coherent
meaningfulness in endless, eventually tiresome iterations of comparison
and contradistinction. Some might find the poem's technique crude, perhaps, in its spasms and crescendo, but for me there is considerable force in
this awkward, mechanical accumulation of long lines, particularly coming
as these do at the end of the poem. British poetry in this century has more
often been noted for terseness than for Whitmanic inclusiveness, or expansive sprawl. Macleod suggests that terseness leads to spiritual squinting
(strabismus).

It is not hard to understand why such a poem would not win Macleod
many readers in England—the long, late poems of MacDiarmid, with
their inoppugnable idioms, their obscure scientisms, did not fare all that
much better there. And if we were to look at other poems in *The Ecliptic,*
even those in couplets, we would find invocations to Dionysus, passages
in Greek, and in general the classical focus of a Poundian modernism—
in short, a very "difficult," challenging poem. As I noted above, just a few
years after publishing it Macleod wrote to Pound in some despair about

the impact of popular poets in Britain and the impossibility of finding a publisher for more recent work. If Empson had found it hard to imagine the accessible, watered-down modernism of a book like *Conquistador* being published in England, how might he have been prepared for poetry like Macleod's? And Empson was no mere reviewer for a London literary paper—with Leavis and others he was soon to define the methods and boundaries of literary study in England.

Uncovering, Recovering Macleod

We would do well, I think, to add Macleod to the ever-growing list of modernist poets American critics are busy recovering in an effort to expand and complicate our ideas of modernist poetry. Discovering the almost forgotten smells a little of "academia" these days; it's part of "expanding the canon." My own interest in Macleod's poetry and story is not driven by the motives most often central (recently) to American recovery missions—the need to explore the literatures of previously marginalized groups, to allow individuals within these categories to speak for themselves. Macleod's work might very well enter into a discussion of the problems of Scottish or Anglo-Scottish literature in England, but that is also not my concern here. I mean to address Americans primarily, and afterwards whatever British readers I might be lucky enough to find, and to convince them that there's a more considerable body of challenging British modernist poetry than they might have come to believe. Mina Loy and Basil Bunting have, in the last twenty or so years, slowly found more and more readers, the latter in both nations more so than the former. David Jones, Hugh MacDiarmid, Ford Madox Ford, D. H. Lawrence, and Edith Sitwell, among modernists of earlier, pre–World War II generations, have their advocates too. But, in England, there is a small but growing effort to recover British modernisms. Peter Riley and Andrew Crozier, among others, have waged small, local campaigns on behalf of poets such as J. F. Hendry and Nicholas Moore.

Crozier has gone back to the first site of British modernism—the Lewis, Joyce, Pound, Woolf era—to "recover" and publish an edition of the work of the poet John Rodker, whose poet's novella *Adolphe* (1920) Pound once regarded as an advance on the methods of *Ulysses*. Opposed to a "monumentalized" modernism, Crozier argues that all such projects of recovery must be justified by their ability to offer complicating pictures of the modernist era. Rodker's work is of value to him not just as a way of filling in forgotten parts of a picture with Pound and Lewis and Eliot at its center—Rodker's Ovid Press published all of them; he succeeded Pound as editor of *The Little Review* in 1919—but because it forces altogether new pictures to emerge. Rodker's interest in theatrical forms (masques) and his affiliations with the so-called Choric school locate him in literary circles less exclusively male and masculinist than those of Pound and Lewis. In Rodker's poetry itself Crozier detects

> neither the erasure of the writing subject, nor the ironic objectification of the dramatic subject in its imputed language: both of them modes which constituted the modernity of Pound and Eliot. Furthermore, we find quite the reverse of Lewis's theoretical dissociation of mind and body. Somatic effect is continuous with psychic affect, in a way which removes the new sensations of the mechanical environment from simple astonishment and intellectual fashion. To an extent Pound was right when in 1914 he classified Rodker as a Futurist. (xvii)

A poetry where "somatic effect is continuous with psychic affect" might also describe much of the work of Mina Loy, who was also much more deeply invested in futurism, Freudianism, and Bergson than Pound, Eliot, or Lewis were, though never uncritically so. "Anglo-Mongrels and the Rose" thematizes mind-body dualisms to reject them, and the earlier and in the more self-consciously "experimental" "Love Songs" the "writing self" is not so much "erased" by Loy's cubistic collage techniques as it is made multidimensional, multivocal. There is some evidence that Rodker knew the "Love Songs," which, like his own work, British critics have been slow to claim for a British modernism.

With the recovery of poets such as Loy and Rodker, new patterns emerge for modernism, and we affirm the British critic Peter Nicholls' good sense in entitling his book on the period *Modernisms*. Wallace Stevens's correspondent Nicholas Moore (son of the famous philosopher), Lynette Roberts and Hugh Sykes David, Mary Butts and Douglas Goldring (who wrote an early and important essay on Vorticism), Robert Graves—inserting or reinserting these names into accounts of literary modernisms will do much to deepen our understanding of modernism in Britain, and not just in Britain but also beyond it. Discussing these writers is more work than I can do here, and anyway it might be argued that such work should be most important to British poets and critics who wish to contest a literary history in which an antimodernist poetry is inscribed as the most significant British tradition. Such a project is well underway in work like Crozier's edition of Rodker. I quoted Crozier earlier naming a Pound-Williams tradition as essential to the poetry of the British poets collected in *A Various Art;* moving beyond that tradition to rediscover and reengage neglected British modernists seems to be the order of the day in the years since the publication of that anthology in 1987, and for understandable reasons. For the work of Rodker and Moore and others, if not pursued in isolation from other modernisms, can help to ground contemporary practice in modernisms that have operated in British contexts.[10]

Finding a more complete and richly diversified modernist practice is an admirable aim, but one hopes also to find poetry that retains its power and surprise. With Macleod, for me, it's only *The Ecliptic,* and not all of that. With Rodker, it's less his first book, a hodgepodge of imagist and symbolist poetry entitled *Poems* (1914) than the second book *Hymns* (1920). Here's a shorter and not altogether typical poem from that second book, without Rodker's signature use of the dash. The poem contrasts the ecstatic sexual union of cold-blooded frogs with an intellectualized, dispassionate male sexuality and, in its critique of male postcoital remoteness, represents a view of sexual relations far removed from what we get in poems like Eliot's *The Waste Land,* where we hear of distracted women happy to forget about sex the minute it's over with; here it is men who are emotionally incapacitated by and in sex:

> I'd have loved you as you deserve had we been frogs
>
> Where did I hear of two smooth frogs
> clasped among rushes
> in love and death:
> rigid and with spread fingers.
>
> And we   men
> all brain, all heart, hot blood;
> turn lightly, then
> 'Ah, weren't we once friends?'

That space between "we" and "men"—that emptiness, that whiteness, that pause—prepares us for the poem's ironic ending. Word placement for onomatopoeiac-rhythmical effect is notable here as well—in the surge of the second stanza's second line, in the lighter, slowed movement of the third, which ends in rhyming men/then delicately, turning to the quoted speech before the rhyme can settle in.

When we contemplate their work over the course of their careers, certainly Loy and perhaps Rodker too are more consistently surprising poets than Macleod, which is not to gainsay Macleod's accomplishments, which are considerable. But the curious fate Macleod's long poem met in the pages of *Poetry* has much to tell us about our Americanized readings of literary modernism, about the extent to which the earliest histories of modernism have at their center American writing and an understanding of literary production permeated by a popularized discourse of avant-gardism; by the need to imagine poets as part of groups offering new directions, "new dawns," a "renaissance." I fear, though, that these are easy lessons to extract from the Macleod-Zabel episode—as if it were enough to echo Marx's famous statement that, if history repeats itself, it does so as farce, or to chortle over the ways in which Zabel imagines he can help reproduce in the early thirties, amid the Depression, and from across an ocean, the enthusiasms of London in 1914. But there is something more to be gained from remembering this episode and recovering Macleod's long poem than a critique of the rhetoric of avant-gardism or American boost-erism. Odd specimen that it is, Macleod's poem and its reception tells us a good deal about the history of British modernism itself, which was the work of individuals largely isolated from one another, barely visible and then often only by virtue of the mediations of Americans such as Zabel. Macleod's post-*Ecliptic* future as the very different poet Adam Drinan shows him searching for a poetry that might reach British, Scottish, and Hebridean working-class communities in a way that the hybrid modern-ism, the Poundian and neo-Augustan mix of the poetry of *The Ecliptic*, could not. Since the thirties, British modernist poetry has been dwarfed by the shadow of American modernist poetry, while simultaneously it has been obscured by the antimodernisms of those who would position the work of the Auden circle or the Movement as more centrally located in a native "English" tradition. Macleod's turn to the folk poetry of Drinan shows him opting to abandon a modernist poetic as if it simply had no viability in Britain, as if internationalized poetic modes were consigned to oblivion in Britain. And, for the most part, they were. Macleod had writ-ten a poem which was destined to find too many of its best readers in the United States or among Americans. This is the story which must be set alongside Loy's romance of American modernity. If America was moder-nity itself, how might one be modern elsewhere?

PART TWO: Readings

4. Mina Loy's "Anglo-Mongrels and the Rose"

In 1922 Scofield Thayer arranged for Mina Loy to meet with Sigmund Freud in Vienna, shortly before she moved to Paris for her most extended stay in that city. According to Loy's biographer, Carolyn Burke, Freud read Loy's stories and pronounced them analytical (313). Loy sketched Freud. By itself such a meeting proves little, but there is good reason to believe that Loy had thought about the significance of Freud's work. Burke's *Becoming Modern: The Life of Mina Loy* (1996) tells of conversations about Freud at the Walter Arensberg apartment in New York in 1916 and of Loy's consultations with a young disciple of Freud, Roberto Assagioli, in Florence several years previously. Here is Burke's summary of Assagioli's "psychosynthesis":

> Assagioli thought that the unconscious was balanced by another dimension, a "superconscious," where one's soul experiences the desire for transcendence. And while Freud saw religion and art as sublimations, Assagioli considered them pathways to this higher self. Like Freud, he believed that we suffer from the repression of our instincts, but he also felt that we suffer as much from the repression of the sublime. Assagioli was particularly sensitive to the spiritual concerns of women: he was perhaps the only man in Italy interested in Christian Science, meditation, and his mother's new faith, Theosophy. . . . One could effect change by becoming aware of the will, he explained, as well as by imag-

ining what one hoped to bring about—a technique now known as "visualization." (146–47)

In assessing the contours of Loy's thought one cannot overestimate the importance of her years among English and American expatriates in Florence, where the American Mabel Dodge helped make it possible for her to read not only Freud, Bergson, Stein, and the Italian futurists—writers regularly discussed in literary histories of the period—but also the British scholar Frederic Myers, author of "a study proving that the spirit survived after death" (144). The people Loy would converse with while living in Florence, Paris, and New York include Stein, Pound, Duchamp, Bunting, Barnes, Marinetti, Man Ray and Wyndham Lewis, among many others well known; in Florence she would also converse with George Herron, a "deposed American minister whose radical interpretation of Christ's word had led him in the direction of utopian socialism" (147). I offer these odd and artificial juxtapositions so that I might be able to suggest the difficulty of sorting out influences when considering large subjects like ideology and religion in Loy's writing. Assagioli, Myers, and Herron are to Loy what Allen Upward is to Pound—figures whose importance is obvious but who also represent discourses nearly off the map of contemporary intellectual life: mysticism, Christian Science, and a revisionary Freudian psychology therapeutic in the agency it offered women.

It would have been almost impossible for a poet of Loy's cosmopolitan credentials not to have developed an opinion about Freud's influence in the Paris of the 1920s, when Surrealism began its long and difficult relationship with the father of psychoanalysis. Loy lived in Paris for thirteen years after 1923, and she was very familiar with Surrealism, as is demonstrated in her roman à clef about the German Surrealist painter Richard Oelze, called *Insel*. The evidence suggests that this novel was written towards the end of Loy's residence in Paris, in the midthirties, and, as Elizabeth Arnold has written, it can be read as a critique of Surrealism, especially of André Breton's figure of woman-as-muse as drawn to obscene proportions in *Nadja* (185). Criticizing Surrealism, of course, is not the same thing as criticizing Freud, as the movement from its beginnings was itself critical of Freud, especially of Freud's failure to recognize instinct and impulse as "the mechanism of an avalanche: ultimately, a revolution" (Chénieux-Gendron 180). However, for all of its quarrels with Freud, the movement would have been impossible without him, its various strategies for liberating subconscious impulses inconceivable. If Loy rejects these strategies in her novel, it is worth exploring the extent to which her major poem, "Anglo-Mongrels and the Rose," written at the beginning of her stay in Paris between 1923 and 1925, is also critical of Freud and the various discourses of instinct then ascendant on the European intellectual scene.

Loy's "Anglo-Mongrels and the Rose" for a long time had at best a legendary status in avant-garde circles, or rather it was only a rumor until Roger Conover included it in its entirety in his Jargon Society edition of Loy's poems, *The Last Lunar Baedeker* (1982). Parts of it had appeared in the twenties in two numbers of *The Little Review* and in Robert McAlmon's *Contact Collection of Contemporary Writers*, and a part of it had been published in Loy's first book, *Lunar Baedecker* [*sic*] in 1923, but the poem was not published whole until 1982. So it is only recently that the excited remarks of Jerome Rothenberg, who once called the poem a lost "modernist master-poem," have been expanded into scholarly analysis, though not in Britain. Though a British edition of *The Last Lunar Baedeker* exists, published by Carcanet, Loy's work has not yet been much taken up by British scholars. Given Loy's English upbringing and the subject matter of her longest poem "Anglo-Mongrels and the Rose," one would imagine that British scholars intent on mapping British modernisms and their intersections with an international avant-garde must soon do so.[1]

"Anglo-Mongrels and the Rose" is among the oddest of modernist long poems, a strange combination of satire, didactic commentary, and lyrical mysticism. It is also autobiography or automythology, and curious in its selection of autobiographical events. Though Loy was forty years old when she wrote the poem, it is largely concerned with her life as a child in London, from her birth to her first efforts as a young adult to leave what seems to have been a rather frightening family. With regard to its status as an autobiographical text, it is necessary to mention what might be a weakness in the poem: without at least some extra-textual biographical knowledge of Loy, the reader is likely to be befuddled by several sections that briefly introduce characters who are not especially integrated into an already cryptic personal mythology. Two people who would become important to the adult Loy—her husbands Stephen Haweis and Arthur Cravan—are represented by the poem, also viewed only as children. Cravan is mentioned (as "Colossus") only in one section. Loy meant to contrast various childhoods, to imagine character in its formative stages. Within their families Cravan is seen as an infant dadaist, Haweis, as an infant aesthete, as if somehow their adult sensibilities were already fully formed by the age of five.

The idea that somehow the childhood of each of the poem's principals has adequate explanatory power to allow Loy to delineate personality traits owes something to Freud, and throughout the poem Freud and Freudianism—by which I mean a range of what I am calling "discourses of instinct"—aid Loy in her struggle to articulate a Christianity opposed to her mother's evangelical Christianity. Loy's Christ has nothing to do with the moral systems erected upon him by Victorian evangelicals, for Loy finds these systems to be grounded in a refusal of the body—or, rather, in a mind-body dualism long familiar in the West. She once wrote that "No man whose sex life is satisfactory ever became a moral censor" (1990, 15). Loy's Christ was "a precursor of the ultimate," an "indication of the ultimate point of arrival":

> Jesus knew that a certain element in human consciousness would inevitably ask where we are going to—towards what are we tending— and presented it with a synopsis of the future. Its utility lay in the fact that although insanely inadoptable to the entire mass world consciousness—it would in some corner of some consciousness keep as the merest scintilla—the torch that will light the future.
>
> It is there for the retrievement of desolation—for those who have arrived at the end of all things of the intellect—as an antidote to extinction. (14–15)

This is the Christ of the mystic who has abandoned all systematic thought, the Christ of the *via negativa*. If "Anglo-Mongrels and the Rose" is to be read as a "religious" poem, as I think it must be, we have to first acknowledge that nearly all forms of "orthodox" religious doctrine—Jewish and Christian—are renounced by Loy on behalf of an experience beyond intellect which she believed to be a direct sensual and intuitive apprehension of divinity. It is Freud or Freudianism that gives her some of the language—the discourse of instinct—she needs to validate her experience against the competing religious practices of her father's Jewish ancestors and her mother's Christianity. But Freud and his influence also represent the reason "Christ's necessity seems to have collapsed into an entire inutility" for many (14).

Some of Loy's most direct statements about Freud can be found among her chaotic notes from some twenty years after the composition of "Anglo-

Mongrels and the Rose," notes I have quoted from in the above paragraph. One note claims that:

> Jesus saw through us far better than Freud—in seeing that our real dilemma was our desperate determination to establish our identity apart from the general mass. While Freud believes man to be moved by instinct—Jesus saw him to be actuated by humbug.
>
> When the gentile world falls over its self it is usual for the Jews to come to the rescue. When it required a savior they nailed up a Christ. When it required a second savior to counteract the effects of the first, Freud was at its service. (15)

Here, twenty years after the writing of "Anglo-Mongrels and the Rose," ten years after *Insel*, is evidence that Loy came to recognize limits to Freud's theories, or at least became skeptical of the central role the understanding of "instinct" plays in these theories. But "Anglo-Mongrels and the Rose" can be read as part of the same conversation with Freud. Against Freud's diagnosis of humanity's efforts to reconcile itself with biological drives, Loy posits a Christ who thinks that it is not instinct but rather distorted values that one must worry about. Loy's Christ is an answer to biological determinism. If one reads the cryptic remark above as saying that the nonsense ("humbug") that drives man *is* "our desperate determination to establish our identity apart from the general mass," our need to affirm our individualism, then Loy's Christ emerges as a valued spokesperson for democratic and communal values, an optimistic voice to counter Freud's conservativism and pessimism concerning the possibilities of social amelioration. Loy's Christ begins to take on the shape of Herron's utopian socialism.

For my purposes here, in reading "Anglo-Mongrels and the Rose," I am less interested in Loy's rejection of Freud (or part of him) than in the enormous respect accorded to him in this pairing of his influence with Christianity's. I do not know the extent to which Loy had read particular works by Freud, but it is not necessary to know this if we understand that the poem is reacting to what Loy perceived as a radical transformation of values in modernity, which the work of Freud and its popularity reflected. "Anglo-Mongrels and the Rose" is a poem about cultural paradigms colliding in an individual—Loy or "Ova." It uses discourses of sexuality and instinct to criticize the Christianity imposed upon Loy by her English mother, and then in its last section turns Loy's own highly idiosyncratic

Christian mysticism back upon modernity to view a post-Victorian world with considerable irony. Ultimately the poem—or so it seems to me—resists both Freudianism and Christian dogma in favor of the mystical experience described in the shortest of the poem's many sections, entitled "Illumination." In a poem brimming with negativity, this section contains the only genuinely affirmative moment, and like all accounts of mystical experience it is impossible to reduce to doctrine.

A few more biographical facts must be mentioned before I begin to look in some detail at the poem. The subject of the poem's first section, "Exodus," is Loy's father, Sigmund Lowy, who, along with his Hungarian Jewish ancestors, is referred to as Exodus. Lowy seems to have abandoned his faith when he came to England without ever adopting the religious practices of his wife. His ancestors apparently were quite successful in Hungary, his grandfather having erected or provided for or been honored by—the poem is not altogether clear on this account—a synagogue in Budapest. His father having been disinherited by this same grandfather, Lowy moved to England, began as a tailor and became quite prosperous through investments. In the poem Loy attributes her intelligence to him, or at least her "brain"—"Behold my gift / the Jewish brain!" (132). As an amateur painter and as an awkward suitor of Loy's mother he often appears something of a fop. In the poem he is sometimes harmless, sometimes definitely not. The subject of the second section of the poem, Loy's mother Julia Bryan, was English, and is called both "Alice" and "Ada" in the poem. In a scurrilous portrait, she comes off as cruel and repressed and manipulating—a stereotypical Victorian matron. She seems to have been a woman dedicated to insular English traditions, much concerned with long-established customs and an ancestry which her husband's heritage violated—or was perceived to violate in anti-Semitic circles. In reading the poem's account of her one must remember that information about her independent of Loy is nearly impossible to obtain. Loy herself, the subject of the third and longest section of the poem, is a "Mongrel Rose" because of her mixed heritage, and is called (in the third-person) "Ova," short for *ovary* perhaps. The other two characters who have small and not especially integrated roles in the poem—Loy's husbands Haweis and Cravan—are called, respectively, "Esau Penfold" and "Colossus."

"Anglo-Mongrels and the Rose" up until its concluding section is a poem written in the third person and often in forms of the present tense, recounting a series of events arranged—with some interruptions—in a roughly chronological order. One might call the poem a lyric sequence, as Jim Powell has, but the poem's reliance on narrative makes it unique among modernist lyric sequences, which more often subordinate narrative events to other concerns—to the emotional conflicts of a central persona, for instance (13). Unlike Loy's own "Love Songs To Joannes," "Anglo-Mongrels and the Rose" is not a collection of interrelated lyrics reflecting and projecting the complex and often conflicted states of consciousness surrounding a central event, in that case a failed love affair (or affairs). Without engaging in arguments about the status of genres in an era that cross-bred them by the dozens, I will only say that for convenience's sake one can call the poem a lyric sequence because of the extreme condensation of the narrative and the emphasis placed upon the witty but more often embittered commentary surrounding key events in the fragments of family history Loy is recording. The poem does not end in narrative but in commentary, in sweeping cultural critique in fact. The events themselves include the parents' courtship, Ova's (Loy's) birth, one of her earliest efforts at understanding the simultaneously empowering and alienating effects of entering into language use, a trip with a governess to a poor Jewish neighborhood, an epiphany in a garden. When chronology is violated it is for a purpose, such as in "Illumination," where Loy states that her mystical experience sustained her throughout a disastrous future which is beyond the narrative time frame of the poem.

One might say that using the third person offers the poem some of the "impersonality" valued by many modernist poets. But impersonality here, if the term applies at all, is less an effect of Loy effacing herself from the poem than a technique for increasing a critical and ironic distance between herself as author of an autobiographical poem and herself as its subject, or one of its subjects. Loy's "incognito" Ova, fragments of whose psychic life are described primarily in forms of the present tense, is surrounded and eventually supplanted by the adult speaker's commentary, which has access to all tenses and (compared to, say, *The Waste Land*) an epistemologically secure perspective. At moments, the poem is didactic enough to view Ova's life as an object lesson demonstrating the results of a British middle-class upbringing. Ova's mother will come to be synonymous with the Rose that is England, or rather its hegemonic values, and her distance from her mother is also her distance from England.

At a more mundane level, the poem's third person proves useful as Loy narrates events she could not have in any real sense witnessed or remembered, such as her birth:

Her face
screwed   to the mimic-salacious
grotesquerie of a pain
larger than her intellect
   They pull
A clotty bulk of bifurcate fat
out of her loins
to lie
for a period   while   performing hands
pour lactoid liquids through
and then mop up   beneath it
their golden residue
A breathing baby
mystero-chemico Nemesis
of obscure attractions

(130–31) [2]

It is something of a convention, especially in the great English novels of
the eighteenth and nineteenth centuries, to attach great significance to
the birth of the protagonist. Loy is having fun with this convention here,
working as she is in a narrative form; from Ova's first moments, as Loy
imagines them, she was pissing on the authorities.

Loy refuses to sentimentalize birth even when it is herself she is describing entering the world. The only vaguely "poetic" diction in the passage
("golden residue") describes an excremental function, and Loy will insist
throughout the poem that it is her special talent as a poet to find poetry
where it has not always been found before—in the mundane and the
fleshly, even in the excremental. The ironic description of the biological
and clinical realities of labor and birth allows her to assert the "mystery" of
life without succumbing to cliché. The baby is both "fat" and a "Nemesis /
of obscure attractions," an incipient personality of indefinable qualities.
In linking the biological and (for lack of a better word) the "poetic" in
the epithet "mystero-chemico" Loy is already on the way to the central
problematic of the poem, forcing a conjunction of the biological and the
spiritual. In terms Assagioli might accept, the excremental is admitted as
the sublime is restored.

While "Anglo-Mongrels and the Rose" is autobiographical, it transcends the autobiographical to offer propositions concerning a range of

subjects: English ideology, gender roles, sexuality, and so forth. For instance, Loy's indictment of her mother's repressed sexuality begins by bemoaning its effects on her own psychic development and then goes beyond blame to explain the mother's personality and behavior as culturally determined. First, the critique of the mother:

> To the mother
> the blood-relationship
> is a terrific indictment of the flesh
>
> . . . . .
>
> There is no liberation
> from this inversion
> of instinct
> making subliminal depredations
> on Ova's brain
>
> She is overshadowed
> by the mother's aura
> of sub-carnal anger
> restringent to the pores
> of her skin—
> which opening
> like leaves for rain
> crave for caressings
> soft as wings
>
> (147–48)

Elsewhere, Loy calls her mother an "armored tower" (140), and suggests that an impenetrable coldness affected not only her marriage but her parenting. The effect on Loy, the passage suggests, was subtle but lasting—a "subliminal depredation." Yet is it Loy or her mother who craves caresses? The syntax is ambiguous, perhaps suggesting that it is both.

If this passage seems to blame the mother, there is also this, from somewhat later in the poem, an abstract proposition moving out from her own experience:

> New Life
> when it inserts itself into continuity
> is disciplined
> by the family
> reflection

of national construction
to a proportionate posture
in the civilized scheme

deriving
definite contours
from tradition

personality
being mostly
a microcosmic
replica
of institutions

(153)

This passage indicates the ways in which Loy attempts to use her family—
especially her mother's English side—as representative instances of the
effects of national ideologies on individual personalities. Throughout the
poem, the insular Victorian "civilization" of her mother is attacked for its
sentimental idealism and its repression of instinct. But to the wounded-
ness of her young self, for which she blames the mother, she adds another
deprivation the sources of which move beyond her; she is "Lacking dictio-
naries / of inner consciousness" (148), lacking the very language needed to
map her consciousness. The poem can be read as an extended effort to find
a lexicon for psychic damage as it occurred within the setting of Victorian
England, and in view of related efforts by Freud and others to understand
the role of instinct and repression of instinct in human development.

And it must be added that Loy's logopoeic technique often deflects attention from the narrative to cultural analysis. The poem's vocabulary is
polysyllabic and abstract, its syntax complex and occasionally ambiguous,
its free verse slow moving and interrupted within and between lines to
allow for the special emphasis of phrasal units and exaggerated and often
ironic rhymes. The rhymes in particular deserve mention, as in this passage from the portrait of the English Rose:

Maiden emotions
breed
on leaves of novels
where anatomical man
has no notion

of offering other than the bended knee
to femininity

and purity
passes in pleasant ways
as the cows graze

(124)

The ironic force of this portrait of the English Rose as bovine is strength-
ened by such rhymes as "ways" and "graze." The sometimes multisyllabic
rhymes (knee/femininity/purity) slow down the movement of the verse,
and force attention to the ironies outlined by line breaks—anatomical
man has no "notion," maiden emotions "breed." Marjorie Perloff has argued that Loy's rhyming, and her verse in general, is a "variant on skeltonics"—the verse form named for the English poet John Skelton. Shorter
lines of two or three stresses, a regular use of parallelism, and "short runs
of monorhyme called 'leashes'" are characteristic of skeltonics (8–9), but
Loy's freedom within the form involves not just the frequent placement
of "leashes" within lines—which Perloff notes—but also occasionally one-
word lines which visually isolate key words to give them a force one might
describe as venomous. Often, as above, these words are verbs. "Grinding
it out," Loy's poem presents a hyperintellectualized, "logopoeic" rhyming
which is also "vulgar," belonging as much to the music hall as to a tradition associated with Skelton. While the verse's parodic moments make
it seem pedantic to describe such work as an effort to renew a British
tradition older than the Keatsian, Wordsworthian, and Tennysonian traditions adapted in Georgian verse, it also does not seem accurate to speak
of an outright rejection of the "poetic." This is no postmodern antipoetic.
Rather the poem merges a constructivist attention to the materiality of
individual words, abstract or concrete—to use a familiar if discredited
jargon—with the thunderous rhymes of folk tradition. These are also pre-
vented from attaining a naturalized status by parodic overemphasis and an
excruciatingly slow pace. Hyperintellectual and folk at once—this is what
distinguished the work from the poems in, say, Edith Sitwell's *Façade*.
This is cosmopolitan Europe and inventive America visiting middle-class
England. It is tempting to read the poem's form itself as a metaphor for
Loy's own particular exile among an international avant-garde. And it is
crucial that we read Loy's technique as a merger of the carnivalesque and
the didactic, of "body" and "mind."

Even the most intensely personal moments in the poem gain their authority from the distance between poet and autobiographical subject. In part this is a matter of verb tenses, especially the recurrent use of the present tense to describe events we recognize as events of the past. Nowhere is Loy's manipulation of tenses more brilliant than in the short vignette describing her religious illumination. As this moment is represented as "timeless," sustaining her from its occurrence through the moment of the writing of the poem, it makes sense that it is cast in the present progressive:

> Ova is standing
> alone in the garden

> The high skies
> have come gently upon her
> and all their
> steadfast light is shining out of her
> She is conscious
> not through her body but through space

> This saint's prize
> this indissoluble bliss
> to be carried like a forgetfulness
> into the long nightmare

> (163–64)

Mystical experience, of any variety, is notoriously difficult to represent. Paradox is one of the most familiar tropes used to suggest the intuition of an ecstatic union with divinity, and Loy employs a kind of paradox here in her middle strophe. There is also the reference to the paradisiacal solitude of the garden to consider. But what distinguishes this most important of moments in the poem is the way Loy suggests the value of the mystical experience by surrounding it with hints of the horrors—the long nightmare—it apparently helped her survive. One can link this with the remark I quoted above: "It [Christ?] is there for the retrievement of desolation—for those who have arrived at the end of all things of the intellect—as an antidote to extinction." This one moment, this "illumination," is frozen in epigrammatic stillness against Loy's desolation, and her access to it in memory is sustaining.

With reference only to the poem, the reader would not know the full extent of the disasters Loy was to suffer—the mysterious disappearance or death of Arthur Cravan, for instance. Yet maybe it is enough to mention the nightmare without having to detail it. Within the poem, this key passage works to explain Loy's dissatisfaction with her "religious instruction," accounts of which follow shortly afterward.

Loy was raised a Christian because "In mixed marriages / it is mostly the custom / for female children / to adhere to the maternal religion" (168). But the poem is critical of both orthodox Christianity and Judaism, and for related reasons:

> there is always a pair
> of idle adult
> accomplices in duplicity
> to impose upon their brood
> ideals erected upon such increate altitudes
> that Man
> in falling from contemplation
> of a mere simulacrum
> has soused himself (in blood
> since Time began)
>
> Jehovah—
> exemplar par excellence
> of megalomania—
> the Whole Old Testament
> of butcherly chastisement
> coerces humanity
> to an "assumed acceptance"
> of an abstract idea
>
> (169)

This seems mostly directed at the father. Several sections earlier in the poem Loy tells the story of a "gift" she once received from her father, a shiny new coin which she took (with her nurse) to buy some flowers. She had been told that it was a "sovereign," only to be humiliated when she learned that it was really a farthing. The pun on "sovereign" is too much for Loy to resist, and in the last strophe of the section her own father, with his cruel gift, mutates into the Father: "How evil a Father must be / to burst a universe by getting / so far into a sovereign" (167). While Loy's father comes off better in the poem than her mother, as something of a victim because of her mother's use of English ancestry as a weapon, Loy's critique of the excesses of his patriarchal authority (as manifested in his economic power as well as in his ironic acceptance of her mother's machinations) is clear enough. The Old Testament God of his ancestors was only a crueler form of the idealism "erected upon such increate altitudes."

Loy's relationship to her mother's Christianity has a complex history. As a child she seems to have had little choice but to accept it, while struggling to find a way around its idealistic dogma toward the kind of direct apprehension of the divine she eventually found alone in their garden:

> Press the cerebellum
> into phantom
> moulds of idealism
>
> and no matter
> what ocular
> and intellectual contact with phenomena
> occur—
> grey matter
> is addled forever
>
> Ova accepts Christ
> as the sacrificial
> prototype of the laboriously elect
> sect
>
> notwithstanding
> that the maternal Christian
> is inflicting
> Him upon her
> as a spiritual bludgeon
> threatening
>
> And the vaguely disgusting
> inquietudes of the flesh surrounding
> her she also accepts
> as she is bidden
> as hidden
> immortalities
> that ripen
> for divine destinies
>
> (167–68)

One thing that can distinguish the mystic from other believers is an insistence on a direct sensual experience of the divine presence. That is, mysticism is not content to accept God entirely "on faith." For various reasons, this has often left mystics at odds with the orthodox among their faith. In part, Loy's distaste for her mother's Christianity has to do with her promotion of this "belief" on no grounds other than faith and dogma. Thus the pun on "no matter" in the second strophe above. Along with this, Loy resents the use of Christianity as a moral "bludgeon," especially in its renunciation of the flesh—always well hidden, as the ironic line break in the last strophe suggests. What Loy adapts from her mother's religion is the idea of Christ as sacrificial prototype, which is something different from the idea of Christ as mankind's savior. Loy's Christ is not historical. As Gershom Scholem has written, "the mystic tries to assure himself of the living presence of God," and "conceives [of] the source of religious knowledge and experience which bursts forth from his own heart as being of equal importance" as the historical occurrence of Revelation. For the mystic, there is a "constant repetition" of revelation throughout history (10–14).

Such a mysticism with all of its confidence in meaningful individual experience also allowed Loy to accept what to her mother was the "vaguely disgusting" body. There is a remarkable passage in the poem where Loy takes up the image of the rose she uses to characterize her mother and suggests its appropriateness as a figure for repressed sexuality:

> The best
> is this compressed
> all round-and-about
> itself conformation
> never letting out
> subliminal infection
> from hiatuses
> in its sub-roseal skeleton
>
> (129)

The hothouse purity of this "armored tower" matriarch heavily wrapped in her "iron busks of curved corsets" (140) bred disease, Loy suggests. Quickly thereafter, the image of the intricate and layered conformity of the rose is then extended to apply to the British empire, so that what is true of the mother is also true of the imperial heritage she admired. To "let out" such "infection," to free a once repressed body, is one of Loy's particular agendas in this poem as well as in most of her work; this poem is unique only for its development of clear analogies between cultural and individual repression, for its use of images as heavily invested in tradition and ideology as the English rose.

While the rose is a familiar image, its use here is not. In an amusing passage early in the poem, Loy imagines her initiation into poetry as having occurred when, as a two-year-old, she hears her mother and her nurse talking over the crib of a younger sister. They are discussing the baby's green diarrhea, a word which the toddler Loy hears as "iarrhea." Because she has been playing with a green ball and watching a gleaming "cat's eyes horse shoe" pin on her mother's bosom she associates this word "iarrhea" with beautiful and beloved objects. This "fragmentary / simultaneity / of ideas / embodies / the word" (141). Obviously, Loy is having some fun in imagining this scene as an initiation into language, though the section ends with the mother once again asserting her repressive control over the child Ova, pulling her out from beneath the furniture to prevent her from pursuing her curiosity about objects with new and strange names. "Simultaneity" might resonate for historians of the avant-garde as a name for those verbal techniques whereby the avant-garde poet would force new perceptions on her reader; Loy is suggesting that her career as an avant-gardist is grounded in new perceptions of the excremental set over against English idealisms.

This is made more explicit in the next section of the poem, "Opposed Aesthetics," which contrasts Loy's own excremental poetic with the sickly aestheticism of her painter-husband, Stephen Haweis:

> As the arrested artists
> of the masses
> whose child faces
> turned upon Beauty
> the puny   light
> of their immobile recognition
>
> made moon-flowers   out of muck
> and things desired
> out of their tenuous soul-stuff
> Until the Ruling Bluff
> demanded a hell-full
> of labor
> for half a belly-full

So did the mongrel-girl
of Norman's land
coerce the shy
Spirit of Beauty
from excrements and physic

While Esau of Ridover Square
absorbs the erudite idea
that Beauty IS nowhere
except posthumously to itself
in the antique

And trains
the common manifestations
of creation
to flatten
before his
eyes
to one vast monopattern

(142–43)

The elaborate simile that begins this vignette is necessary because Loy has
been comparing her own more humble origins to Haweis's. Her childhood
surrounded by such spectacularly repressed sexuality explains her need to
take up the body as her subject matter. Haweis, on the other hand, whom
we see earlier as a five-year-old surrounded by Ming vases, comes to believe that beauty simply cannot be found among the new, the common, or
the living. These are only repulsive to him, and thus the future husband
and wife are seen to be "opposed," their marriage eventually to fail.

The narrative of "Anglo-Mongrels and the Rose" ends in the poem's
penultimate section with a brief notice of the fact that Loy would eventually set out "to seek her fortune" in literature and a cryptic account of
what seems to have been several attempts to run away from home. That
she equated the whole environment of her mother's English "civilization"
with repression is proved by the concluding strophe of the section:

Oracle of civilization—
"Thou shalt not live by dreams alone
but by every discomfort

that proceedeth out of
legislation"

(172)

The final section of the poem largely transcends autobiography to proffer a discursive statement of the theological issues at stake in the entire poem. It begins by announcing the exhaustion of religious discourse:

Out of the hands of God
the aboriginal
muscle-pattern
with its ominously
cruciform completion
in view of propagation
indulged   its uniform
imputation
of the image and likeness
of Deity
to satiety

and through varying civilizations
experimented in deformations
of contour
while fashion
and fanaticism disputed
with passion
the incompatibility
with his dignity
of exposing man
to the contemplation
of the insignia
of his origin
and continuity

(172)

This might be read as a condensed summary of the history of religion up to its contemporary crisis. The "cruciform completion" of the "muscle-pattern" refers to the unity of body and spirit which various religions have sought to deny by erecting (upon "increate altitudes" Loy would say) hierarchical systems, dualisms of body and spirit. Loy believes all of these systems are incompatible with human "dignity," and the next few strophes shift to jingling rhymes to reduce them to nonsense:

> Theological tinkers
> and serious thinkers
> attacked the problem
> of dissubstantiation
>
> Some said
> "It were better to cast it off from us utterly"
> And some took a plank of wood and set it
> about with nails and lay upon it
> saying "This will make us forget it"
>
> Spiritual drapers
> Popes and fakirs and shakers
> decked it
> out with oblivion
> and let it
> appear
> to disappear

(173)

The awkward coinage "dissubstantiation" takes its cue from the concept of transubstantiation, the Christian doctrine that the bread and wine of the Eucharist are transformed into the true presence of Christ, while their appearance remains the same. If transubstantiation is bread and wine becoming flesh, then "dissubstantiation" is (real) flesh becoming pure idea, symbol. The "problem" of dissubstantiation is the problem of the flesh, or, in the terms Loy uses earlier in one section's title, the problem of "Christ's Regrettable Reticence"—his failure to appear in a contemporary world. Ultimately, the "problem" is one of proof: how does one prove the reality of a nonmaterial Christ or God? One can try to suggest that material evidence is not important, just as one can try to deny the body on a bed of nails. But the body's reality and the fact of carnal desire will not disappear. As Loy writes several strophes later, "the 'unprintable word' ['sex'?] / is impossible to erase from a vocabulary" (173). This has always been the case, she implies, even before the triumph of Darwin and Freud and the rest of them. There has always been the dispute with "passion" to trouble both the orthodox and the fanatics.

And then suddenly, without transition, the poem turns to announce
the birth of another "greater than Jehovah":

> And there arose another
> greater than Jehovah
> The Tailor
> the stitches of whose seams
> he is unworthy
> to unloose
>
> (173–74)

Who is this one greater than Jehovah? Christ? Freud? The passage is impossibly cryptic, ambiguous. Is the Tailor Jehovah? To whom does "he"
refer? Perhaps the next passage will give us a clue:

> Out of the hands of Exodus
> the Oxonian
> seeming
> a sunbeam that has chanced to stray
> into a cut-away
> (Gentlemen
> wear
> clothes
> with an easy air
> of debonair
> inevitability).
>
> (174)

If we remember Loy's suggestion that gentiles had used Freud to "counteract the effects" of Christ, we might want to read Loy's "Tailor"—with a
capital *t*—as Freud, a Jew ("Out of the hands of Exodus") who had cast
light ("a sunbeam") upon the old strictures of Jehovah. Such a reading
would seem to be justified by the following strophe, where Loy writes that
"Clothed and shod / the tailor's concept of a man-made God . . . / peoples
the sod" (174). Freud, of course, would insist that God was a projection of
human desire and need, an illusion without a future.

And yet we must also remember that, in the poem itself, Exodus is the
pseudonym for Loy's father, who had shed the religion of his ancestors,
thereby passively subordinating himself to his wife's Christianity. Finally,
Loy seems to be arguing that her father's secularism—his apathy before

matters of the spirit—is typical of modern middle-class Britain, where religion can be less a matter of deep belief than of genteel social conventions:

> Under the shears
> of the prestidigitator cutter
> (who achieves
> the unachievable Act of the Apostles)
> the cruciform scourge
> of conscience
> disappears
> in utter
> bifurcate dissimulation
> leaving
> only those inevitable yet more or less circumspect
> creasings
> in the "latest thing in trouserings"
> or serge
> And man
> at last assumes his self-respect
>
> (174–75)

There is surely irony in Loy's metaphors, which equate the renunciation of Christian conscience with the choice of a new pair of pants. Since in this part of the poem Loy is especially interested in moving beyond autobiography to a diagnosis of the fate of Christianity in the modern era, we should note her ambivalence about the condition of Christianity. The "cruciform scourge of conscience" may have become little more than a "crease," but that also means that we have gained a new "self-respect."

But if there is any doubt that a modernized Christianity did not altogether "suit" Loy, the next passage removes it:

> And man with his amorphous nature
> who defied
> the protoform of Who made him
> but has not denied
> Him   obeyed
> the tailor who remade him
> and denies him
>
> (175)

I read this as saying that the evolution of human culture has left us in a position to deny the protoform of God, which is to say the historical Christ, but not divinity itself. Without the ethical and religious dogma of a credible Christianity (or Judaism), it is "the tailor" (now reduced to a small "t") who offers direction for living. The tailor—whom we might read as a figure for a secularized Christianity or just simply as modernity—has remade humanity, but he also denies us, or at least that part of us which is spiritual, our "cruciform" nature.

Loy then concludes the poem by noting that Christ, that "fancier of travestied torsoes / . . . who staked the plot / of mankind in his nobler form" is despised and ostracized by the "gently born," who "turn away" from him (175). Ironically, this is because he chose an occupation "all too feminine"—the giving birth to new men and women. But that is not the reason the gentlemen and ladies give for ignoring him, she says. They believe that "Thou shalt not look upon the fact of God and live!" (175). *Fact* is the key word here. The gentlemen and ladies would take their God on faith, and not have him subjected to analysis or the test of experience. They would rather not look too closely at Him, preferring instead to trade for a set of moral propositions which might encourage good cheer and proper English behavior. A popularized Freudianism would want to connect such gentility with the mechanisms of repression; Loy's Freudian but finally more Assagiolian—or Blakean, if we require a canonical figure— argument anticipates A. Alvarez's famous assault on gentility by nearly forty years. "Anglo-Mongrels and the Rose" professes a figure of Christ that had survived an English upbringing, a Christ that could look Freud in the eye without blinking, a Christ who might gather the inexpressible experience of a woman whose will and imagination made her uneasy with the forms of Christianity she knew.

5. *Briggflatts*, Melancholy, Northumbria

Like many modernist and postmodernist works, Basil Bunting's *Briggflatts* (1966) is partly a self-referential poem, reflecting on all that makes its composition difficult. In the poem's second strophe the figure of a mason precisely carving upon a tombstone the name of "a man abolished" (43) links writing and death, thematizing writing as funerary inscription. "The word gives me the being, but it gives it to me deprived of being" (42), Maurice Blanchot once wrote, thinking of Hegel's remarks on naming, and it is writing *as* naming that will be called into question in a poem ending with a series of questions, poised between the need for an "acknowledged land" (58) and the fact of "fields we do not know" (63), toward which we blindly go, "earsick" and towed by "strong song" (63). The mason will be careful with "letter's edge, / fingertips checking" (43), ideally working in harmony with natural processes to the extent that he might "time" his mallet to the "lark's twitter." But the poet will also be like the lark, whose song is set against the mason's mallet "naming none": "Painful lark, labouring to rise!" / The solemn mallet says: In the grave's slot / he lies. We rot." (43). Anthropomorphized like that bull implored to brag and "descant" and dance in the previous strophe, this lark, like the mason himself, is a figure for the poet. Between the "naming" of the mason and the "painful" song of the bird a space is opened, a tension created. This writing would rise above inert inscription into the transient being that is song, but it will understand that effort as difficult, its chances of success involving a future beyond the poet's control, which he can at best resign himself to stoically.

In his defense of lyric, Allen Grossman writes that "whereas selves are found or discovered, persons and personhood is an artifact, something that is *made,* an inscription upon the ontological snowfields of a world that is not in itself human. . . . And the distinction between person and self is that the *person* is value-bearing: the person is that fact in the world which we are not permitted to extinguish, which has rights" (20). "Person," Grossman argues, is inhuman, ideal, value bearing; the "word *person* does not specify a static or isolated state of affairs, but a profound interaction, a drama always going on, of acknowledgment and presence" (21). Grossman's late modernist values sit well beside Bunting, I think, and in discussing *Briggflatts* here, I want to acknowledge that one might read the poem in sight of its claims as "an autobiography," as Bunting called it, without losing sight of Grossman's modernist sense of "person" as a made thing. In textures of writing which seek to synthesize an identity, to sound the conflicts and dimensions of a "person" or "voice," we confront again and again the poet's realization that the poem's relationship to identity—to what he is—is elegiac. "An autobiography" Bunting called his poem, but it is not a chronicle of fact, of a "self." It is rather autobiography as extended lyric, autobiography as *"the image of the person* that is encoded in the very language-matter of the poem itself" (19). The poem's central concern is giving the melancholy accompanying the diffuse memories of an old man (Basil Bunting) form—in order to disperse them, to fix them here as the image of a person whose voice will be credible enough to merit acknowledgment, to make present an identity. Our hearing that "voice" (and its conflicts, its struggle to emerge) will do work on behalf of identity more important than our struggle to grasp or wrestle a more conceptual understanding from the poem.

Briggflatts has come to be a key text for some poets and critics in England precisely because it is for them unmistakably an English—or, more precisely, a Northumbrian—poem, full of passages lush in their hard alliterations and stress rhythms. As Tony Lopez notes, Bunting's "habits of language use, and stories of ancient Welsh and Norse heroes, help to construct Northumbria as a proud and hard kingdom that has understandable attractions in a time when the old industrial basis of the North East's economy has been undermined" (114). In his notes to the poem Bunting is careful to gloss Northumbrian words "strange to men used to the koine or to Americans who may not know how much Northumberland differs from the Saxon south of England" (210) and suggests that "southrons" will mispronounce others. But at the same time he was given to speaking of

Scarlatti's sonatas when discussing the larger structures and movement of the poem, and thought that the densely woven patterns of Northumbrian art which are imitated in the poem's patterning of vowel and consonant sounds and images were a characteristic of classical Persian art as well. The very decision to write an "autobiography" which would not be "a record of fact" or a "chronicle," a poem whose "truth" would be of "another kind" (210) bespeaks an "impersonal" modernist aesthetic with an international pedigree, though the most important task of the poem, it might be said, is to offer that modernism a Northumbrian signature which might distinguish it from, say, *Four Quartets*, equally an autobiography but one content to rest in the certainties gathered into a more rotund, public language.

The poem's composition was made possible in part, as is well known, by the flowering of regional arts movements and fundings in the 1960s. Bunting's friend Denis Goacher has speculated that new activity among younger poets in the north of England prompted Bunting to show what an older poet, a one-time companion of Pound and Yeats, could do. It was also written at a moment when Britain's belated recognition of economic decline and the end of empire was breeding parochialism and romantic nationalism among some of England's political elite. In 1964, as Bunting was completing the poem, Enoch Powell—a neo-Georgian poet and classicist himself as well as one of the most important oracles of British racism and nationalism—was arguing that "England underwent no organic change as the mistress of world empire. So the continuity of her existence was unbroken. . . . Thus, our generation is like one which comes home again from years of distant wandering. We discover affinities with earlier generations of English, who feel no country but this to be their own. . . . We find ourselves once more akin to the old English."[1] Bunting's poem too is about wandering and "coming home," but his is a home reached only after a vision of apocalypse. While at least one section of the poem does seek to imagine "unbroken" continuities in Northumbria, this is a home where one arrives suddenly and without transition as a "dazed" woodman awakening and suddenly lucky to hear the pastoral song of the slowworm, a home one finds after meeting the accidents of fate and the limits of ambition. Bunting's home is "post-imperial" and inhabited without regret or irony.

The moment of Powell's speeches on behalf of reimagining English national identity was also the moment of newly vigorous national movements in Scotland and Wales. "Politically speaking, the key to these neonationalist renaissances lies in the slow foundering of the British state, not in the Celtic bloodstream," Tom Nairn wrote in his polemically titled *The Break-Up of Britain: Crisis and Neo-Nationalism* (1977), a book written too soon for Nairn to have witnessed the full consequences of a redeployment of Powell's rhetoric of one nation in Thatcherism's populist assault on Britain's liberal intelligentsia. Bunting's poem works with materials of "cultural ancestry," uses them to appeal sentimentally to regional consciousness, but in referring to "Baltic plainsong speech" (44) together with "a galliard by Byrd" (51) and "Schoenberg's maze" (51), in taking the narrative of his poem's middle section from Firdosi's Persian epic, and in grafting Welsh, Norse, and Northumbrian bardic traditions onto modernist collage and *condensare,* it is a hybrid structure. Its Northumbrian core is set in a field of international influences and traditions, confronting the parochialism of the English center with continuities beyond its view — the bardic hero and the Northumbrian saint with the modern Northumbrian, once-alienated poet; the British imperialist with Alexander.

But I am getting ahead of myself here, and need first to map the development of the "person" this poem would project or embody. In the first half of the poem, as Bunting works the poem toward an emotional climax, we hear often of a difficulty in bringing a "resolution in feeling" to the page.[2] At one point the poet refers to the impossibility of finding the right words, to dissatisfaction with the words found. The poem alludes to discarded text: "Brief words are hard to find / shapes to carve and discard" (46). At another moment we hear of a pressure that inhibits composition, cast in a metaphor alluding to an English sport: "What twist can counter the force / that holds back / woods I roll?" (47). We encounter the same motif expressed in a musical metaphor: "But who will entune a bogged orchard, / its blossom gone, / fruit unformed, where hunger and / damp hush the hive?" (51). And at one point near the end of the first section, Bunting declares straightforwardly and despairingly, "It is easier to die than to remember" (46).

In a letter to Peter Makin written in the last year of his life, Bunting remarked in the course of discussing his poetry that he felt himself to be "much inclined to" the sin of *accidie,* and if we are to understand what it is that *Briggflatts* is struggling against, what it is that is inhibiting the poet's remembering, his "naming," we might begin by understanding what is involved with this "sin." In Bunting's letter to Makin, he explains that it means essentially "hopelessness":

In the Commedia, Medusa makes her appearance just after Dante has made acquaintance with the "accidiosi." Chaucer had the word, but it has vanished from modern English and all its very complex meaning is forgotten and no one takes any notice of it. It is essentially hopelessness, no longer a cardinal sin, perhaps because the industrial revolution has condemned so large a proportion of our population to wallow in it. In the Well of Lycopolis I have tried to turn Dante's contempt for it around, where I have Styx "silvered by a wind from Heaven"—ultimate hope rising from the helpless victim of accidie. You may reasonably conclude that it is a sin I feel myself much inclined to, to be cured or nullified by the epicurean slowworm rather than by Alexander's heroics, though both have a place.[3]

Dante fixes the *accidiosi* in the fifth circle of hell in his *Inferno*'s seventh canto, where as the "sluggish" or the "sullen" they are among those whom anger has defeated, wedged in a swamp. Two cantos later, Virgil and Dante will encounter the fates, who are asking for Medusa—agent of castration, enforcer of impotence. Bunting thought the Medusa did little more than underscore the accidie. Within the larger narrative of the *Inferno*, cantos VII through IX record a second major crisis in Dante's journey, a moment when he fears he will not be able to go on. No part of Bunting's beloved Dante mattered more to him, as is evident in "The Well of Lycopolis" and "Attis," which translate parts of the *Inferno*'s cantos VII and IX. The problem of *accidie* is central to these poems, but, as Bunting's letter explains, it is *Briggflatts* and its "epicurean slowworm" which presents its "cure."

The complex history of *acedia*—a variant of *accidie*—is well documented in Reinhard Kuhn's brilliant book, *The Demon of Noontide,* where Kuhn traces at great length the evolution of the word from the fourth century, when it first became "the recognized designation for a condition of the soul characterized by torpor, dryness, and indifference culminating in a disgust concerning anything to do with the spiritual" (40). According to Kuhn, the first literature on acedia coincided with the inception of monasticism; it was a malady monks and hermits felt themselves prone to in the deprivations of their lives. Described by Evagrius of Pontus in the fourth century as one of the eight capital sins, the "torpor" of *acedia* eventually acquired a rather ambiguous valuation. For later mystics such as Bernard of Clairvaux, John of the Cross, and Theresa of Avila, the spiritual aridity of *acedia* is "almost a precondition for a life of eternal bliss"

(45). For them, *acedia* is a psychic condition one must pass through—as Dante does—to attain bliss, a kind of way station on the *via negativa*. Within the monastic movement itself, as represented by Evagrius (and also perhaps by Cuthbert, the seventh-century Northumbrian saint who figures so importantly in *Briggflatts*), acedia is the last of the sins to conquer and the most dangerous.[4] Having vanquished other vices, having replaced gluttony with generosity and so forth, the monk is still exposed to pride in his own accomplishments. But in transcending acedia he entertains the highest of virtues, joy in all creation.

Looking backward for related discourses, Kuhn compares the literature on *acedia* with the equally complex classical literature on melancholy. In his view, the two terms *acedia* and *melancholy*, for all their different valuations, describe a similar psychic condition. Perhaps the most fascinating classical text on melancholy is Aristotle's treatise on the humors, the *Problemata Physica*, where he broke from the Hippocratic idea of four humors by removing melancholia from pathology to locate it in nature. In Julia Kristeva's study of melancholia, she writes that

> this Greek notion of melancholia remains alien to us today; it assumes a "properly balanced diversity" (*eukratos anomalia*) that is metaphorically rendered by froth (*aphros*), the euphoric counterpoint to black bile. Such a white mixture of air (*pneuma*) and liquid brings out froth in the sea, wine, as well as the sperm of man. . . . The melancholia he invokes is not a philosopher's disease but his very nature, his *ethos*. . . . With Aristotle, melancholia, counterbalanced by genius, is coextensive with man's anxiety in Being. (7)

For Aristotle, melancholy is neither sin nor psychosis, but rather an indication of the balance in both man and nature of splenetic and ecstatic energies. Kristeva sees this Aristotelian melancholia as a "forerunner of Heidegger's anguish as the *Stimmung* of thought" (7), and for his part Kuhn thinks we cannot overestimate the "incalculable influence" of Aristotle having linked melancholia and genius in philosophy, poetry, and the arts (19). It is partly due to medieval interpretations of Aristotle's text, especially Ficino's *De Vita triplici*, that the cult of the suffering artist emerged in the Renaissance.

With this in mind we might ponder the "epicurean slowworm" as "cure." We know that Bunting admired the Roman poet-philosopher Lucretius, disciple of Epicurus; *A Note on Briggflatts* lists "Lucretius and his masters" among the philosophers he has most sympathy with (3).[5]

Whereas Aristotle tries to link melancholy and genius, Lucretius understands it as a more typical psychic condition; his discourse concerning it will be an ethical one:

Men feel plainly enough within their minds, a heavy burden, whose weight depresses them. If only they perceived with equal clearness the causes of this depression, the origin of this lump of evil within their breasts, they would not lead such a life as we now see all too commonly—no one knowing what he really wants and everyone forever trying to get away from where he is, as though mere locomotion could throw off the load. . . . Since he remains reluctantly wedded to the self whom he cannot of course escape, he grows to hate him, because he is a sick man ignorant of the cause of his malady. . . .

What is this deplorable lust of life that holds us trembling in bondage to such uncertainties and dangers? A fixed term is set to the life of mortals, and there is no way of dodging death. In any case the setting of our lives remains the same throughout, and by going on living we do not mint any new coin of pleasure. So long as the object of our craving is unattained, it seems more precious than anything besides. Once it is ours, we crave for something else. So an unquenchable thirst for life keeps us always on the gasp. (11)

Lucretius is describing the *horror loci,* the feeling of limitation that is one of the symptoms of melancholy (and ennui, as Kuhn would have it). In Lucretius's description of a Roman gentleman we have one of the first diagnoses of the restlessness and the perpetual wandering that constitutes the plot of so much "melancholy" literature, especially among Celtic and northern European peoples. Bunting adapts one part of this passage in several lines in *Briggflatts* which describe his (youthful) abjection: "He lies with one to long for another, / sick, self-maimed, self-hating" (47). Lucretius would have one confront restlessness and desire with what sounds like a recipe for quietism—with study and the search for knowledge, resignation to the limits of life and the inevitability of death. Such a "pastoral" remedy would not have been unattractive to Bunting, especially if, as *Briggflatts* will suggest, the end of "wandering" might be possible with integration in the traditional practices of a specific Northumbrian community, the keeping in step with "fell-born men of precise instep" as they "follow the links" (61). An epicurean but also a Wordsworthian cure.

Some of Bunting's earliest poetry—three short odes written between 1924 and 1926—announce the concerns that will be his in *Briggflatts* in ways that the longer sonatas written later do not. Here, for instance, is the earliest poem of his to survive:

> Weeping oaks grieve, chestnuts raise
> mournful candles. Sad is spring
> to perpetuate, sad to trace
> immortalities never changing.
>
> Weary on the sea
> for sight of land
> gazing past the coming wave we
> see the same wave;
>
> drift on merciless reiteration of years;
> descry no death; but spring
> is everlasting resurrection.
>
> (79)

How "conventional" this poem is in its subject matter! And yet melancholy never knew a more precise, condensed articulation, five stresses (four of them strong) among the poem's first seven syllables, the long vowel sounds of "weeping" and "grieve" surrounding "oaks" without subsuming it, much as affective experience surrounds the thing or event without exhausting its mystery. A generic theme—the eternal sameness of natural cycles—meets the singular torsion of Bunting's syntax—its turning, the way the third line in the middle strophe is lengthened almost as if mimetically to suggest a straining for sight of land, a straining the next line recognizes as vain. In "mournful nature" we have possibly the first precursor of "painful lark" to be found in Bunting's poetry.

A more "Aristotelian" representation of melancholy is found in "I am agog for foam," where the pace of the iambic pentameter—first surging, then slowing—mimics a nearly manic-depressive struggle between euphoric bliss and cataleptic stupor. Students of melancholy from Aristotle to Kristeva have noted that the melancholic is often simultaneously a sensualist, and this most erotic of Bunting's poems makes the same metaphorical equation of froth and sexual discharge one finds in Aristotle:[6]

> I am agog for foam. Tumultuous come
> with teeming sweetness to the bitter shore
> tidelong unrinsed and midday parched and numb
> with expectation. If the bright sky bore
> with endless utterance of a single blue

unphrased, its restless immobility
infects the soul, which must decline into
an anguished and exact sterility
and waste away: then how much more the sea
trembling with alteration must perfect
our loneliness by its hostility.
The dear companionship of its elect
deepens our envy. Its indifference
haunts us to suicide. Strong memories
of sprayblown days exasperate impatience
to brief rebellion and emphasise
the casual impotence we sicken of.
But when mad waves spring, braceletted with foam,
towards us in the angriness of love
crying a strange name, tossing as they come
repeated invitations in the gay
exuberance of unexplained desire,
we can forget the sad splendour and play
at wilfulness until the gods require
renewed inevitable hopeless calm
and the foam dies and we again subside
into our catalepsy, dreaming foam,
while the dry shore awaits another tide.

(81)

In this poem, which happens to have been a favorite of that scholar of
Celtic melancholy, W. B. Yeats, all that Bunting takes to be characteristic
of melancholy—"indifference," "restless immobility," "casual impotence,"
"hopeless calm"—is counterbalanced by the "exuberance of unexplained
desire." The sea in its rocking and surging motion proves to be an apt
metaphor for a recurrent desire for the new which is always also the same.
There is something terrifying about the poem's relentless refusal to posit
any escape from the cycles it describes. If the sea, as a figure for the repeti-
tive "alteration" of desire and indifference, is "hostile" and does nothing
more than force us to recognize our "loneliness" or singularity, there is no
comfort either in the poem's other figure, the sky. Its static permanence
is equated with sterility, the pun in "bore" identifying boredom with destructive invasiveness, as in a drill opening a hole in something previously
intact. Later in the same sentence boredom "infects."

Among the three early Bunting odes which might be described as odes "on melancholy" the one that is closest to *Briggflatts* is "Farewell ye sequent graces," where melancholy is represented not so much as a general psychosexual condition of "man" and nature but rather as the result of a particular event—the lost love that will figure in the later poem both within an autobiographical frame and synedochically as Bunting reconsiders his place within Northumbrian life. It ends as follows:

> Airlapped, silent muses of light,
> cease to administer
> poisons to dying memories to stir
> pangs of old rapture, cease to conspire
> reunions of inevitable seed
> long blown barren sown gathered
> haphazard to wither.
>
> (80)

What this poem shares with "I am agog with foam" is Bunting's fear that no willful act of forgetting will be able to supplant desire sustained by memory. There is no possibility of escaping the past; the very effort to "poison" memory only revives it. Altogether, the poem is less a statement of the need to reconcile oneself to the past, to a history of psychic pain, than a prayer that the pain might be forgotten—hence the address to the muses. Even the poem's opening suggests as much: "Farewell ye sequent graces / voided faces still evasive." *Briggflatts* will extend this poem's farewell but in a voice more reconciled to it.

In the letter to Peter Makin I quoted above, Bunting suggested that his "The Well of Lycopolis"—one of the longer sonatas written some ten years after the poems above—had tried to reverse Dante's more orthodox valuation of *acedia,* and I will complete this survey of Bunting's early representations of melancholy by quoting from the last section of that poem:

> Stuck in the mud they are saying: 'We were sad
> in the air, the sweet air the sun makes merry,
> we were glum of ourselves, without a reason;
> now we are stuck in the mud and therefore sad.'
> That's what they mean, but the words die in their throat;
> they cannot speak out because they are stuck in the mud.
> Stuck, stick, Styx. Styx, eternal, a dwelling.
> But the rivers of Paradise,

the sweep of the mountains they rise in?
Drunk or daft hear
a chuckle of spring water:
drowsy suddenly wake,
but the bright peaks have faded.

. . . . .

Join the Royal Air Force
and See the World. The navy will
Make a Man of You. Tour India with the Flag.
Out of the ragtime army,
involuntary volunteer,
queued up for the pox in Rouen. What a blighty!

. . . . .

muttering inaudibly beneath the quagmire,
irresolute, barren, dependent, this page
ripped from Love's ledger and Poetry's:
and besides I want you to know for certain
there are people under the water. They are sighing.
The surface bubbles and boils with their sighs.
Look where you will you see it.
The surface sparkles and dances with their sighs
as though Styx were silvered by a wind from heaven.

(26–27)

Throughout its first three sections "The Well of Lycopolis" is a poem which satirizes the "abject love" and "infamous poetry" of modern England. Bloomsbury is the prime target as Bunting depicts a decadent and impotent society subject to the "cunnilingual law" (25)—there is considerable misogyny in the poem. The use of the plural "we" throughout the poem suggests that Bunting did not mean to exempt himself from the critique he forges out of a collage of fragments from Dante, Villon, and other sources, although, as is often the case in the works of this northern poet, it is the cultural center in London that takes the worst beating.

In turning to Dante in the fourth section of the poem Bunting broadens the scope of the poem in order to explore the underlying causes of cultural impotence and abjection. Thus the first section quoted above, which begins with a translation of lines from Dante's canto VII, seeks first to relate the impotence of modern society to *acedia*. The next strophe sarcastically offers bogus remedies for psychic crisis—join the army, tour

India—available to citizens of the empire. While these "career options" are clearly mocked, it should be noted that at the time of the composition of this poem Bunting himself was pursuing a kind of escape from England, trying to find a living in the Canary Islands. One might argue that the sarcasm of the strophe hardly disguises Bunting's own dilemma; there were few options, none which allowed the Englishman to escape his culture's pervasive despair. The strophe which follows this (I have omitted it here) rather predictably relates this despair to World War I, referring to self-inflicted wounds, mustard-gas ulcers, and other horrors. Then we return to Dante's hell in the poem's final strophe, historical specificity giving way to poetic analogues.

What can we make of the poem's last line given what Bunting said about it to Makin? It is true that Dante has nothing but scorn for the sullen sinners stuck in the mud, but Bunting does not understand *acedia* as a "sin" in the manner of medieval theologians or poets.[7] In writing that the surface of Styx bubbles with the sighs of the sullen as if "silvered by a wind from Heaven," Bunting perhaps reads *acedia* as a stage in the journey to spiritual enlightenment, after the fashion of the mystics of the *via negativa*. The "people under the water" might, as it were, emerge, once they recognized the source of their plight. Such optimism is not characteristic of Bunting, however; still it is clear that, moving towards satire, the poem has a didactic moment. This is culture poetry, mining the Western archive in order to launch an ironic critique of contemporary British society. It resembles Pound's *Mauberley,* some of the earlier Eliot. *Briggflatts* will have little to do with this model of poetry. It will offer us, instead of critique and ironic proposition, a model of a Northumbrian voice that would be acknowledged.

For readers unfamiliar with it, I might briefly describe the parts of the poem. *Briggflatts* has five sections and a coda. Except for the middle section, which has two parts in what Bunting thought of as a dream sequence, the poem follows the order of the seasons, beginning with spring. The first section offers all we need of the "plot" of the poem—a tender and erotic vignette of two young lovers which ends with several references to this young love having been willfully abandoned, "murdered." It is notably without first-person pronouns; these will enter the poem only at that point in the second section when the poem expressly addresses the difficulties and belatedness of its composition. The second section of the poem finds the youthful protagonist of the first now a poet, wandering in London and then abroad in Italy, awash in corruption, alienated from urban and foreign experience. The third begins in the mythical landscape of the Persian poet Firdosi's *Shahnameh;* we are among Alexander's men watching the conqueror push toward Gog and Magog, the end of the world. After Alexander confronts the angel of death, Israfel, we are transported suddenly and without transition back to Northumbria, where a "woodman dazed by an adder's sting" (55) is listening to the slowworm's song of pastoral bliss. The "I" enters the poem again, with a vengeance, as the voice of the slowworm. The fourth begins with a cryptic summary of Northumbrian history and then moves on to say goodbye to the long abandoned love that has haunted the protagonist. The fifth returns us to pastoral Northumbria, a Northumbria opening out into the protagonist's cosmic perspective, where time's irrelevance presses upon him, where "Then is Now" (62). The coda then concludes the poem with a series of questions which suggest the limits of human knowledge and the power of emotions we barely understand.

Just a few words now on the architecture of the poem's symbols and autobiographical screens as they might be related to Bunting's melancholy. The poem appropriates several historical persons — conquerors, saints, and bardic poets. All are important to the poem — Saint Cuthbert representing a simple and contented life which is the opposite of the ambition and turmoil that was the life of Eric Bloodaxe and Alexander the Great. Bloodaxe, a ninth-century Norwegian king, was granted Northumbria by Athelstan, and journeyed through the Orkneys and Dublin and back to Northumbria. He was murdered at Stainmore, which Bunting refers to several times during the poem when he is thinking of the end of journeys and of death. Bunting's Alexander, as I noted above, is taken from Firdosi's *Shahnameh,* from the section of that epic poem that describes Alexander pushing to the edge of the world against the wishes of his army. At the edge of the world Alexander confronts Israfel, the angel of death and resurrection. In the complexly interwoven logic of the poem's "symbols" or autobiographical screens, Alexander supplants Bloodaxe; while the latter's "flight" ends only in death, the former recognizes the terminal point of all ambition and turns back. The poem leaves him questioning Israfel about the day of judgment, and then shifts suddenly to the woodman's dream, the lesson of which is that satisfaction might be found in humility within the order of the natural world. That is where Cuthbert comes in, though in the poem he is alluded to rather than appropriated as an autobiographical screen.

In the heroes Bloodaxe and Alexander and the hermit Cuthbert, Bunting means to delineate the full range of his "person," ambition and will as well as knowledge of their limits. Within a less explicitly autobiographical frame, Bloodaxe and Cuthbert also allow Bunting to contest prevailing definitions of "Englishess" by "harnessing north-south divisions" and mapping "completely different boundaries: Dublin—York—Orkney" (118). Perhaps Firdosi's Alexander is intended to stand for both British imperial adventure and for its endpoint in the Middle East (the Suez crisis). Bunting is not without admiration for the ambition of Alexander, just as, despite his record of criticizing actual imperial policies, it is possible that he might once have thought that "a decent British empire" might have been the best system of government in the world.[8] Bunting's admiration for Alexander and empire is by no means simple, for the ambition they represent exists at considerable cost:

> Brief words are hard to find,
> shapes to carve and discard:
> Bloodaxe, king of York,
> king of Dublin, king of Orkney.
> Take no notice of tears;
> letter the stone to stand
> over love laid aside lest
> insufferable happiness impede
> flight to Stainmore.
>
> (46)

Too often the conqueror renounces love, abandons happiness. Read in an autobiographical context, Bunting's bitter self-reproach in this passage is obvious. We are indeed to notice the tears, the sacrifice of a possible happiness, ironically called "insufferable." What was he escaping in Northumbria except love? What was he running to except death? Read in the poem's most immediate national context, the poem joins many other voices outlining a postimperial morality.

Along with the legendary heroes and saints, Bunting's poem uses an extensive bestiary. Too numerous and carefully interwoven for me to reduce to any one-to-one allegorical correspondence, the semantic role of the most important creatures within the autobiography must be mentioned. There is the bull who opens the poem in Bunting's wistful invocation of spring's phallic power and his own youth in Northumbria. Another incarnation of this bull appears in one of the poem's most important passages, Bunting's adaptation of the myth of Pasiphae's rape by Poseidon's bull. In

Bunting's version, Pasiphae willingly submits to the bull, standing "with expectant hand / to guide his seed to its soil; / nor did flesh flinch / distended by the brute / nor loaded spirit sink / till it had gloried in unlike creation" (52). Their "unlike creation" was the Minotaur, a monster half brute and half man, and an emblem for the poem itself. Those who are "resolute to submit," Bunting says in his posthumously published note on the poem, "may bring something new to birth, be it only a monster" (1). In the intersection of the bull and Pasiphae, of willfulness and resignation, we have *Briggflatts,* which is a "monster" one supposes because it tells the truth of a man who views himself as such. Within the larger structures of the poem, the poet's subjectivity can be identified with both rapist and raped, with the violence of form (the mason) and the experience (the lark) that submits to it or attempts to rise above it.

That leaves us with the two other primary creatures in Bunting's bestiary—I'll save mention of a cormorant for later. There are, in abundance, rats, not the Jacobean machinery of horror they are in Eliot's poetry, as Thom Gunn has noted, but rather symbols of a life of cunning, secrecy, poverty, and filth (151). The rats are figures for Bunting's adult life in the Canaries, Iran, and England; more generally, they are figures for the life of a "Poet appointed," who dares "not decline / to walk among the bogus, nothing to authenticate / the mission imposed" (47). We must recognize (as M. L. Rosenthal and Sally Gall do not) that none of Bunting's references to the *poète maudit* in *Briggflatts* are handled with the romanticism of predecessors such as Verlaine; it was only youthful arrogance, he seems to believe, that led him to think the poet's life romantic and heroic; the ambition that sent him abroad cost him happiness and love in Northumbria.[9] The rat is a perfect figure for a difficult, impoverished, and solitary life, where one's only recourse is to be "evasive to persist," where the best one can hope for is to "reject the bait / yet gnaw the best" (59).

The most important creature in Bunting's bestiary is the slowworm, the most recurrent symbol in the poem and the figure for an epicurean sensibility reconciled with the orders of the natural world. As an autobiographical screen, this limbless lizard whose eyelids have given him the name "blind-worm" suggests anything but the beautiful or heroic. He represents a part of the poet that has abandoned willfulness and recognized the error of his earlier ways. He appears at the beginning of the poem, hidden among the mayflowers cast off the hide of the dancing bull, and he appears in the idyll that follows Alexander's vision of Israfel:

Ripe wheat is my lodging. I polish
my side on pillars of its transept,
gleam in its occasional light.
Its swaying
copies my gait.

Vaults stored with slugs to relish,
my quilt a litter of husks, I prosper
lying low, little concerned.
My eyes sharpen
when I blink.

Good luck to reaper and miller!
Grubs adhere even to stubble.
Come plowtime
the ditch is near.

Sycamore seed twirling,
O, writhe to its measure!
Dust swirling trims pleasure.
Thorns prance in a gale.
In air snow flickers,
twigs tap,
elms drip.

Swaggering, shimmering fall,
drench and towel us all!

                                    (55–56)

This is the "slowworm's song," a song of contentment and prosperous harmony in nature. If there be any doubt that these things had become virtues to Bunting, I can refer the reader to an interview Bunting granted Jonathan Williams. Asked "If you did have virtues, which would you want?" Bunting replied, "Inconspicuousness, combined with enterprise" (132–33). That describes the slowworm, but it must be noted that the remark is offered as a description of the virtues Bunting *wants,* not those that he has. Poetry might construct an identity; it does not necessarily reflect one, and *Briggflatts* is *an* autobiography, not *the* autobiography.

There has been much discussion of Bunting's use of developmental principles analogous to those that structure a sonata.[10] Along with a modulation of emotional registers and rhythmic patterns, Bunting's "sonata form" is able to restate themes in a new key, to build upon first motifs to give them greater complexity and denser texture. Thus one early motif—the ambition of Bloodaxe as it meets its bloody end in the last journey to Stainmore—is related to but also different from the story of Alexander in the poem's third section. Thus the bull who is dancing to a phallic hymn in the first of the opening section's twelve 13-line strophes is beef in its last, and so on. One of the things that discussion of the poem's musical model must emphasize is the way in which sonata form allows the poet to resist linear development and narrative; *Briggflatts* is essentially a lyric poem, and a poem skeptical of the relevance of knowledge claims based upon an examination of history, as is evident in the opening lines of the fourth section, where the changes in Northumbria from pagan days through the Christian settlement of Cuthbert are represented as a "shuttles thrown / like drops from a fountain" (57). Cultural origins and historical patterns and continuities are not easily traced in the scattered and complex signs available.

As its symbolic motifs are constantly being mixed and remixed throughout the poem, so are its verse rhythms. Among its five sections (excluding the coda) the first and the last are the most rhythmically consistent; the middle three sections consist of a collage of various accentual, free verse, and song rhythms. All of this gives the reader the impression that no lyric utterance in the poem is final, no emotion simple—all might be revised until the very end. At the same time the poem labors against the very fluidity suggested by sonata form and indeed valorizes the mason's craft as he chisels his words on gravestones: "The mason stirs: / Words! / Pens are too light. / Take a chisel to write" (45). The attainment of such clarity and permanence is surely the desired goal, but the reality is, even for the mason, that "Name and date / split in soft slate / a few months obliterate" (46). One moment melts into another, one second into the next, and even art has only a semipermanence.

We know from biographies that the story of abandoned love that haunts the poem takes part of its shape from Bunting's memories of his youthful romance with Peggy Greenbank.[11] In the opening section we learn that "Her pulse [was] their pace," with "palm countering palm" (45). Introducing the section is the poem's most often quoted strophe:

> Brag, sweet tenor bull,
> descant on Rawthey's madrigal,

each pebble its part
for the fells' late spring.
Dance tiptoe, bull,
black against may.
Ridiculous and lovely
chase hurdling shadows
morning into noon.
May on the bull's hide
and through the dale
furrows fill with may,
paving the slowworm's way.

(43)

Set in the first line's descending vowels and the chiasmus of its conso-
nants, this bull, figure for the young male poet, is up on his toes dancing
in sexual frenzy and bellowing a song against the music of the river rush-
ing over pebbles. But death is already near. We begin to sense that Bunting's opening may be concealing considerable pathos beneath its ecstatic
surface when the bull is given two adjectives: "ridiculous" and "lovely."
While he may be in harmony with nature in so far as his song counter-
points the spring music of the engorged river, he is, however innocently,
chasing shadows, probably his own. Flowers cover him like a laurel crown,
but they also have fallen off in his own excitement, preparing the way and
easing the movement of the more inglorious slowworm. Presumably the
mayflowers will rot in their furrow, and by the next strophe Bunting is
able to name death directly: "In the grave's slot / he lies. We rot" (43). By
the third strophe he will be able to suggest that the procreative energy of
the bull is inextricably entangled with death: "Decay thrusts the blade, /
wheat stands in excrement / trembling" (43).

If the first section of the poem begins with a kind of idyll, where procreative energy and natural decay are perfectly in balance, by the end of
it we have learned that this harmony was to be violated by the willfulness
of the protagonist. Thus we are prepared for the dissatisfaction catalogued
in good Whitmanian fashion by the second section. Bunting describes his
venturing forth into the world as poet:

Poet appointed dare not decline
to walk among the bogus, nothing to authenticate
the mission imposed, despised
by toadies, confidence men, kept boys,

shopped and jailed, cleaned out by whores,
touching acquaintance for food and tobacco.
Secret, solitary, a spy, he gauges
lines of a Flemish horse
hauling beer, the angle, obtuse
a slut's blouse draws on her chest,
counts beat against beat, bus conductor
against engine against wheels against
the pedal, Tottenham Court Road, decodes
thunder, scans
porridge bubbling, pipes clanking, feels
Buddha's basalt cheek
but cannot name the ratio of its curves
to the half-pint
left breast of a girl who bared it in Kleinfeldt's.
He lies with one to long for another,
sick, self-maimed, self-hating,
obstinate, mating
beauty with squalor to beget lines still-born.

(47)

In three condensed sentences driven by verbs detailing his melancholy
detachment from events ("gauges," "counts," "decodes," "scans") Bunting
summarizes the events of his adult life. His poverty, his short career as a
spy, his work with Kamo-no-Chomei's reputedly Buddhistic narrative, his
whoremongering, even his dissatisfaction with his poetic production—all
of these are covered. His was a sensualist's life, hungry for experience,
especially sexual experience. But it was also the life of a melancholic, "self-
maimed, self-hating." The vigorous language of the passage, with its heavy
alliteration, heightens the self-contempt Bunting feels in thinking about
this past. "Self-contempt" is not the right word, though; there is a sense
in which no other life would have satisfied the poet.

As the second section reminds us over and over again, the melancholy
sensualist is condemned to perpetual dissatisfaction as he wanders from
here to there, first of all in this case to Italy's coast. All the while he is half-
aware that "something is lost":

It tastes good, garlic and salt in it,
with the half-sweet white wine of Orvieto

on scanty grass under great trees
where the ramparts cuddle Lucca.

It sounds right, spoken on the ridge
between marine olives and hillside
blue figs, under the breeze fresh
with pollen of Apennine sage.

It feels soft, weed thick in the cave
and the smooth wet riddance of Antonietta's
bathing suit, mouth ajar for
submarine Amalfitan kisses.

It looks well on the page, but never
well enough. Something is lost
when wind, sun, sea upbraid
justly an unconvinced deserter.

(49)

Bunting catalogues the senses only to bemoan their insufficiency. Perhaps the melancholic, with his divided ego, feels most the desirability of wholeness. He is "unconvinced" even amid happiness and romance, feels that somehow he deserves to be chastised. As Freud writes in his famous essay on melancholia, it is "fruitless from a scientific point of view to contradict a patient who brings these accusations against his ego" because he is convinced that such accusations are just and that "he is giving a correct description of his psychological condition" (246). Returning to the Blood-axe motif near the end of section two, Bunting describes a king "Loaded with mail of linked lies" with "nothing on Stainmore to hide / void" (50–55). The movement of the second section's various fragments, considered in their totality, presents Bunting's effort to try and try again to hold this void up to the light. Only in the section's closing lines, remembering the rape of Pasiphae, will he begin to hint at the resolution of psychic crisis that informs the entire poem, the decision to forcibly give up the burden of the past by fixing it on the page, to relinquish the self to a writing which can never be adequate. Bunting will be reconciled to his past only through the act of violence that is the composition of this poem commemorating what has been lost, and the figure for that violence is the rape of Pasiphae.

The third section of the poem, which interrupts the seasonal movement with a long description of Alexander's journey to the end of the world, the brief account of a woodman's dream, and the slowworm's song I quoted above, is the transitional moment in the poem. Rosenthal and Gall have described the first of this section's three parts as a journey through hell (293), but it might be more accurately described as a journey through an excremental world. The opening of section three, based upon Firdosi's version of the Alexander legend in his *Shahnameh,* is narrated by one of Alexander's soldiers who does not share his leader's ambition and wants only to go home to Macedonia. The soldier is tired of conquest and adventure and foreign wars. In strong stress rhythms faintly reminiscent of Pound's "The Seafarer" and several of Pound's cantos, Bunting adapts Firdosi's vision of a world corrupt enough to seem a hell:

> Down into dust and reeds
> at the patrolled bounds
> where captives thicken to gaze
> slither companions, wary, armed,
> whose torches straggle
> seeking charred hearths
> to define a road.
> Day, dim, laps at the shore
> in petulant ripples
> soon smoothed in night
> on pebbles worn by tabulation till
> only the shell of figures is left
> as fragile honeycomb breeze.
> Tides of day strew the shingle
> tides of night sweep, snoring;
> and some turned back, taught
> by dreams the year would capsize
> where the bank quivers, paved
> with gulls stunned on a cliff
> not hard to climb, muffled
> in flutter, scored by beaks,
> pestered by scavengers
> whose palms scoop droppings to mould
> cakes for hungry towns. One
> plucked fruit warm from the arse
> of his companion, who
> making to beat him, he screamed:
> Hastor! Hastor! but Hastor

raised dung thickened lashes to stare
disdaining those who cry:
Sweet shit! Buy!
for he swears in the market:
By God with whom I lunched!
there is no trash in the wheat
my loaf is kneaded from.
Nor will unprofitable motion
stir the stink that settles round him.

(53–54)

In his notes to the poem, Bunting somewhat disingenuously identifies Hastor as "a Cockney hero" (210), a southerner who would be distinctly out of place in this Persian fable.[12] Maybe this is wit aimed at southerners, or perhaps Bunting meant merely to acknowledge and criticize the behavior of English colonialists in Persia. The passage contrasts those who want to turn back (the narrator) and those who do not (Alexander), those who arrogantly and preposterously insist upon their own purity (Hastor) and those who recognize the corruption and defilement that surrounds them (the narrator). Though the narrator sees the shit covering Hastor's eyebrows, Hastor is heard uttering a proper oath: "By God with whom I lunched!" In general, knowledge of one's own corruption and the recognition of limits that follows upon this knowledge is the theme or "point" of section three. Alexander encounters his limits in Israfel. And the woodman, dazed and numb and dreaming, comes to recognize that he is "neither snake nor lizard" but "the slowworm" (55). He must abandon the slithering companions, then, and go home. Autobiographically, this section marks the end of Bunting's journeys—his last stay in Persia—and his decision to return home and attempt to reconcile himself with his past.

The fourth section finds Bunting at home again, and begins appropriately with the history of Northumbria. Knowledge of this history is not sufficient for self-understanding and self-forgiveness, however; one can "follow the clue patiently" and still "understand nothing" (57). Bunting looks not to history but to music in order to confront his past and "acknowledge" his present, acknowledgment being something other than understanding:

It is time to consider how Domenico Scarlatti
condensed so much music into so few bars
with never a crabbed turn or congested cadence,

never a boast or a see-here; and stars and lakes
echo him and the copse drums out his measure,
snow peaks are lifted up in moonlight and twilight
and the sun rises on an acknowledged land.

(58)

Scarlatti's music is as different from the boastful noise of the bull as the
more relaxed and prosaic rhythms of this passage are from the strong accents at the beginning of the poem. Like the bull's descant on the river
Rawthey's madrigal, Scarlatti's music helps Bunting imagine an order or
purpose in the natural world, but it does so in a measure of humility.
While the bull's music is instinctive, full of strong stresses, Scarlatti's represents a quiet and more fully sentient embrace of natural order.

It is in this section that Bunting will once again summon images from
his youthful romance, this time in order to be able to say goodbye for
good to a love fifty years gone:

> My love is young but wise. Oak, applewood,
> her fire is banked with ashes till day.
> The fells reek of her hearth's scent,
> her girdle is greased with lard;
> hunger is stayed on her settle, lust in her bed.
> Light as spider floss her hair on my cheek which a puff scatters,
> light as a moth her fingers on my thigh.
> We have eaten and loved and the sun is up,
> we have only to sing before parting:
> Goodbye, dear love.
>
> Her scones are greased with fat of fried bacon,
> her blanket comforts my belly like the south.
> We have eaten and loved and the sun is up.
> Goodbye.

(58)

Had Bunting begun with such passages, or had they been located somewhere else—they are in the middle of the fourth section—they might
have lost much of their tenderness and poignancy. As it is, this is the
first appearance of the possessive form of the first-person pronoun in the
poem. The present tense temporarily erases the space of fifty years, projecting the erotic vignette memorialized in the poem's first section into a
fourth section where the narrative and lyric frames are more plural and

disjunct. The reader sees what is involved in a "goodbye" difficult enough to require repetition: "Goodbye, dear love" at first, and then, with more finality, "Goodbye."

Having worked through its melancholy, having come to understand the root causes of *horror loci* and the virtues of a life of humility and acceptance of death at home in Northumbria, the poem's autobiographical perspective becomes a cosmic one, meditating upon time's ultimate insignificance. The fifth section opens with an image of time's passing, using one of the most condensed images in the history of English verse: "Drip— icicle's gone" (60). Soon after, Bunting offers us the image of a "gruff sole cormorant / whose grief turns carnival" (60). The cormorant everywhere graces the pages of the Northumbrian art of the Lindisfarne Gospels, and his appearance here helps to fix Bunting at home. Then, after a vision of a contented and peaceful pastoral life in the north of England, of the "Shepherds follow[ing] the links" (61), the poem concludes by meditating upon the starlight of a northern constellation, the source of which is gone or changed even as the light persists for us. In our human observation of starlight, "Then is Now":

> Sirius glows in the wind. Sparks on ripples
> mark his line, lures for spent fish.
>
> Fifty years a letter unanswered;
> a visit postponed for fifty years.
>
> She has been with me fifty years.
>
> Starlight quivers. I had day enough.
> For love uninterrupted night.
>
> (62)

The image of the "spent fish" gives a uniquely coherent force to Bunting's collected sonatas, the first of which, "Villon," concludes with his description of himself as an "unseasonable salmon" (11). To the melancholic now resolute in confronting the sadness of his past, the past remains a "lure," still powerful in its intermittent "sparks," but the decision has been made to give it up. Now, in the last line's adaptation of Catullus's "nox est perpetua una dormienda," his early love is abandoned to uninterrupted night.

A coda follows, confessing ignorance and vulnerability to forces beyond understanding, to a "strong song" (63). Despite the resolution of personal psychic crisis, the poem has little in the way of knowledge to offer us, and Bunting's own description of the poem can speak only of "commonplaces":

> Commonplaces provide the poem's structure: spring, summer, autumn, winter of the year and of man's life, interrupted in the middle and balanced around Alexander's trip to the limits of the world and its futility, and sealed and signed at the end by a confession of our ignorance. Love and betrayal are spring's adventures, the wisdom of elders and the remoteness of death, hardly more than a gravestone. In summer there is no rest from ambition and lust of experience, never final. Those fail who try to force their destiny, like Eric; but those who are resolute to submit, like my version of Pasiphae, may bring something new to birth, be it only a monster. What Alexander learns when he has thrust his way through the degraded world is that man is contemptibly nothing and yet may live content in humility. Autumn is for reflexion, to set Aneurin's grim elegy against the legend of Cuthbert who saw God in everything, to love without expectation, wander without an inn, persist without hope. Old age can see at last the loveliness of things overlooked or despised, frost, the dancing maggots, sheepdogs, and particularly the stars which make time a paradox and a joke till we can give up our own time, even though we wasted it. And still we know neither where we are nor why. (1–2)

For what it's worth, this seems to me "Lucretian" in its generalizations about the human condition, opening onto quietism and resignation. In his *Note on Briggflatts,* Bunting follows these remarks by referring to their "cottage wisdom" (2). "No poem is profound" (2), he writes. This means that we would do better to consider Bunting's notorious efforts "to consign meaning to the margins of poetry," his struggle to "foreground [poetry's] formal aspects, its formal properties, in order to rescue it from its official identity and function as discourse" as a political gesture aimed at avoiding "a centrist monologic utterance characteristic of installed power." By this logic *Briggflatts* puts "intelligibility" at "risk," intelligibility being a "social and cultural phenomenon," a "matter of unspoken agreement, of convention," as Peter Quartermain has written (11). But the poem is neither unintelligible nor purely a matter of its formal properties, those noises it makes that Bunting would have us take note of first of all. We do not have to know what the poet means, or means to name, to understand that it is an "identity" that is being offered us. Bunting would seem to follow

Grossman in thinking that "the first announcement that a poem makes is the announcement not of a world or a meaning, but of the credible fact of a speaking voice" (19). That emphasis on "presence" will locate the poem at some distance from other "innovative" poetries to follow it in England and the United States.

Within the larger context of the English poetry of its era, *Briggflatts* is very much a special case. The English poetry of its era is predominately ironic, suburban in its sensibility, cautious and unambitious in its subject matter. There are exceptions, but few so completely at odds with prevailing modes as *Briggflatts,* which is neither cautious nor suburban. It is not hard to understand a substantial part of post–World War II English poetry as struggling with the collective experience of England's diminished role in the world, and, while *Briggflatts* is autobiography, it too can be read as a response to sociohistorical changes that elsewhere contributed to the little-englandism and irony of so much post–World War II poetry. If we want to read the poem in this way, we will note how exceptional it is. There is almost nothing about the first and the last three sections of the poem that is ironic, neither its account of the ambition of conquerors nor its resignation before the limits they must eventually accept. And Bunting may be giving us some license to ponder the broader implications of his own story when he turns to the collective "we" in his coda:

> A strong song tows
> us, long earsick.
> Blind, we follow
> rain slant, spray flick
> to fields we do not know.
>
> Night, float us.
> Offshore wind, shout,
> ask the sea
> what's lost, what's left,
> what horn sunk,
> what crown adrift.
>
> Where we are who knows
> of kings who sup
> while day fails? Who,
> swinging his axe

> to fell kings, guesses
> where we go?
>
> (63)

The question in that last strophe's first line might be read not as *who knows where we are* but as *from here, where we are, who knows*. Mention of "kings" restores the Bloodaxe narrative but also broadly alludes to the fate of the British—day fails, the sun goes down on the British empire, but what will the world be beyond it? "Who knows" in its stressed position articulates a profound uncertainty while sustaining a communal "we" which knows itself if not its future.

For years I had read the ending as an expression of the same unevasive resignation with which Bunting had forced himself to confront his and Northumbria's past, but it also seems possible to read that last, open question as an expression of political optimism. Read in this light, we can link *Briggflatts* with a remark Bunting made in his stint as president of the Northern Arts Association some ten years later, about the time Nairn was predicting the breakup of Britain:

> the central task of this institution should be to encourage not of course imitations of ancient [Northumbrian] models, but whatever seems to be conceived in their spirit. It is useless to import southerners, however skilled they may be in their art. They can only steer us further from the course that agrees with our deepest nature. And we should try to recall our . . . schools to the study and the habit of specifically Northumbrian art.[13]

For all of its lyric intimacy, *Briggflatts* participates in this work on behalf of regional, postimperial Northumbrian identity. That it does so primarily in its music and idioms does not distinguish it from related efforts on behalf of *national* identity, such as the poetry of Hugh MacDiarmid or Kamau Brathwaite, but Northumbria is neither Scotland nor Barbados, and Bunting's poem has none of the public urgency of these poets. Nevertheless, there is little question that its movement between melancholy and resignation can be read as reprimanding a British center intent on covering over the collapse of an old system with new assertions of the homogeneity of "Englishness." *Briggflatts* would acknowledge a local world its poet had almost forgotten and now sought to preserve against the eventual and inevitable extinction of his part in it.

6. Alternative British Poetries

The first thing to be said about the British poetry my title means to describe is that it remains largely unknown in Britain, though reviews of the anthology *Conductors of Chaos* (1996) offer some hope that broader recognition might be forthcoming.[1] The second thing, unsurprisingly, is that the poetry is equally unknown in the United States, even among writers and readers who might be expected to be curious about it. The third thing is that it constitutes a field of contemporary practice wherein serious differences and a wide range of poetic practices obtain — the field is far from homogenous. The small-press publications that come and go largely outside of the purview of the cultural institutions of a British public sphere — publications largely unavailable in the United States — have sometimes been the site of an admirably rigorous and energetic critical exchange. Alternative British writing represents a field too vast and diverse to do justice to here; I can offer only a crude outline of some of its more vital areas before I turn to a closer examination of the work of several of the poets who are part of them — work selected to call attention to the size of the field as well as to pertinent differences within it. What the work in this "field" shares is not much to speak of — opposition to or lack of interest in the prevailing modes of British poetry, an engagement with various international poetries, including exploratory poetries of the United States. Even that last statement must be qualified, however, as among these British writers there are poets more and less concerned to define the space within which their work becomes meaningful as first and foremost a British (or even English) space. And among these poets there are those who would seem to want to position their work as explicitly at odds with some of the more recent manifestations of a "mainstream" British practice, and others who are less willing to condemn any "mainstream" *en masse,* seeking acknowledgment from or dialogue with poets and critics from whom it has rarely been forthcoming, or a means of breaking out of a partly self-willed isolation that has for too long been the fate of British exploratory writing.

At the moment of this writing the "mainstream" in British poetry might be defined as the range of poetries on show among the so-called New Generation, its most recent constellation. According to David Kennedy, who has coedited the Bloodaxe anthology of New Generation poets and written the most lengthy study of its poetry, the New Generation represents a "reoriented consciousness about poetry" in Britain (14). In Kennedy's narrative of postwar British poetry, which does not so much as mention any of the poets I will discuss here as "alternative," the New Generation represents a third generation among postwar British poets. A first generation consists of the poets of the Movement, foremost among whom is Philip Larkin. A "middle-generation" names the work of Tony Harrison, Douglas Dunn, Geoffrey Hill, and the Irishman Seamus Heaney, among others. The New Generation itself includes in its more dispersed fold poets such as John Ash, Frank Kuppner, Peter Reading, Selima Hill, Jo Shapcott, David Dabydeen, Carol Ann Duffy, W. N. Herbert, and, most visibly, Glyn Maxwell and Simon Armitage. Kennedy's sense of the continuities and developments among these three "generations" will serve to outline the shape of prevailing practices in postwar Britain, though it must be acknowledged that his account of the "mainstream" largely ignores several poets with substantial reputations who are harder to locate among his "generations"—Peter Redgrove, Charles Tomlinson, and Roy Fuller, for instance.

Kennedy understands the relationship between Larkin's generation and the next to be one of continuity. In Larkin's poetry, he writes, "the relations between poet and subject, dialect and dominant pronunciation and speaking voice and cadence can be said to represent the belief that while individuals may have varying backgrounds, attitudes and aspirations such differences can be smoothed into a common style and forgotten in a set of shared values" (14–15). To understand how Larkin's "beliefs" as defined by Kennedy are evident in Larkin's practice, we might examine "Nothing to Be Said":

> For nations vague as weed,
> For nomads among stones,

Small-statured cross-faced tribes
And cobble-close families
In mill-towns on dark mornings
Life is slow dying.

So are their separate ways
Of building, benediction,
Measuring love and money
Ways of slow dying.
The day spent hunting pig
Or holding a garden-party,

Hours giving evidence
Of birth, advance
On death equally slowly.
And saying so to some
Means nothing; others it leaves
Nothing to be said.

(138)

The persistent particularity of local customs is not to be echoed by the verse. Nothing is to be said because everything is understood. Those who are outside of this discourse will not hear it anyway and are to be left ("dying") there; those who already understand the melancholy and nostalgia which it steels itself against do not require it. A consensual, nonconflictual public sphere is represented as a *fait accompli,* Larkin's role within it that of the ventriloquist ironically expressing what is already known—as if the poet were the one with the gall to remind "us" of what we had rather forget. The first and most important sign of the poetic here is a public "voice" secure in its abilities to utter propositions which will be exactly refined so as to take on the force and tone of platitudes—the multifariousness of life experience reduced to the knowingness of common wisdom, the speaker standing apart from and above the processes he would describe in order to summarize their meaning and consequences. With resonant epithets ("cobble-close families"), selective images appropriately representative rather than particular ("The day spent hunting pig"), simile and metaphor ("nations vague as weed"), and the stark turns and balancing of this syntax (the poem's ending), the poem's address is such that the reader understands that it might pertain equally to all localities. If this is a public, "common" style, it also demands little of its reader and promises no information, content, or perspective that it does not take as already fully understood, given, agreed upon. The poet is representative man distinguished only by the skill with which he expresses what is already known, and what is already known can be contained once and for all in polished, finished utterance. The poet's perspective is epistemologically secure; his utterance has the summary function of the obituary.

Both the "successes of an all-purpose social realist style" (15) and the mode of civic address evident in Larkin's poetry can be said to have exerted a continuing influence among the work of the "middle-generation," Kennedy argues, but in these poets Larkin's often thematized anxiety about the ability of a common style to speak to and sustain cultural and national consensus has been replaced by the desire to "write poetry whose strengths are based on a lived 'truth to origins.'" In Harrison, Dunn, and Heaney, Larkin's invitation to consensus, his desire to transform the experience of what he often viewed as the decay of meaning attendant upon the passing of an older England into new and debased but nevertheless shared values and perspectives is replaced by "a recognition that the individual and acts of culture are defined by issues of access, ownership, property, and rights; and this recognition is, in turn, combined with some elements of the confessional mode's autobiographical poetic and cult of the authentic self" (15). The self-consciously regional and class-specific particularity to which Kennedy refers has one of its most famous voices in Tony Harrison:

> That summer it was Ibsen, Marx and Gide.
>
> I got one of his you-stuck-up-bugger looks:
>
> *ah sometimes think you read too many books,*
> *ah nivver 'ad much time for a good read.*
>
> *Good read! I bet! Your programme at United!*
> *The labels on your whisky or your beer!*
>
> (141)

Here we note the entrance of the autobiographical—Harrison has made a career, most successfully perhaps in *V* (1985), in representing negotiations between what he might conceivably owe his origins and what he needs and obtains from a broader public sphere. These negotiations typically involve a kind of "liberal guilt" and considerable anxiety, sadness, and frustration. However, while the speaker in Harrison's poems has access to memories, voices, and idioms that distinguish him from Larkin's more remote and confident ironies, "he" is meant to be no less representative. It is *what* or *who* he represents that differs, but the poetry is no less vessel for the expression of a recognizable and coherent identity, albeit one set dialogically among other voices. Were we to look at other poems we would find that the signs of the poetic are much the same in Harrison as in Larkin, though the former's poetry is less given to idioms and tones vacillating between irony and cynicism—nor is it so prone to the nostalgia Larkin often struggles to negate and thereby preserves.

In their use of regional idioms and "previously excluded voices, histories, classes and genders," Dunn, Heaney, Hill, Anne Stevenson and others of a "middle generation" prepared the ground for the multicultural poetics of the New Generation, Kennedy writes, at least as this newest group of "mainstream" poets might be viewed entire, framed by its defining anthology, *The New Poetry*. Because of the diversity of its poets and the fact that none among them has yet risen to the acclaim of Larkin and Harrison, generalization about them will necessarily be more precarious business. However, Kennedy adds, in some of these poets the "battle" of Harrison and others on behalf of particular identities has been replaced by an "aestheticizing impulse toward culture, history and politics" and the belief that "any cultural origin or position is available and equally valid" (18). The prevalence of dramatic monologues constructing divergent personas in the work of Carol Ann Duffy might stand as an example of a practice that moves easily among different identities. Because Kennedy understands that "the structural problems of British culture and society still remain and, many would argue, have been made worse in the last ten to fifteen years" (19) Kennedy worries that abandonment of the pursuit of authenticity and "truth to origins" among the New Generation risks being read as complacent aestheticism. That need not be the case, he is concerned to show, and it certainly is not the case with a writer such as David Dabydeen, whose engagement with the politics of racialized identities in Britain is exemplary.

Kennedy's narrative of postwar British poetry is the story of the gradual decentering of cultural and national identity in poetic practice. Insofar as he is concerned to discuss the formal conventions of poetry, he wants to read them within these narratives of identity. His favorites among the New Generation represent a "development" in British poetry not because they have rejected a poetics of identity but because they have abandoned the pursuit of origins and authenticity in favor of what one might call "performing identity," a poetics of fluid subject positions. Inheriting many of the formal conventions of its predecessors while turning them to the purposes of the theatrical, the grotesque too, often gives this poetry a pervasive air of diminished ambitions, desperate or campy futility—or at least that is the case with some of the poets. Glyn Maxwell's "Thief on the Cross" will serve as an example of a persona adopted only to have its (in this case historical) authenticity immediately and self-consciously discredited:

> How are you doing on yours, my pal
> in crime?

These are the first lines of the poem; they serve to identify a speaker who is already identified by the poem's title, and to construct a cynical mode of address that ultimately flatters readers of the poem. Thief speaks to thief and, in overhearing, we are allowed the space to deploy our moral compass in judging him and exonerating ourselves. The banal phrase "pal of mine" projects the poem into the present, destroying any illusion that this will be a poem interested in the historical identity of its supposed speaker, or in the realist surface of Larkin. It is the kind of dramatic representation of the crucifixion we might see on *Saturday Night Live*. As the poem unfolds, going through the motions of offering the discourse of this hard-boiled fictional speaker to his companion in crime with a wordless wink to us, we hear the speaker accuse his companion of "flapping away," complaining that his companion has "barely cracked a word in our lingo." He speaks of a "squawking dawn" and "wailing wives" and eventually chides his companion for asking Christ for "help":

> I tell you,
>
> feckless snivelling rascal whelp:
> we're only smack bang where our blessed old dears
> predicted, all those years
> gone: but this one isn't one of us lot.
> he's innocent; he can't help.
>
> (91)

The ironic force of the speaker's concluding proposition—innocence sets Christ apart, thereby making him useless—is not lost on the reader. So familiar is this morality play that it might be argued that the poem does not in any real sense depend upon it; rather the poem's success or failure turns upon the reader's engagement with the speaker's venomous epithets. Are we satisfied by figures such as "squawking dawn" (with its token allusion to Homer) and "feckless snivelling rascal whelp"? Well, such rotund insults are amusing, as they also are in some of the Bob Dylan songs Maxwell has named as an influence — "Positively Fourth Street," for instance. The credibility or authenticity of the speaker is not at issue here, as in the poetry of Harrison; still, the conventions of dramatic monologue as deployed here do not take us very far from the models of poetic subjectivity and expression at work in Harrison or Larkin.

Kennedy is intent on demonstrating that the diversity of the New Generation involves more than the various regional, ethnic, and class origins of its poets and also that, by and large, their work can be read beside some of the propositions of postmodernist and post-structuralist "theory." In writing of Jo Shapcott's "Phrasebook," for instance, he argues that "the artful confusion of discourses in the poem invites the reader to speculate on the relation between the impossibility of a bourgeois poetry of commodified confession and the uncertainty of Britain's role in the postimperial age. The continuities provided by ideas of nation have been replaced by the flickering realities of the media" (22). Identity in Shapcott's poetry would not only (as in Maxwell) abandon the authentic but also singularity and containment; the boundaries of the self are altogether permeated by the media. In its abandonment of romantic and neoromantic models of lyric interiority, the poem Kennedy bases his claims upon has all of the subtlety of *Invasion of the Body Snatchers*. Here are its first two and last stanzas:

> I'm standing here inside my skin,
> which will do for a Human Remains Pouch
> for the moment. Look down there (up here).
> Quickly. Slowly. This is my own front room
>
> where I'm lost in the action, live from a war,
> on screen. I am an Englishwoman, I don't understand you.
> What's the matter? You are right. You are wrong.
> Things are going well (badly). Am I disturbing you?
> . . .
> Where is the British Consulate? Please explain.
> What does it mean? What must I do? Where
> can I find? What have I done? I have done
> nothing. Let me pass please. I am an Englishwoman.

(204–5)

Surely Kennedy is correct to think that the appeal to "Englishness" made by the deracinated speaker of this poem is an empty gesture; the poem's entertainment of opposite, conflicting propositions in its jerky phrases and parentheses means to suggest the extent to which the agency of its "I" has been overwhelmed by the noise and power of the media, set afloat among binaries and contradictions. And yet the experience of reading the poem is hardly one of disorientation or surprise; by the end of the second stanza we understand that this "I" is a robotic ventriloquist for the aforesaid media, a word processor, a machine without a mind of its own; the irony of that desperate insistence on her status as an "Englishwoman" is one-dimensional and obvious, suggesting an implied perspective from which that irony might be confidently launched. The poem can even be said to have a "speaker" whose identity—as robotic nationalist, say—is clear and contained. The repetition of the poem's most resonant phrase offers the poem a predictable closure, with the preceding phrase ("Let me pass please") suggesting an overt if ironic editorializing on the part of the poet Shapcott, working this robot behind this scene, fairly secure in her distance from and superiority to the sad fate that has befallen such a representative "I." Much as in the Maxwell poem, the reader is flattered, asked to join the poet in mocking the speaker.

Shapcott's poem exists at some distance from Larkin's, but there is much too that it shares with it. Poetry for both the Movement and the New Generation poet looks very much the same on the page; it is arranged in lines and stanzas more or less faithful to the canonical forms of British tradition, with a distinct preference for the shorter, self-sufficient lyric or dramatic monologue. Forms of so-called "free verse" are slightly more common among some of the poets Kennedy admires, and sometimes they are given to working in lyric sequences which allow more matter to be shovelled into the poetry. There is—generalizing here—less emphasis on economy of presentation than is typical in Larkin. When Kennedy writes that "the most important poetry of the last fifteen years is distinguished by a dominance of the discursive mode" (14), he means to suggest, perhaps, that the poetic modes of the New Generation have been more expansive than those of Larkin and some of his immediate contemporaries, allowing for a poetry more essayistic and—to be less kind—more glib than Larkin's distilled ironies, but in the end the basic assumptions and conventions of this poetry are not so far removed from the Movement poetry which, for better or worse, has cast a long shadow over postwar British poetry, largely obscuring more exploratory poetries which have nevertheless persisted, sometimes without bothering much to challenge the machinery of reputation- and audience-making which has been so kind to the Movement and its heirs and so ignorant of alternatives present in the British field, alternatives altogether invisible in Kennedy's book and hardly more visible in others like it.[2]

Let me be clear about this last point. Among the many reasons for the invisibility of the poetry I mean to notice here is what R. J. Ellis has called a "convention of critical silence" (74), a reluctance on the part of these poets and their supporters to carry on the struggle on behalf of those poetries in the face of widespread indifference or hostility. As I suggested above, it is not exactly that good, informed, intelligent criticism and exegesis of various alternative poetries has ever been altogether lacking; small, ephemeral publications such as *The English Intelligencer, The Grosseteste Review, Poetry Information,* and others have come and gone over the last thirty years and have been sites of lively contestation and dialogue. However, since the midseventies, after the events surrounding Eric Mottram's tenure at *Poetry Review* (discussed in chapter 1), efforts to engage a broader public sphere have been few and far between. Mottram's own efforts are still viewed by some who otherwise share at least his position on the margins of British poetry as an "entryism" which is futile or which poets should be above. But even Mottram's supporters have noted the strangely passive response to the events of the middle and late seventies. In the words of Cris Cheek, "We abandoned the site of conflict in disgust and distaste, we resigned and opted for forms of resistance which have yet to impinge sufficiently exquisitely onto the rewritten agenda as to need to be addressed. A recent crop of ironic Mottram obituaries in the national press revisit such sites by calling him perhaps the best known of the 'unknown poets' here. I can still remember, with a chill, Lee Harwood being surprised that the powers of reaction within the British establishment didn't behave 'like gentlemen.' . . . We sat by and shrugged and we got what we deserved."[3] This is admirably direct and honest; there's no weeping about the unjustly neglected. In his pursuit of an audience for some of the poetries I will soon turn to, Cheek, like Robert Sheppard and a few others, has taken on (and been let go from) work as a reviewer of poetry for broad-circulation newspapers. Other efforts to forge new audiences by forming alliances with musicians and artists, moving beyond the traditional practices of the "poetry world" in cross artform performance, mixed-media, and intermedia, are also noteworthy and, together with renewed initiatives in pedagogical institutions, represent a means of broadening the audience for exploratory poetries and more generically hybrid writing.[4] Given the visibility of the New Generation—their sudden, orchestrated, and perhaps temporary projection into a position whereby they can be said to represent the direction of British poetry, it would be easy for the British poets I value most to stew in their own resentment or to publish manifestoes attacking what sometimes looks like an easy target. But, somewhat to my surprise, there seems to be very little of either going on in Britain today. Indeed, as the long letter from Cris Cheek I quote below indicates, it is possible to believe that there is room for more conventional and "accessible" poetry and exploratory work *both*.

A map of British alternative poetry and writing as it appears from some distance—a map which, in the words of Michel de Certeau, offers us the "fiction of knowledge" in its "lust to be a viewpoint and nothing more," its "exaltation of a scopic and gnostic drive"—is something I would rather avoid here. I ask the reader's patience, then, in offering just such a map in the crudest of forms.[5] For some observers in Britain and beyond it, Cheek and Sheppard are grouped with London-based writers, though like many of the poets gathered in Sheppard and Adrian Clarke's anthology *Floating Capital* (1991), which was instrumental in defining said "group," neither presently resides in London. These London writers, including Bob Cobbing, Allen Fisher, Gilbert Adair, Paul Brown, Kelvin Corcoran, Ken Edwards, Virginia Firnberg, Maggie O'Sullivan, Peter Middleton, Hazel Smith, Sheppard, and Clarke, are sometimes supposed to be at odds with writers affiliated with another cultural center, Cambridge. Such tensions as exist between the two "groups" were no doubt exacerbated by an issue of the magazine *Angel Exhaust* containing, among other notes on a purported London/Cambridge divide, editor Andrew Duncan's essay "The Cambridge Leisure Centre: Traits." Identifying four generations of Cambridge poets—some of the names are J. H. Prynne, John Riley, John James, Peter Riley, Michael Haslam, Denise Riley, John Wilkinson, Veronica Forrest-Thomson, Rod Mengham, and himself—Duncan went on to caricature Cambridge life and to propose affinities, common histories, and influences among these poets, sketching some of the poetic practices evident among various subgroups while acknowledging that nearly all of these poets had been reluctant to admit the existence of anything like a Cambridge school.

The essay has its fair share of provocative gestures, many of them entertaining—the abandonment of expressivist models of poetry among some Cambridge poets, for instance, leads Duncan (who thinks of himself as a socialist realist) to imagine a rationale for such practices. He imagines a vignette where Cambridge poets are seen to be pedantically mulling over the skeptic's tired problem of "other minds":

> One of the characteristics of Cambridge poetry is to be language with no inside. It just doesn't seem to contain a human with a state of mind. I'm afraid this comes from the presence of a supercilious and hypercritical audience. What exactly do you mean by a state of mind? How do you know other people have states of mind? I mean, we aren't writing folksongs, are we. Isn't identification a rather imprecise and premodern concept? Is *I'm unhappy* a defensible statement? (8)

Applied to particular cases, such rhetoric collapses, but of course its purposes are far from dispassionate scrutiny of individual poets and poems or their epistemological assumptions. This is criticism meant to prod and insult rather than show the fly the way out of the fly bottle. Elsewhere, Duncan's analysis is more subtle, as for instance when he remarks that, despite its reputation as "the school of Prynne," few of the poets associated with the Cambridge "group" and its publications, Andrew Crozier and Tim Longville's anthology *A Various Art* (1987) for instance, write poems that much resemble either the early or the later Prynne. Similarly, Duncan writes that, while the "reputation of the group is for hermetic complexity . . . looking at the page shows that many of them have chosen an exaggerated simplicity" (5). Duncan's noting of "a remarkable density of serious Marxist politics" (5) and "key influences" such as Ashbery, O'Hara, Olson, Lefebvre, Debord, Foucault, Deleuze, and Brecht, among the Cambridge school, allows the reader guideposts to begin negotiating this terrain, though the particulars of these "influences" are only barely discussed. Predictably, the mandarin critic suggests that the most important poets—Tom Raworth, Roy Fisher (who anyway is present in *A Various Art*), Barry MacSweeney, Brian Catling, among others—belong to no group (6).

The gambit of Duncan's essay—and he can be a brilliant critic—must certainly have involved his hopes, shared by others such as Drew Milne, that he might force dialogue among British exploratory poets by having the temerity to step in and do some of the mapping and theorizing others had been reluctant to do.[6] Acknowledging that no generalization will hold up under much scrutiny, and adding that any London/Cambridge opposition leaves altogether out of the picture significant poets based in other regions of England, we might continue our rough view of British alternative poetry from a distance by relaying what seems to be the common understanding concerning differences among the London and Cambridge groups. One stereotype has it that the poets of London are more prourban, outward looking, engaged with everyday life, while Cambridge poets are more self-consciously literary, more sentimental and romantic, more reflective, their urbanity poised against the London group's rudeness, their radical pastoral utopianism against a nonviolent anarchism. Such a stereotype probably owes something to the contrast in personal styles between the acknowledged patriarchs of both groups, Eric Mottram in London and J. H. Prynne in Cambridge. While Mottram was endlessly energetic in organizing readings and events, Prynne is seen as leading the more cloistered life of a scholar, refusing to give public readings. More sustainable distinctions might be made by noting the investment in performance and cross artform collaborations among the poets affiliated with the London scene; few of the writers linked to Cambridge have shown much interest in performance, in extending their practice beyond the most traditionally literary sites. Many of Prynne's books, including the early and influential post-Olsonian books such as *Kitchen Poems* (1968) and *The White Stones* (1969) as well as more recent and hermetic work, show that the design of the page and book are meaningful to him, but primarily as contributions to a literary artifact. Tom Raworth, whose *Logbook* simulates "pages" within the actual pages of the book, surrounding the "pages" we are to understand as surviving fragments of a logbook with the psychotropic drawings of Frances Butler, resists the pristine seriousness of poetry's book culture just as he mocks the conventions of the colonial travel narrative (see fig. 1). This, like another Raworth mixed-media collaboration with Jim Dine, represents the kind of aesthetic production few Cambridge poets have employed; perhaps such work smells a little too much of the comic book or children's book to them, or of mass culture; perhaps it seems merely a distraction from the high seriousness of poetry confronting the austere whiteness of the page. At any rate, recently, it is (formerly) London-based writers like Cris Cheek who have been among those most active in promoting and publishing some of the newer "performance writing" now appearing in England, writing intent on maximizing the possibilities of the page and book as performance spaces. In Caroline Bergvall's *Éclat* and Forced Entertainment's *Speak Bitterness,* both published by Cheek's Sound and Language, the avant-garde tradition of the "visible word" is extended so that even the extralinguistic—such as the latter text's heavy black "erasures," the underlining and circling of phrases as these enter into play with the tonalities of a postpunk manifesto reproduced in primitive typeface—has complex semantic possibilities. Conventions are

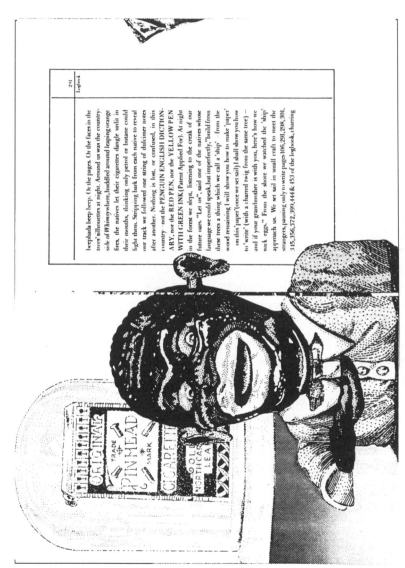

Figure 1. Tom Raworth, from *Logbook*

established and then undermined, or they might allude to the processes to which texts are regularly subjected—in the latter's case to an editorial process that draws lines between phrases to make us examine their relation (figs. 2, 3).[7]

Other important differences between London and Cambridge groups involve the latter's regard for the artifactual status of the poem as a resolved and "finished" object; this will be evident in the discussion below of an exchange between Allen Fisher and Drew Milne in the latter's journal *Parataxis,* as well as in my quotation of various of Peter Riley's remarks on the poem as "an object between poet and reader which is both a means of communication and a barrier to communication" (93) and on Riley's sense of the importance, within poetic sequences, of offering individual poems an "utter completion." Finally, there is the question of the relationship of both groups to international and especially American poetic models. Here we are on dangerous ground, as there is no question that both groups have been seriously engaged with all of these poetries in a way that their peers among the so-called mainstream often have not, and transatlantic correspondence and personal contact has been important to many poets among both groups as well. Charles Olson, Frank O'Hara, Jack Spicer, among others, have been influential, if often in different ways—Prynne's Olson does not much resemble Mottram's, for instance. But it is equally certain that some of the Cambridge poets have, at times, seemed more intent on identifying continuities among their work and specifically British traditions, modernist or otherwise. Moreover, the most significant critique of some of the propositions advanced in the name of that recent North American practice called "language poetry" has emanated from Cambridge, from Prynne himself and several of his students.

It is these last two matters—the desire among some in Cambridge to identify continuities with British traditions and the critique of "language poetry"—that I want to take up here, albeit briefly. On the first of these matters—the desire to identify and extend British traditions—the thing to do would be to speak of the presence of British traditions in the poetry itself and of critical and editorial efforts on behalf of known or unknown British writers. I have done the latter in an earlier chapter in speaking of the need for British poets to identify a British modernism as a way of countering the parochialism of the British public sphere in its post-Movement formations, and I will do the former below in reading the excavations of English madrigal verse performed by Peter Riley's *Distant Points.* For now I'd like only to quote some off-the-cuff remarks from an

At any rate: The orderly fashion of starting points would (at this stage of your genital outlook) make you roughly locatable as one apparent over →

[heere] It's

a small dynamic silo we've prepared for you in the physical ambience.

Indeed (it must be said) we figured that (at a push) you'd currently be looking like [so] (well, more or less). Hardly a mouthful I agree. Still a great improvement on. Now leave this spot: your features might start drooping. Now stay here: your bone structure might dehydrate. 4. The choice is yours not entirely.

16

You're thinking about a small object something stable something stable and precise something stable precise and accurate

. . . . . . You've decided to follow on through?
(Well done). *Leave the r....* . . . .

Figure 2. Caroline Bergvall, from *Éclat*

We're guilty of heart attacks, car crashes and falling off bridges. We agreed with Albert Einstein the scientific genius. We [■] asleep, eye-witnesses, minor clerics, prostitutes, and baseball fans. We dreamt of heat and solitude. We wished for peace, or a cease-fire at least. We put the head of a live rooster and drank the blood, we thought it would help. We fucked our brother. We were smugglers, heathens or pirates. We lied about our age and then hoped for better things. We showed a gun in the first act, in a drawer hidden under some papers; the central character kept staring at it and mumbling, crying almost, but we weren't prepared to let her use it, the dramatic tension was all wrong and so by act four the audience were still wondering what the gun thing was about. We burned effigies of trade negotiators. We were fraudulent mediums, working the crowd. We were not beautiful, or especially bright, but we had the strange gift of being remembered. We were hate filled children with ice in our veins. We ... came to the place where the tape says POLICE LINE DO NOT CROSS and then we crossed it.

We're guilty of dice, of teletype and needles. We spread(true rumours and wrote false receipts. [■] We made the heartbreak face and then we smiled. We stank of chlorine and fists fell on us like the rain. We made a mockery of justice and a mockery of the american/english language.

We sacked the town, we painted it red. We slipped thru customs at Nairobi International, without even being seen. We were exiled kings, useless princes. We revenged our image, we were really working class. We made the crowd blush, we were driven by demons whose names we couldn't even spell. We were white collar criminals, haunted by our pasts. We told Mrs. Gamble that Helen wasn't with us when she was. We were ex-cons trying to go straight. We thought that Freud was probably right about laughter. We had no moral compass, or if we did have one it had been badly damaged during the frequent electrical storms. We're guilty of heresy and hearsay, of turning our backs to the wall. We saw Arthur Scargill's blue movie cameo. [■]

Figure 3. Forced Entertainment, from "Speak Bitterness"

interview conducted with Riley, who is not only a remarkable poet but very useful in being given to colorful opinions which show that the anxieties accompanying recent British-American relations in poetry are not solely confined to the poets of one or another "mainstream."

Asked whether he still regards American poetry highly, Riley responds as follows:

> There's been a lot of fuss about it these last twenty years, to the extent that, well, by some accounts it's been the only English language poetry there is, and the best we can do over here is copy the accent and hope to latch on to some of the novelty. This has been abetted by American poets and critics themselves to quite a large extent: to them England is a psychologically difficult area connected with senses of familial authority and parental pressures, so that to gain an independent newness at the expense of an English staleness is a kind of *de rigeur* step of adolescent rebellion for the young American poet. They don't understand English poetry and can't read it, and this goes right back to all the absurd things Pound and Olson said about Wordsworth and Milton. Actually I think the English achievement in poetry this century has been just as impressive as the American, and that's counting Eliot, Pound and Auden as Americans. (5)

Elsewhere in this same interview, Riley openly wonders about the point of reading, say, Ted Berrigan when the light-verse poet Gavin Ewart is homegrown and available, offering pretty much what can be found in Berrigan: "a species of deliberately wasteful or 'light' poetic which had a terrific bite at times" (15). He also says that "an American moment" in British poetry was over in 1965 (6). He notes that the tradition that is meaningful to him is the whole of English poetry and utters a passionate defense of writers outside of British canons, arguing that, for the writer as opposed to the critic in the Leavis tradition, it is important that there be many rather than few poems that matter (14–15).

One can understand Riley's remarks here. The writer in Britain faces different or differently shaded issues—negotiating postimperial realities, the parochialism of the center, and so on—and others more sympathetic than Riley to recent American exploratory poetries have stressed the need to speak to the British contexts British exploratory poetries emerge from.[8] No doubt Riley has in mind numerous statements by American writers, including Olson, about space being the most important reality in American life, but his evidently psychologized narrative no longer persuades, if it ever did even so long ago as the moment Pound penned *Hugh Selwyn Mauberley*. It is blissful ignorance rather than anxiety that accounts for casual opinion about British poetry among some Americans, and Riley was closer to the truth when he wrote in 1970 of the "withdrawal" of English poets before the brute machinery of American cultural imperialism: "It is quite obvious to them [i.e., the English poets of a Cambridge variety] that a very large machine is in operation, probably centered on America, and that anyone's cautious discriminations as to cause an effect *or* niceties of critical acumen *or* announcements of the 'truth' are going to impede this machine's progress about as much as a trail of snail-slime." [9] In the more recent interview, "America" comes to stand one-dimensionally for all those poetic practices Riley would reject: "for one thing Americans have a lot of difficulty distinguishing between truth, and statement, which they think is English and feudal or something. [Karl] Shapiro said that truth was a component, that truth goes into the making of a poem rather than residing in its result or essence. And a lot of avant-garde stances about poetry, about fragmentation and open-endedness and all those anti-formal concepts of the poem as a network or vibrations or a bag of chips or whatever . . . they're all insisting on avoiding manifest truth at the centre of the poetic discourse. But it won't do" (9). Here we have a caricatured America—site of the open-ended, preeminent home of the avant-garde. Here we have a rhetoric which allows Riley and others the chance to add another dimension to their critique of poetic practices also to be found among certain British poets by implying that they are in some sense properly "American."

A rhetoric turning upon blunt oppositions is not uncommon in the casual setting of the interview; indeed most evaluative criticism, in reviews and elsewhere, will eventually fall prey to it. We can take as an example the American language-poet Charles Bernstein's brief review of recent British exploratory poetries. Despite efforts to respect the difference(s) of British contexts, Bernstein proceeds to contrast the London-based poets of *Floating Capital* with the poets of *A Various Art,* many (though not all) of whom have or had some affiliation with Cambridge. Poets committed to "open and new forms" are contrasted with those who manifest "a tenacious commitment to an unobtainable lyric." These latter poets, some of the Cambridge poets, are only "ostensibly dedicated to alternative poetics," Bernstein claims, because they "display a corrosive dismissiveness toward exploratory works that are radically skeptical of the rhetorical grounding of both sprung and traditional lyricism" (206). Bernstein acknowledges the "renovations (or refashionings) of lyrical and pastoral (or postpastoral) forms" in Cambridge poetry, but his enthusiasm for *A Various Art* is not great. Nor does it have to be; if my own preferences can find room for both poetries, it might make me more eclectic but it doesn't make me somehow "better." If Bernstein's tent is only so big, so is Riley's, and the point is not to belittle either poet-critic but to demonstrate how easily even the most sophisticated British and American readers fall into deploying simple critical opposition that can only increase transatlantic static when they are translated—as they sometimes are—into the binary America/England.

The critique of language poetry in Cambridge might very well be part of what Bernstein is responding to in his review; certainly poets and critics associated with London, such as Ken Edwards and Peter Middleton, have been much more responsive to language poetry. But responsiveness here means reviewing and writing on the work, and in some cases publishing it. It makes less sense to speak of a British "language writing." The use of Gilbert Adair's awkward term *linguistically innovative poetries,* which has had some currency in England, suggests that there are a few near approximations, but there is no poetry of which I am aware specifically indebted to the writing Ron Silliman has spoken of as the "new sentence." Silliman's fellow practitioner Bob Perelman describes the "new sentence" as a "more or less ordinary" sentence which "gains its effects by being placed next to another sentence to which it has only tangential relevance: new sentences are not subordinated to a larger narrative frame nor are they thrown together at random. Parataxis is crucial: the autonomous meaning of a sentence is heightened, questioned, and changed by the degree of separation or connection that the reader perceives with regard to the surrounding sentences" (61). The "new sentence" is only one mode employed by language poets, and one could go on to discuss some of the prosodic and generic issues it raises. But the critique of language poetry in Cambridge and elsewhere in England has taken comparatively little interest in particular poems or practices and instead has attacked a number of propositions extracted from a critical prose.

The "theory" of language poets has been vulnerable in its discussions of the politics of form and the purportedly newly empowered role of the reader responding to "antiabsorptive" techniques—to use just one critical idiom for an emphasis specific "language poetry" practices place on the resistant surfaces of the nontransparent word and texts which acknowledge their constructedness while challenging the limits of semantic and syntactic conventions.[10] Some British readers have rejected "the notion that writing can be instrumental by virtue of its mode" and the idea that "modes of writing are more or less (or not at all) empowered to require of the reader an active hermeneutic role."[11] J. H. Prynne opts out of the utopian hopes of Steve McCaffery's poetics, indebted as these are to the essays of Bataille and Baudrillard, rejecting the premise that language poetry's "de-referenced sign system" will leave the reader "free to opt for useful waste or wasteful utility." Prynne poses the "classic freedom to eat cake" and the illusory freedoms of the supermarket as apt analogues for language poetry's promise to require of the reader a (newly) active role in constructing meaning. Anthony Mellors's argument that particular phonic and typographic practices merely "*represent* the priority of libidinal drives instead of actually effecting libidinal praxis" (86); D. S. Marriott's much more contentious assertion that language poetry fetishizes the signifier and presents an "aesthetics of disavowal" which should be understood as a "phobic" response to "the traumatic excess associated with referential markers of sexual and racial difference" in American culture (77) — these critiques offer a contextualism in response to what is taken to be a formalism.[12] But the Cambridge critiques are themselves vulnerable on the same grounds — that is, they typically read what are in fact performative critical texts intent on re-directing contemporary poetic practice as a series of truth-claims and/or "theoretical" propositions about language, reading, politics, and so forth. Much language poetry "theory" — especially the prose of Charles Bernstein — acknowledges its situated agendas and motives, the fragility and contextualism of its terms.[13] One can find truth-claims uttered with Althusserian authority here and there, but the permutations and incoherence of much of this "theory" needs to be taken into account also.

There really is no cure for the misunderstandings and decontextualizing that I am speaking of here — the history of the dissemination of the word is, in good and bad ways, the history of misunderstandings and recontextualizations. Nevertheless, when these take place under the sign of nation, the results are nearly always devastating. Perhaps it is a utopian dream to imagine that some transatlantic static might be altogether cleared up. In the name of such a dream, however, I mean to give over the last words of this part of the chapter to Cris Cheek. He will offer a brief insider's narrative and analysis of the course of particular British alternative poetries in the wake of the events surrounding Eric Mottram's tenure at *Poetry Review*. I find his optimism commendable.

Some brief observations on what happened once those fourteen poets and editors — Barry MacSweeney, Peter Hodgkiss, Jeremy Adler, Peter

Finch, Bill Griffiths, Cris Cheek, Lawrence Upton, Allen Fisher, Bob Cobbing, Jeff Nuttall, Tom Pickard, Pete Morgan, Ian Patterson and Ken Smith—resigned from the General Council after the Poetry Society had adapted the [Sir John] Witt report. Eric's editorial tenure was curtailed. Kings' College, through his energies, became a focus for readings alongside places such as the Acme Gallery but activity began to thin. While I was in Baltimore typesetting Ron Silliman's "Sunset Debris" political crises brought Thatcher into power. Rapid deterioration began. For the best part of a decade from 1980 there was only really occasional Kings' readings, the Subvoicive series curated by Gilbert Adair, and Bob Cobbing's Writers Forum workshops. Allen Fisher ran workshops at Goldsmiths' College which generated a focus and produced the Robert Sheppard, Adrian Clarke axis, and there were occasional programmes such as the RASP session in South London put together by Reality Studios and Spanner [two small presses]. But really the scene, which had been a steaming scene, went flat.

During the second half of the 80s a different tendency had been developing. Its public face was a roots resurgence of cabaret and alternative comedy. John Hegley, for instance, one of the most successful of contemporary popular poets, came up through that scene, nourished as a comedian whose act revolved around short, comic, often self-effacing ironic poems—many of which in performance explored images of masculinity, being visually challenged and so on. I'm sure this all sounds very familiar. There were heirs to punk poet John Cooper Clarke such as Joolz, Attila the Stockbroker, who were formed into a performance-based movement (called "The Popular Front of Contemporary Poetry" by its most successful curator Paul Beasely) through the organization Apples and Snakes. Importantly Apples and Snakes managed to create the bridge to Black Poets out of the rap and dub traditions such as Linton Kwesi Johnson, Jean Binta Breeze and Benjamin Zephaniah together with exiled poets from Azania such as Pitika Niuli. The oral tradition became dominant; occasionally Bob Cobbing, or myself or Aaron Williamson, Peter Finch, Tom Leonard, Geraldine Monk would be taken into that scene but hardly ever on a mixed bill. They always had their "experimental" poetry night but never Jean and Geraldine say. I've talked with Beasely a lot about this aspect. They were worried about crossing audiences and losing everyone as a result. Programming was niche identity oriented. Sound familiar?

Now the Poetry Society had meanwhile renamed itself the National

Poetry Centre and was having pressure put onto it by its funders (the Arts Council again, but that's a long story—[Charles] Osborne had liquified literature funding and then left to pursue his career as opera critic; Literature has been revived under Dr. Alisdair Niven who was keen on the Commonwealth) to represent the implementation of equal opportunities in contemporary poetry. Cultural minorities and the culturally disenfranchised were to be represented. I, and I wasn't alone, was particularly concerned to break out of what was looking increasingly like a male-dominated white modernist poetry ghetto. But the National Poetry Centre, seeking to capitalise on the evident success of Bloodaxe Books and exploit a renewed hunger for poetry (this is all relative you understand) formed an alliance with publishers to launch the New Generation and regain the ground for the printed rather than the oral.

New Gen presented an acceptable "literary" collection for the 90s. It got masses of publicity but then it was a publicity exercise. It included a healthy tranche of Scots and a decently pc balance of female/male. Black poets were really not much more than token presences (although of all the New Gen crop Dabydeen arguably has most to offer) and they were being appropriated by the white literary establishment as "proper" writers as opposed to the more difficult to publish oral poets. Performance poets were embraced into the publicity thrust of the year's events through the aegis of the First National Poetry Day in October which got significant TV coverage and through which Adrian Mitchell and Zephaniah could be "incorporated." Even Stephen Spender was wheeled out and there was representation from the Nuyorican cafe (here's where the current connection between English and American poetics seems most connected—at least for the public eye). This was a cynical but certainly in the short term successful exercise in the imposition of a cultural hegemony for the times. Glyn Maxwell is held up as the acceptable face of post-modern poetic practice within the English English as opposed to American English traditions. Even though he, like many other younger poets wishing to blur pop and high culture in these countries, takes his cue from Bob Dylan. How successful this whole strategy will prove to be in the long term is obviously difficult to assess. I feel strangely positive about it. It creates space. Many might be curious about poetry. Hopefully some will want to go beyond the immediate surface they find much as those who have an interest to find out more about challenging music will pursue behind the charts. In this sense there is a conduit being opened. On the down side it does have the potential to further paper over the cracks and prevent a deepening crisis of confidence within the literary establishment. Poetry is certainly ascendent as opposed to prose in sales more recently. Its bit size chunks feed the hungry market. Poets are cheap to present in your theatre and don't necessarily bring in any less of your core audience. They're the stop gap flavour of a bankrupt infrastructure.[14]

In an effort to show something of the diversity of poetic practice outside the British "mainstream," I present in what follows brief readings of single volumes by five poets. These poets are chosen partly for the contrasts they allow, partly on the basis of my own preferences, and partly because of the nature of the critical commentary that has grown up around their work, or the comparative absence of the same—Peter Riley having received much less critical attention, for instance, than his Cambridge peer J. H. Prynne, whose work is discussed in numerous critical articles and now a book-length study published in England.[15] Limiting the discussion of each poet's work largely to one volume naturally distorts the development and differences within a poet's work, and in several instances I will have occasion to refer to other poems and books, but the purposes of this abbreviated survey require limitations of scope. Whole books might be written on each of the poets I discuss, but my first purpose here is a detailing of some of the terrain crudely mapped above as a means of indicating the limitations of any view of recent British poetry such as Kennedy's. It is the case, I think, that whether we are talking about identity, subjectivity, language, politics, or poetic form and practice, there are more possibilities represented by British alternative poetry, and more differences among these possibilities, than in the work of the three generations Kennedy names. Whatever contrasts may be evident in the juxtapositions which follow—between, say, a late modernist poetry of the sublime and varieties of postmodernist practice—should not obscure the fact that *all* of these poetries have for too long been invisible to or dismissed by the institutions of a British "mainstream" or, in a few cases such as Roy Fisher's, viewed as somehow idiosyncratic with regard to it. Given the fate of these poetries, it is really small wonder that an early hopefulness such as that expressed by the "pastoral desire" of Prynne's "Moon Poem" (*The White Stones,* 1969)— "the wish is gift to the spirit" (54)—should sometimes give way in more recent and often more hermetic poems to the sentiments which end *Down where changed* (1979): "sick and nonplussed / by the thought of less / you say stuff it" (313).

Peter Riley

Opening to the first page of Peter Riley's *Distant Points* (1995), the first volume of an ongoing series of what the book's jacket describes well enough as "prose-poems in which any singular voice is constantly interrupted by itself in another guise, and a whole theatre of masks jostles for position around the central condition of meditation," we find two "poems" or passages which look like this:

I.
the body in its final commerce : love and despair for a completed memory or spoken heart   *enclosed in a small inner dome of grey/drab-coloured* [river-bed] *clay, brought from some distance* (from the valley bottoms)   and folded in,   **So my journey ended**   moulded in the substance of arrival   **I depart**   *and a fire over the dome and a final tumulus of local topsoil*   /benign memorial where the heart is brought to the exchange: death for life, relict for pain/ double-sealed, signed and delivered — under all that press released to articulate its long silence, long descended * tensed wing / spread fan / drumming over the hill.

C39.
folded in river clay, the boat on the hilltop   *lying East-West facing upwards Right hand on Right shoulder Left arm across the body* gradients of sleep, to die, to dream, or mean/   *beyond his feet to the East a row of three circular pits or stake-holes*   dawn trap as the compass arc closes southwards and the heart is secured by azimuth, all terrors past: **She only drave me to dispaire**/dead child, cancelled future in a satellite cloak hovering to SE. Yet the loss, folded into history, sails adroit in the clay ship over commerce and habit, bound for (to) this frozen screen where [cursive] we don't live, but do (love) say, and cannot fail. (7)

How might the reader negotiate such a text? A first sentence fragment juxtaposes two phrases on opposite sides of a colon, perhaps to offer an initial articulation of the poem's concerns — the body in "its final commerce" (what could that mean?), the emotions attendant upon the desire to speak and in some sense "complete" memory and emotion. Clearly, we know at least that we are on some of the most traditional grounds of lyric, seeking a language adequate for our mortality, remembering the anguish of the word that would redeem while memorializing. But that's to get ahead of myself, reading the last lines of the second passage, where loss, "folded into history," is taken as the ground that not only enables but in some sense requires a writing that "cannot fail." Our first reading of the poem must take account of the disjuncture between that first sentence fragment and a next set in italics, that strangely affectless description of what (at first reading) we do not know. With brackets and parentheses, this phrase itself is interrupted, as if by qualifying or clarifying commentary. Then a third, bold typeface makes its first appearance, together with the first person. A journey's end is declared, to be followed after the return of the normative typeface which describes "arrival" as "moulded" (like clay?) by another boldface fragment declaring the beginning of a journey. An ending before a beginning. Reading down below in the second passage we note that this boldface font there presents antiquated spellings, indicating perhaps that such language has been imported from another source. It reads like lyric poetry, like renaissance song.

But of course I am being willfully naive here. We think we know from *The Waste Land,* from Pound's *Cantos,* and from many another modernist poem, how to negotiate the poetics of collage and juxtaposition — we have experienced these texts and read the commentaries over the course of time. Moreover, in the book's notes, Riley provides more help in explaining that his "meditative" texts are "concerned with the human burial deposits of the so-called Neolithic/Bronze Age culture of what is now the Yorkshire Wolds," and are based upon "late nineteenth century tumulus excavation accounts by J. R. Mortimer (1905) and Canon William Greenwell (1877)" — though the volume we are reading here uses only the Mortimer text (60). Mortimer's massive book is a painstakingly detailed narrative and description of the process of excavating the Yorkshire gravesites, and of what was found there. It testifies to the Victorian imagination in the wake of Darwin and Ruskin; the latter's suggestion that "the greatest thing a human soul ever does is to see something, and to tell what it saw in a plain way" is quoted to begin the book's introduction (xvii). Periodically, Mortimer will interject a statement which excretes some of the more bluntly ideological content of the cultural frames within which he operated; at one point in the introduction he writes that "As regards the Britons, let us hope that they may have been partially civilized and seldom resorted to cannibalism except in their revered funeral customs which would be the last to disappear" (xxiv). But the great virtue of his book involves its exhaustive detail, and the comparatively dispassionate objectivity with which that detail is typically presented. Here is part of the "excavation account" which Riley is "using" in the first passage above:

> The upper portion (E) [the letter refers to a drawing of a burial mound], to a depth of 16 inches, consisted chiefly of the surface soil of the neighborhood, the bottom part of which was reddened as if by the action of fire. Close below this was a stratum of wood and ashes and other dark matter, 2 to 3 inches in thickness; and then a lenticular bed of tough drab-coloured clay, 29 feet in diameter, and 12 to 14 inches thick in the centre, gradually thinning towards the circumference. The upper part of this bed of clay, which was in contact with the stratum of wood ashes, was reddened by fire; its under surface had a similar appearance, and rested upon what seemed to be a second stratum of burnt and decayed matter, 2 to 3 inches in thickness, similar to that already described. The clay forming this lenticular bed contained numerous small fragments of grey flint, characteristic of the chalk of the neighborhood. It must have been obtained from one of the valley bottoms. . . . in which are exposures of the Kimeridge clay. In these places angular pieces of flint and chalk crumble from the hillside, and mix with the clay, imparting a greyish colour to it. (1–2)

This is fairly typical. But the relationship of Riley's prose-poems to the Mortimer text is complex.

When I first read *Distant Points* in light of Riley's note about his sources, I assumed that his italicized passages, nearly all of which consist of this same affectless descriptive language detailing the arrangement of skeletal remains and the other contents of the gravesites, had been imported as blocks of text into his poems. I thought, in other words, that this italicized writing was "excavated" text, as it were, and that its prosaic qualities served not only to remind the reader of the site of these meditations but also as a refrain, a bass line against which a more animated if fragmentary lyric expressiveness might press. This in italics was information, all that we know for sure; we die and this is what they do with us, or what they once did owing to rituals whose meaning is a matter only of speculation now. This initial reading seemed confirmed by the knowledge that the phrases printed in boldface consist of fragments largely retrieved from the archives of English madrigal verse, snatches of song though also occasionally borrowings from more recent "literary" writers such as Pound, Kierkegaard, and Prynne. These were other excavated textualities, different in kind; somehow the two were to be brought into relation. Fragments of a descriptive prose detailing with clinical precision the dead and their places and then these excavated fragments of a lyric tradition wherein one generation after another has poured out its heart and tried to make sense of life and death, mediated and traversed by Riley's "own" writing seeking a meditative space between the extremes of lyric poetry and the deathly objectivity of Mortimer's prose. I couldn't escape the pun locked in Mortimer's name and set about pondering again the famous texts by Hegel, Blanchot, and many others articulating the relationship of writing and death: "The word gives me the being, but it gives it to me deprived of being" (42). Lyric, some have said, crossing over into a permanence of form, and paying for its admission there with "an eternity of stillness," desires the condition of our own mortality — that embodiment in temporality which is the voice breathing air into song and words.[16] I wanted to read the collision of discourses in Riley's text as an effort to create a postpastoral, postlyric space wherein the contortions of the syntax presented here in normative typeface enacted the struggle to reconcile lyric emotion and brute facticity, the silences and blank spaces cutting between the different registers of language representing the "real" across which these conflicting registers are sprung as unpresentable abundance confronting the gaps of desire.

I still think that many of my first impressions are accurate, but, as the passage above shows, it is not the case exactly that Mortimer's writing is imported in whole chunks into Riley's meditations, as fragments of "found language" or "textuality" for instance. The italicized passages do pick up phrases from Mortimer (for example, "drab-coloured") but these are invariably rearranged, condensed. Moreover, in other passages outside of the italics, Mortimer's language can be recontextualized, metaphorized (or literalized), and extended. The "boat" in the second passage, for instance, owes its existence to a phrase in Mortimer describing a "grave being partly filled with a boat-shaped block of clay" (93). If we are interested in the habits and meanings of neolithic burial customs (and it remains to be suggested to what extent and how Riley is interested in these) we might speculate about the meaning and purposes of "boat-shaped clay" or whether Mortimer is even accurate in describing this particular mound as such. But Mortimer's "boat" in Riley's "C39" is decontextualized — we have no idea it is a boat of clay — allowing Riley to launch a series of metaphors concerning the ability of the prospect of death and loss to set us (with compass) sailing beyond everyday commerce and custom towards whatever meaning we can find. Writing is the boat's destination, as it is the body's, the boat itself as "folded" in clay a figure for that everydayness writing might somehow transform. The point is that the "standard" typeface here moves in and between all the available "sources" for the poem, extending Mortimer's prose here, echoing and revising *Hamlet* elsewhere. In moving back and forth and around and between the "excavations" of Mortimer's prose and of more traditionally "literary," primarily poetic sources, Riley's prose poems finally manage to confuse or invert the relationship between one and the other genre of writing, so that the deathly description undertaken in the italicized fragments over the course of the series of prose-poems can seem to gain an affective weight one would think to be reserved for the fragments from the English lyric archive. This works much in the same way, say, that the reportage style employed by Charles Reznikoff in the "Massacres" section of *Holocaust* offers horrors a more florid style cannot.

The ontological concerns of Riley's poems might call for glosses from any number of modern philosophers—Heidegger's discussions of the relationship between the being-with-others that is everydayness (read "custom" in Riley) and the being one's self toward death might be one place to start, as would Merleau-Ponty's writing on the body in *The Phenomenology of Perception*. But such arsenals of terminology aren't really necessary in reading this poetry, and anyway Riley has resisted an appeal to philosophy in the past. Nevertheless, Riley's poetics were once described quite astutely by John Hall as "a hesitant self-contradictory and doomed transcendentalism" (16). Hall begins by quoting a passage from Riley's earlier book *Tracks and Mineshafts* that reads, "It's easy enough to focus on nothing like a missing pilot and set absence into the text just to have it before us, newly reflective: but you are *elsewhere* and it's very uncertain that something human is actually there at the end of this dispersed line wanting or waiting for anything on earth. Surely the fire is getting low: if we don't signal our love there will be no reason for dying" (12). The "inadequacy of saying" and "the inadequacy of the need to say," the dialectical relationship between "the 'I' who desires and the 'I' who knows what it is (he) desires" (13)—such characteristic concerns of Riley are very much evident in *Distant Points*. Thus one might say of that book what Hall says of the earlier one: "through it all, despite everything, runs the hope of a redemptive power of (a notion of) selfhood and language. As so often when there is the idea of 'self' at work, there is a strong and consistent metaphor of redemption, with its implied loss or failure—that gap that pertains to desire rather than an easily redeemable lack, and there is that familiar questing self, burrowing it seems into otherhood out of sheer ontological destiny" (15). Riley's sense of the purposes of poetry has all of the urgency of Rilke writing on "the bees of the invisible," on the need for the poet to "imprint this provisional, perishing earth in ourselves so deeply, with such passion and endurance that its reality rises again in us 'invisibly'" (Powell, 145). At times Riley's discourse of an ever elusive redemptive word approaches the apocalyptic: "The very fabric of our perception rests delicately on our love. If we lost its purpose, even in the gloss of a leaf, horror is let loose on the world" (92).

The poem itself, conceived by Riley "as an object between poet and reader which is both a means of communication and a barrier to communication" is also in his view a "body of light . . . constructed out of paradoxical or conflicting motivations within a tradition: desire crossed with fear, envy crossed with confidence, the need to say and be revealed crossed with the need to remain silent and secret." Riley is careful to note that there is nothing "modernistic" about this view of the poem, except perhaps that the poem has "more usually" been thought of as "a grace of transfer rather than as an obstacle to transfer" (93–99). Insofar as Riley is willing to articulate distinctions between poetry and prose these concern not the "form" of the writing involved—line and measure and so forth—but the intended relationships between writer and reader. Prose is rhetorical, directed communication: "If there is a sharp distinction between poetry and prose it is that poetry omits all the headings and footnotes and says what it says in stark isolation, leaving you to make the most of it in the knowledge that it is certainly not meant for you in an exclusive sense. . . . I argue that this is what poetry is: essential writing. Writing which is essentially of its own nature. Prose I take to be in imitation of non-writing, thus bypassing parts of what it is (such as its disposition on the page and its constantly nascent ambiguity) by mechanisms of conventional omission and by the furnishing of constant specifying sub-directives" (94). Prose, in other words, bypasses consciousness of its "body"—a dubious claim these days.

Riley's poetics see the poem as an unpredictable, mysterious, but altogether self-contained artifact, the relationship of poet to poem as "impersonal." "The poet is anonymous, and poetic language comes from an unknown source," Riley writes; the "poet dies constantly into the poem" (102). As he notes in the interview, the finished, perfectly at rest wholeness of the "true" poem applies even to individual poems within the poetic sequence, where, ideally, "the sequence of the book is carried forward *be-*

cause of the utter completion of each poem in it. Poetic completion or perfection is more than a closure, it implies a furthering and continuity, and the book realises that" (8). Riley understands that this view of poetry is explicitly at odds not only with a shriveled neo-Augustan "mainstream" poetry of "anecdote and self-distancing, wry observation of conditioned reflexes, wistful delineations of trappings of the heart" (96) but also with various process-based, procedural, and aleatory poetries which often appeal to heightened reader engagement but which in his view abnegate "the poet's duty to truth," leaving "the reader helplessly alone" (103).

As this survey of Riley's statements on poetics suggests, Riley's poetry, including *Distant Points,* might be thought of as late modernist—if categories are required. *Distant Points* is as much a book about the possibilities of lyric and specifically the continuities of English lyric—about the grounds for and the traditions of lyric—as it is a book about archaic gravesites. In Cambridge, Riley might very well know Ian Hodder, whose essays on neolithic houses and tombs, in resisting a general unified theory of material culture, argue that the "referential and metaphoric nature" of tombs " 'meant' in different ways through time" (75). We cannot assume, Hodder argues, that "through the . . . centuries and even milennia of tomb construction in north-west Europe people gave the tombs meaning by reference to houses. Even if the tombs were called houses of the ancestors and were built on house or settlement sites, they presumably came to have meaning in their own right as associated with a specific set of activities" (85). Such a contextualism applied to the material culture that is language would not seem to appeal to Riley, for whom the meaning of the "poetic" would seem to be stable, as permanent as the reality of death which leaves one to ponder "the hole in the ground and the human entirety it no longer holds, but which continues to exist in the history of script"—to quote again from the book jacket. The syntax is just a little ambiguous— is it the hole or the human that exists in script? Are these meditations that would offer the reader some insight into the identity and practices of this neolithic culture or do they instead represent the contortions and difficulties of trying to make sense of the past in the present? Tomb to house to text—is language, for Riley, the house of being, the house of death, or both? These are questions not easily answered. One might at least read this poetic series incorporating fragments of the description of gravesites as an exploration of the "origins" of lyric in that domus which is also a tomb, in the life which is built on the back of death. Ironically, lyric takes its most recent form in what most would call "prose," as the dislocations and syntactical gaps of this writing, its silences, suggest that "Meaning spills, over the edge. The vortex has stabilisers, contingent but discontinuous" (51). It is the ability of this text to work against definitions of "poetry" like some of those Riley has himself advanced, propositions which suggest a certainty about poetry's nature and purposes, that is one of its virtues. The redemptive word, the essence of lyric itself—a "completed heart"— remains unobtainable.

Allen Fisher

In deciding to navigate the extensive terrain of Allen Fisher's work with the book *SCRAM: or The Transformation of the Concept of Cities* (1994) as a first compass, I am engaged in an act of self-preservation. Fisher's published work is now of such bulk, some ninety pamphlets and books, that one's ability to speak confidently about his accomplishments and purposes must immediately acknowledge that the work in its abundance and diversity outruns and outwits the scopic drive that would produce a fiction of knowledge concerning it. By no means am I the first critic to notice this much about it. Robert Sheppard, introducing a selection of the work printed as part of the book *Future Exiles* (1992), declared that Fisher's "heterogeneous, overlapping works" were "initially overwhelming in their bulk and baffling in their complexity" (11). Similarly, Drew Milne, initiating an exchange with Fisher following upon the receipt of materials from Fisher and the publication by the latter of an essay on *A Various Art* outlining the aesthetic principles shared by a number of that anthology's poets and poetries, stated that "many people find your work both unapproachable in its size and diversity, and are suspicious of the internal coherence of particular poems and sequences" (29). Luckily, *SCRAM* is produced as if in response to such concerns. The book's preface explains that *SCRAM* is "a book of parts" selected from works published between 1971 and 1982, up the point of initiation of Fisher's current work in progress, *Gravity as a Consequence of Shape,* the several volumes of which published to date represent for this reader some of Fisher's most significant work. Along with the fact that its texts are more easily excerpted than those in *Gravity, SCRAM*'s critical commentary, written in the third person by Fisher, presents temptations too great to resist. Here this highly conceptual work is framed by its producer, even as he insists that the book offers "glimpses" rather than "synopsis" of the poetic projects it excerpts and even as we must admit that this permutation of the project represents but one (perhaps broken) new frame (7). The commentary at times seems perfectly serious, although, as we proceed, we note too that the convention of the third person has been chosen purposefully, allowing Fisher the opportunity to mock the pretension of such an exercise as the one he is attempting. For instance, after speaking of the "lack of subsequent availability" of parts of the sequence *Blood Bone Brain,* he writes that "it is thus, with initial relief, that the reader comes upon *Paxton's Beacon*—the only extensive selection to be published from the long *The Art of Flight* sequence which coherently tables the agreement between procedural and processual techniques in the form of an artifact that all too often gives pleasure to read" (12). Consider the unravelling of such a sentence, which begins by promising the reader relief from her labors and ends by criticizing whatever pleasure such relief might bear in hand. Fisher, with a reputation as difficult king of a crumbling postmodern mountain of multiple systems and discourses, is too rarely given credit for the alternately devious and carnivalesque wit regularly a part of his projects.

Fisher's prose commentary in *SCRAM* might also be read beside the questions asked by his Adornean interlocutor Drew Milne in an exchange in *Parataxis.* After beginning by distinguishing a "restricted" and "more dispersed sense of poetic relation to linguistic manifolds," the former of which is said to manifest assumptions about "a poetic relation to language, and an overdetermined sense of what constitutes formal beauty and coherence" and the latter to risk a "more unsettled" and "improvised dance above the manifolds of language" and a "range of possible discourses, languages and texts" (28), Milne distinguishes a poetic practice which maintains "a core belief in what might be called the persistence of lyric" from Fisher's procedures, which he thinks have combined "an Olsonian kind of open field together with procedures drawn from *language* poetry" (29). Having framed his interests in this fashion, he asks Fisher if he had considered the possibility that chance operations, improvisitory techniques, and so forth might alienate the reader; how Fisher conceives of the relationship between the improvised and the formally controlled; and how he knows "when a poem is finished" (29). Aggressive questions, these, and perched on a faultline some might describe as a part of a London/Cambridge divide in British poetry. But Fisher had hardly been less aggressive in reviewing *A Various Art,* arguing that the bulk of the poems in that book (Prynne's work is bracketed) factured a "constructionist aesthetic with, in the main, a consequential emphasis on ideal limits, self-referral and autonomy common to late modernism; a reliance on direct perception (itself a construction) usually through autobiographical or domestic descriptions . . . ; a rhetorical surface that has been self-parodied, or is a pastiche from conventional usage . . . ; an address that aspires to the civic, rather than public" (69–70). Fisher's response to Milne's queries began with the insistence that, despite conventions indicating the need for one, he had no single or consistent "aesthetic stance" (30) and that, indeed, there would be no one answer to any of these questions, that rather one would have to know exactly what one was talking about. This is a blow to Poetics with a capital *p:* "An overview of the projects, of which my published works are 'showings,' would require recognising a multiple aesthetic programme: it would involve a recognition that each project had been conceptualised and specifically designed." As for the desire for "finish" and "coherence," Fisher continued, these had been critiqued by Courbet and Baudelaire in the nineteenth century, by "many physicists concerned with acuity and more recently by Bela Julesz regarding texture, Oliver Braddick on spatial analysis in vision and K. W. Yau and others researching the effect of ions on light-sensitive current in retinal rods" (30). (Fisher's pursuit of "structural homologies in the sciences" has been noted by Sheppard.) As for the question of Olson's influence, yes, some of the earlier work had combined constructivist and open-field methods, in the process of following but also critiquing Olson. As for language poetry, which of that work could Milne possibly mean in such a sweeping and seemingly dismissive remark? While, like some language poets, he had found the work of Jackson Mac Low, Clark Coolidge, and Louis Zukofsky instructive, he had not "drawn from" language poetry per se. As for the notion of a "persistence of lyric," that was surely no more "than a phrase from a weak critical apparatus" (32).

It should be more than evident by now that Fisher will not easily be pinned down. The legacies of Blake, of Situationism, of Fluxus and Fluxshoe (in which he participated), and of other avant-garde and neo-avant-garde traditions of site-specific performative aesthetics and aesthetic theory, help underwrite what is in much of his work a perpetual and perpetually renewed commitment to the revolutionary, a dedication to what he calls in the last volume of his *Place* series, *Unpolished Mirrors* (1985), "a coming English revolution":

> I am in the garden of a coming English revolution
> rid of the pole
> the tethering

without loss of homeostasis
        wanting strength enough to hold Goodness before
        any malignity of genetic fate

I have come to increase my liberation
        through the dynamegalopolis
        Urthona rise from the ruiness Walls.

                                                        (1)

Few poets—Blake would be one, Hugh MacDiarmid another—have been
engaged in work which pursues so many avenues seeking exit from the
ghettos of aesthetic autonomy and commodity status within which art
resides as a leisure activity. For Fisher, poetry must rather be "necessary
business," as one manifesto puts it. In prose such as that of the manifesto,
Fisher's tone can be dogmatic, Debordian almost, as here in rejecting a
class-conscious and representational practice:

> The new pertinence read art as an affirmation of life as distinct from
> the attitude of the State and its entourage. To paraphrase Augusto Boal,
> art is immanent to all people and not to a select few only: Art is not
> sold, no more than breathing, thinking or loving. Art is not merchan-
> dise. For the new and the old bourgeoisie everything was a commodity:
> People were commodities. All things people made were commodities.
> What the bourgeoisie failed to comprehend was that pertinent art arose
> from the same crisis as that of the proletariat. This art did not exist for
> the proletariat as such because this condition of "an art" for "a class"
> was the product of the thinking of a class, the bourgeoisie, who insisted
> on the separation of art from the process of life.[17]

Personification of the state—it has an attitude—allows this rhetoric to
represent the state as a monolithic entity. And in what sense is it true that,
for the "bourgeoisie," everything—even the person—is a commodity?
Among the many simplifications of this post-Marxist rhetoric is the fact
that the desire to transform the relation of art and "the process of life,"
to transform leisure (and also work)—these familiar motivations of historical and neo-avant-gardes—have themselves lately been the product of
a "bourgeoisie," or rather they have been incorporated within it much
the way music has become part of the mall. In rejecting class politics
per se, Fisher nevertheless demonstrates the greater purchase these have
in British discourse, preserving the idioms of a Marxism he would reject
or transform. We're left to wonder—to enumerate just a few concerns—

to what extent art still exists as separate from "the process of life," and by what agency a cure of consciousness and praxis enacted and demanded by avant-garde activity might engage (not to mention transform) political institutions. This is a politicized aesthetics which has largely abandoned the idea that the political efficacy of artistic practices is a relevant question.

But the poetics that have grown out of Fisher's revolutionary desire are far more plural, unstable, and contradictory than the prose might suggest, embracing nearly every available technique in the arsenal of a politicized aesthetics, from the post-dadaesque distortions and erasures which grew out of the "Destruction in Art" symposium to the discursive didacticism of MacDiarmid, from the poetics of defamiliarization to varieties of historiographical and documentary practice, and beyond these alternatives too in tonal registers as different as the first lines of "Birds Locked in the Roof" in *Unpolished Mirrors:*

> Walked out into borne disease
> release compressed nitrogen headache in fall-out
> propelled anti-bodies juicing a harm
> fuming odorous courage penetrating ozone unload
> with relay-sprung deodorants
>
> (13)

are from the first lines of "bending windows: 2" in *SCRAM:*

> because of economic chaos we're not going to make the lift-off
> 50, 000 in orbit won't be enough to ease the load
> my calypso shirt switches into a playsuit or a bag
> I'm in the territorial army but dislike militarism and violence
> went off weekend camp with the 71 Signals
> pirate-style pants convert into trousers my mate calls 'em zouvre
>   but they're not
>
> (74)

Fisher's divergent methods of "facture" are evident in the microparticulars of sonic and visual "style"; one could account for the different "tones" in these two passages by speaking of differences in the speed, stress-patterns, grammar, and idiom of their lines, the first poem more monologic in its cataloging of an ecological nightmare, the second a more dispersed series of dramatically ventriloquized banalities, as if overheard media noise and street babble. It should be clear also from the above samples that Fisher's poetry can be, in its politics, "content-specific" — to borrow a word from Peter Barry.[18] It is never sufficient to speak of the "politics of form" in discussing his work, though a critique of existing modes of (constructed) perception and normative poetic practice is implicit in all of his procedures.

After writing in the preface to *SCRAM* that "a strong inclination in the bulk of the work has been against the finite poem as statement and shifted towards a clearer understanding of contemporary possibilities" (7), Fisher then introduces the book's first section, "conceptual framed constructions" from 1971 to 1982. Admitting that an earlier work showed "an apparent strain of division between lyric ego and idealist construction," Fisher sets the more conceptual work undertaken later in the context of the events of 1968 in Paris and London, just as, in the introduction to the book's second section displaying works produced as "conceptual frame-broken construction" he refers to the "turn-around in the Portuguese Revolution of 1974–75, and the forbidding excitement leading into the first public conflagration at Brixton in 1980" (29). The first category means to describe work manifesting "a struggle between procedural programmes and processual plans" (11) — between the use of what Joseph Conte calls "predetermined or arbitrary constraints" — and a fully conscious, strategic improvisation.[19] Not Mac Low on the one hand and Olson on the other but some ongoing contestation between them. The second category names work that takes on multiple and "self-interfering" frames and procedures. This is the category, Fisher explains, that might contain the several works of the major project of the 1970s, the *Place* project. *SCRAM*'s third section/category, "structured thematics," contains a fragment pulled from *Place* and also "provides examples of the grounding" of the later series *Gravity as a Consequence of Shape* (55). A fourth and last category/section entitled "dramatic and other monologues'" endeavors to show some of the possibilities of "voice" and ventriloquism, Fisher having begun the use of quasi-Blakean, archetypal narrator-figures such as the "Gardener" and the "Artist" (the Burglar, etc.) in the last volume of the *Place* project and increased their use in the more narrative-based poems of the more recent project.

Sampling *SCRAM* one finds post-Zukofskyan word presentations such as the following, from "defamiliarizing":

> paint
> happens
>
> bar

norm

window   glass air
                  (26)

Isolated from its series, this has in its presentational immediacy, in its symmetrical music, exactly the artifactual "finish" Milne might seem to desire as a norm, even as the three words which are the poem's middle include two that seem to ask the reader to "bar" the normative—if we read "bar" as a verb. The "glass air" that resolves the poem's music might be said to ask for an aesthetic other than the representational one "window" remembers. Like a good number of the book's poems and other Fisher productions of the period, the "conceptual" work of this poem is a matter not just of form and procedure but of the ability to articulate as metadiscourse propositions about form and procedure (as elsewhere epistemology, consciousness and so forth)—propositions usually contested elsewhere.

"Paint/happens" hears behind it "shit happens" perhaps? Anyway there is a "hardness," a refusal to rest satisfied in any configuration of identity, sentiment, proposition, idea, or idiom in many of Fisher's poems, such as the following from "interjacents":

> the birds in your hand are invisible
> until you grasp them
> in your hands you cup them
> and your dream is death
> because you hold it
>
> The nameless uncarved block
> is freedom from desire
>
> brings
> peace of its own accord
>
> and you will hate it

                                        (64)

Unlike some postmodernists who recognize that "multiple theories overlap, complicate and evade Theory, Control, Money, Law, the State, and sometimes the Reader," Fisher doesn't buy the postmodernist hypostatization of desire" (418), Andrew Lawson argues in a passage that might be productively juxtaposed with the torqued syntax of this little fragment, where freedom from desire isn't the answer either. The deployment of multiple, self-interrupting frames in Fisher's work is impossible to represent here without the ability to quote entire some of the longer poems of the *Gravity* books or the whole of *SCRAM*, so I will conclude simply by quoting the second stanza of a poem as unlike either of the two above as any I can find, one of Fisher's "four novels" where the interest is partly in narrative, partly in persona and voice as Fisher makes his sarcastic contribution to British travel literature:

> Duckfoot Johnny made me till I got the tune with enough vigour
> and emotion to satisfy him. Let's embroider this produced
> little fiction. The chance to get in, wander round a little.
> In my opinion what we should do is dance—
> the only way to create the proper atmosphere for such an occasion.
>
> (31)

This seems a proper ending for such an occasion, where I have only begun to wander around a little in a work whose circumference is beyond single vision.

Geraldine Monk

Pity poor Geraldine Monk, extracted here from a whole host of British women experimentalists—including Denise Riley, Wendy Mulford, Caroline Bergvall, Maggie O'Sullivan, Grace Lake, Paula Claire, Carlyle Reedy, and Fiona Templeton—inevitably to be made to carry a discussion of the issues confronting feminist poetry in Britain. She might equally well be made to represent some of the possibilities of performance and performance writing in that London tradition discussed by and with reference to Cris Cheek above. As Cheek notes, British alternative poetry scenes have sometimes seemed a white-male ghetto, despite the ongoing work of the writers named above, all of whom are part of the invaluable multinational anthology edited by O'Sullivan, *Out of Everywhere: Linguistically Innovative Poetry by Women in North America and the United Kingdom* (1996). Male-dominated poetry scenes in Britain are nothing new, as a perusal of most anthologies, "mainstream" or otherwise, demonstrates. However, the sparse representation of women in many mainstream anthologies— the recent Bloodaxe *The New Poetry* is an exception in this regard— and the sociocultural reasons for the same have attracted less attention than the more abstract question of whether or not, in an era of identity politics, "experimental" poetry can be made to carry or enact a feminist politics of significant force. Contrasts are drawn between a poetics of the "expressive voice" wherein "part of the political impetus of [the] work lies in representing female experience within the institution of literature, and thus within the 'public' sphere" and a poetics which rejects "dominant expressive modes" because they risk "co-option by the dominant literary establishment."[20] Such arguments go back into the deep past of modernism, raising a number of familiar spectres—the idea that experimental poetry is elitist, for instance.

The critics Clair Wills, Linda Kinnahan, and Helen Kidd have written provocative essays on these questions as they pertain to the British context, taking their cue from an extensive feminist critical literature that has not regularly sought its examples in Britain. By focusing on the changed relationship between the private and public, Wills deconstructs the binary formations that have often reigned in discussions of the relationship of "dominant" expressive poetic modes and a "postmodern" work that seems to reject these:

> it is not that "expressive" poetry naively falls back on a stable individuality, and experimental work explores the radical absence of subjectivity. Both are responses to the reconfiguring of the relationship between public and private spheres which makes the "private" lyric impossible, and in effect opens it out toward rhetoric. While the private sphere has been invaded by the public, or the social, at the same time the social has opened up to take note of formerly private concerns, and both modes of poetry reflect in their form the changing nature of this relationship. (39–40)

In writing of the "experimental" work of Denise Riley and Lyn Hejinian, Wills argues that

> despite their use of experimental poetic forms, which question the coherence of the poetic "voice" and the consistency of the speaking "I," their poetry is nonetheless strongly weighted towards articulating questions of interiority and emotional inwardness. But that identity is defined less as a fixed identity than as a series of processual identifications with elements of both the private (familial) sphere and the public world, in which language comes to us already moulded by the media. Far from recording the radical hollowing out of subjectivity, this poetry suggests that it is through the productive appropriation of elements of mass-culture that a meaningful subjectivity can emerge. (51)

Following Wills here, one might demonstrate the variety of ways in which a "productive engagement" with mass culture occurs in experimental women's poetry. This would be more than a matter of asserting the agency of irony in parodic mimicry of the media-speak all of us are fed daily (as in the Shapcott poem quoted above); it is also the case that fragments of media-speak and media imagery can be de- and recontextualized to be used in any number of ways—to bespeak with the utmost seriousness passion and sentiment, to locate autobiographical and historical meaning, and so forth. Denise Riley's work is a good example of a poetry in which the discourses of mass culture function in unstable and sometimes ambivalent ways. Is that line from that pop song meant to be ironic or not? More so than that line borrowed from the English canon? Is that an allusion or an inclusion? Is that *my* beautiful house?

In a manifesto she coauthored with O'Sullivan, Monk has written that "ultimately, the most effective chance any woman has of dismantling the fallacy of male creative supremacy is simply by writing poetry of a kind which is liberating by the breadth of its range, risk and innovation."[21] This is admirably direct and pragmatic. And the first thing to be said about Monk's poetry is that while it does not use the "dominant modes" of expression, neither is it difficult. Playful, rhetorical, feminist, it also can be as "expressive" as an insult. Here is the whole of "Molecular Power Progressives" from her selected poems, *The Sway of Precious Demons* (1992):

STATUS

Flouncing insignia hearts on sleeves

CULT HUGGERS

BOOT CRUSHERS

Leather boys strategically studded

Soldier boys swallowing uniformity

Heavy boys banging blue denim metallics

City boys pin striped and tied

Law boys robed and wigged

Holy boys cassocked and collared

FIngers WAggers   THumb SCrewers

RanK

MEN

TALITY

Boys in all of their costumes then, punks and lawyers gently mocked in an ecstasy of verbal and visual playfulness. The debt is equal to oral traditions and concrete poetry. The structure is simple. Capital letters will indicate "status" in short phrases exploiting sonic affinities (cult huggers/boot crushers) or conceptual ones (fingers waggers/thumb screwers). Lower-case lines will name "insignia"—the roles identified by dress—in grammatically parallel lines a little longer. The middle of the poem, from line 3 to line 11, is symmetrical, the last line breaking down the visual opposition between caps and lower case. With the double meaning of "rank" and the next two lines we are offered the resolution of summary commentary. Nothing profound at all about the poem, its typography its only (precarious) claim to raging innovation. We could speak of avant-garde traditions of the "visible word" and bardic catalogs, but the fact is that most of the techniques employed in this poem are available to Monk on the flyers advertising rock shows and in the music they advertise. It is in this sense that mass-culture enters her work and is transformed in her alternately eroticized and politicized expression—not as allusion but as material form.

For all of the mountains of academic discourse concerning the fluidity of postmodern subjectivities, the end of interiority and such, there is little that's been said about subjectivity that wasn't said nearly as well by the first lines of "I Am the Walrus," which is perhaps distantly echoed in lines from "La Quinta Del Sordo," a sequence of love poems that—with its echoes and allusions to Mina Loy and fairy tales, nursery rhymes and the Bible, Gertrude Stein—has as its last section a collapsed, fragmented prose. For this reader it is Monk's best poem, and I'll end this discussion by quoting part of it:

> You will go where I go where I and you go twinning
> this siamese disease forming bunches of limbs
> fused in trepidation
>
> You remain me and I and you with these taunting
> ligatures of skin binding mutual
> assailants
>
> Inextricable

we are
compulsory chaperons
a nexus of stretching
nerve
drained currents and
overheated desires

. . .

And here more hooks more eyes and this
fleshless wet bandaging of loneliness with black marrow grape

Come now
Let us beckon
Let us reckon hard
with this block vengeance

Tom Raworth and Roy Fisher

I conclude this brief survey of alternative British poetries with this strange pairing for a number of reasons. For one thing, Roy Fisher and Tom Raworth are now, together with J. H. Prynne, elders among an "avant-garde"—not that either of them has been much given to writing critical prose or manifestoes of any sort or would accept the pretension of such a phrase. I'll quote only from Fisher's *A Furnace* (1986) and Raworth's *Catacoustics* (1991) here, but both men have moved across a broad terrain of experimental modes in their distinguished careers. The earlier poems of Raworth, for instance, bear comparison with (and in my view surpass all but the very best) poetries associated with the so-called New York school, engaging as well the practices associated with several Black Mountain poets. Roy Fisher's earlier work owes a similar debt to American experimental poetries, to Williams and Zukofsky, and several of his prose poetry publications make their contribution as well to traditions associated with European avant-gardes, particularly surrealism. In an essay on the two of them alongside Allen Fisher, Andrew Lawson writes, "Like Roy Fisher, Raworth combined at the outset of his career a broadly surrealist ontology with the aesthetic concerns of modernist American poetry as represented by the short-lived but influential Black Mountain school which included Robert Creeley, Edward Dorn, and Charles Olson, as well as Willem de Kooning and John Cage: the interface of perception and language, the indeterminacy of the speaking subject, the register or graph of 'a mind moving'" (420–21). A second reason for the pairing is their having managed to avoid being altogether claimed by one or another of the factions or pseudo-factions in alternative British poetry, while being respected by all of them. They might even be said to be the most "successful" of nonmainstream poets, though of course success is relative. Fisher was eventually published by Oxford University Press, which potentially offers him more visibility than most of his peers though it doesn't necessarily keep his books in print. Raworth is surely the most "famous" British avant-garde poet in the United States, where he has lived for extended periods, and where many of his books have been published, sometimes before he was able to publish them in England. Finally, I juxtapose their work because, despite shared influences, despite our ability to speak abstractly of matters such as "the interface of perception and language" and "the indeterminacy of the speaking subject" with regard to some of the work of both poets, in the end Raworth's work doesn't much resemble Fisher's, which tells us something about the value of such language and more about the size of the field of alternative British practice, which I have only barely sketched.

Catacoustics—the words run together in its title suggest cacophony rather than harmony—is a forty-one-page poem written partly in a version of the disjunctive style Raworth has been working variations on since the early seventies, in books like *Ace* (1974), *Writing* (1982), and *Eternal Sections* (1993). Kit Robinson describes *Ace* as

> an exploration of discontinuous language in continuous time. The language of the poem is composed of bits (short lines) which, by virtue of a polyvalent syntax, can point forward and/or back. There is no punctuation. Meaning is dependent on where the mind locates its attention within the continuum and how it groups the particles. Each language event (line) qualifies what has come immediately before and violates any totalization prior to it. Time destroys fixed ideas. (467)

Among a number of possible interpretations of the significance of Raworth's syntactic practice the cottage wisdom of that last sentence will serve our purposes perfectly. Raworth's poetry in this one mode self-consciously sets the fixity of the printed word, as per our poetic conventions in lines printed on a page, against the temporality of reading. Meeting each new line in the present of our act of reading the poem, we are forced to revise our sense of the last one. Our desire to stop, to settle in the grammar of a proposition, exclamation, or question is constantly frustrated; our memories of the immediate past suddenly become memories of something seen incompletely, words which have turned out to be other than what we imagined by virtue of our turning to the next line, moving down the page to set them in yet another combination.

Easiest to show how this can work by quoting a particular example, in this case the opening lines of the poem:

> should i begin again
> almost with a capital
> i catch to memory a car
> seen from the back seat
> moving past stone walled fields
> lambs
> a cheval glass, bevelled, at a bend
> showing nothing
> but depthless shadows
> i knew his motionless eyes
> meant he was paying attention
> but things look slower
> in peripheral vision
> something is thinking back to me
> enjoy those relegated motors
> that is your thumb
> it feels for you
> it is you
> pay it some attention
> bell rings
> so a current
> is running through the circuit
> up a stair
> round by a window
> your car
> is a very advanced baby
> don't get any ideas
> we share eyes
> we are all
> imagined
> tempting fate

almost fixed
the heir to the throne
so anyverb

(1–2)

This first block of text continues until we come to six lines that might, if we wish, be isolated and read together as an admonition or plea: "come back pulsing / to life / hell to be thought / tastes / to be retraced" (3). The bulk of *Catacoustics* consists of blocks of text that look a lot like this one, though there are lines (sometimes treated text) arranged in smaller groups ("theme" sits all by itself atop one page), blocks of lines that run all the way to the edge of the page like prose usually does, and last but not least a few doodles and graphics. The word *search* is followed by what looks like an exclamation point except that the period at the bottom has been changed to a comma (the number 1 sits at its upper right corner.) After the lines "the mirror badge / upon her breast / that reads" (11) there is a flat oval "badge" which one guesses has its words (two of them arranged cross-wise) printed backwards or flipped, until one is pedant enough to hold the book up before a mirror and see that, while the word printed vertically is indeed *man,* the one printed horizontally reads (in your mirror) *lacanic,* which is *cynical* misspelled backwards or a typo for *laconic.* It is not that the sign is opaque but that it might be read any number of ways depending on how it is seen and in what context one chooses to place it. Hold it up before a mirror? Figure it says something about the "woman"? Think that its scrambling is a defamiliarizing act, in the same way that putting a comma instead of a period at the bottom of an exclamation "point" makes us lose a little respect for the conventions associated with that punctuation mark? We learn that it matters what we do with and to this writing, matters in the extreme, at the fundamental level of syntax. There are other graphics, including a baroque heart, three "pages" with script—more of one of the doodles below.

If we are the kind of readers Raworth probably requires, the playfulness of the lines above is one pleasure that pushes us through his text. We've already gathered most of the principles of the work we'll need if we find ourselves thinking, "But you *have* begun!" while reading the poem's first line. Such activity is potentially licensed by the second line, which might be construed as looking back to comment on the lower case *i* of the first, as if we were to notice that there was some purpose in it—perhaps this *i* isn't thought to be important enough to be a capital "I." Then we're not in the car but reading about the memory of a car—the phrase is awkward or colloquial (compare "call" or "bring" to memory) and in the present tense. Then we learn that the car is as seen from the back seat. The same car? Another car? Is the memory *of* a car, of a car as seen from the back seat—*its* back seat maybe—or of something seen *from* a car, some event involving a car? Rearrange the second through fourth lines to read "i catch to memory lambs seen from the back seat of a car moving past stone walled fields" and you'll understand one of the procedures by which what Kit Robinson calls "polyvalent syntax" might encourage attentiveness while destabilizing interpretation. What is moving? The car or the lambs? Whatever it is, it's moving fast maybe, or as fast as Raworth tends to read such lines in performance.

We're only through the first six lines now and won't be allowed to stop yet. Just down below we encounter the "cheval glass," the "bevelled mirror," at a "bend"—in the road? (The line "bends" here.) It shows nothing, and then it shows "depthless shadows." Is it a figure for this text? What about the next three lines? Is attentiveness really a consequence of motionlessness or are we to take these lines, extracted and isolated, as ironic—given our own motion in reading them? We're being made fun of? Then there is the play with the deictic functions of language in the line mentioning a thumb, the banal deadpan of noting that, an instrument of your use and one often used to distinguish you from lower orders of being, the thumb also *is* you, your body. Again we're asked to pay attention and, as if to wake us, a bell rings. And so on down the page—is it fate that is almost "fixed" or the identity of the heir to the throne? And what would "fixed" mean here? We might continue to construct our fictions of interpretation.

Writing about works like this by Raworth, Andrew Lawson notes the "painterly" quality of this writing, which views language as "intractable material . . . a set of resistances from which expression has to be wrested." This is an aesthetic, he argues, in which "bafflement replaces sublimity as the aesthetic emotion *par excellence,* as sublimity replaced religious awe. But the bafflement is constructive, part of a thoroughgoing scepticism about the coercive logic of definition, of models of understanding, which does not stop short of the self" (421). The disjunctive gaps in Raworth's syntax might be contrasted with the white spaces cut between Peter Riley's fragments in the poem quoted above. In the latter, I think, we are to understand those gaps as negative presentation of an unpresentable "absolute" or "real." Riley's is a poetic of the sublime. In the aesthetics of indeterminacy or "bafflement" in Raworth, our attention devolves not into a terrifying "real" altogether beyond us and unknowable, calling for our inevitably desperate and failed efforts to acknowledge if not grasp it, but rather into the abundance of material particulars which obstinately refuse any effort to gather them, positively or negatively, into depth or coherence. The pleasure one takes (or doesn't) in reading Raworth's texts then will be a matter of engaging the temporal processes of defamiliarization and destabilization and—equally—in our ability provisionally to configure the detail and nuance we pass in our motion through the text. Detail in the text must be such as to allow us (in the words of the poem) "THE EDGE OF RECOGNITION / nothing anyone can't handle" (27). Raworth's is not an aesthetic of nonsense, nor is it nonrepresentational; tone, idiom, and narration all allow us our temporary certainties. Detail is crucial.

As it turns out, the shards of *Catacoustics* contain some of Raworth's most overtly politicized "content." It is one thing to speak of this text, as of the poetry of any number of American poets who have learned from Raworth, as Wittgensteinian, as rejecting a "picture-theory" of meaning for the contextualism of meaning as use.[22] But here the purposes as well as the set of possible consequences of these Wittgensteinian views are also entertained. Raworth goes the duck-rabbit one better toward the end of the poem:

hats   meringues   eggcups
constant cancellation
repeated emotion
dependent messages
soldier in a silo
unable to be brave
makes ghosts from shadows
threats from moving air
we could like forever
in no air up there
you can have the bombs
if we can get away

> time to leave this planet
> before it's all the same
>
> (40–41)

And so on, ending with "he sulks." "Constant cancellation" and "dependent messages" offer the reader descriptive metadiscourse about the production and reading of the poem. Beyond these lines Raworth presents a case study we might construe as having ethical weight. Is the nuclear soldier confronting the instabilities of interpretation likely to be a soldier we will admire for his inability to be brave—perhaps he will not be macho enough to want to destroy people? Or is it that he, in his paranoia, might very well imagine a ghost or threat and put the finger to the button? It is impossible to say. And how are we to take the next lines? Surely the idea that we could "like forever" (as we like, say, candy) is ironically expressed, given the prospect of nuclear annihilation and the fact that, in "forever," there is "no air." Surely too everyone desires abundance—of meaning, of things—rather than a condition where everything is the same. Celebrating abundance and difference would seem to be one of the purposes of such an aesthetic as it is poised against the sublime—including the nuclear sublime—and intent on avoiding dogmatic and fixed meanings. Yet the intellectual honesty of Raworth is such that he will hold before us the possibility that the collapse of some of our certainties will mean turning from our responsibility to the world. This is the "sulking" that accompanies the debunking, playful imagination at work elsewhere in the text. Both tonalities ultimately require of us, as of the soldier, increased attentiveness.

Like Tom Raworth, Roy Fisher is a poet whose syntactic practices (plural as in Raworth) might be exemplary for poets and readers seeking resources. While one suspects that, for many younger poets, it is the earlier postsurrealist books such as *City* (1961), *The Ship's Orchestra* (1966), and *The Cut Pages* (1971), which offer the most challenging models, pointing the way toward new work in a hybrid "prose poetry," the very different syntactic procedures of *A Furnace* should not be overlooked:

> Whatever breaks
> from stasis, radiance or dark
> impending, and slides
> directly and fast on its way, twisting
> aspect in the torsions of the flow
> this way and that,

                                    then suddenly
over,
            through a single
glance of another force touching it or
bursting out of it sidelong,

doing so
fetches the timeless flux
that cannot help but practise
materialization,
the coming into sense,
to the guesswork of the senses,
the way in cold air
ice-crystals, guessed at, come densely
falling from where they were not;

and it fetches
timeless identities
riding in the flux with no
determined form, cast out of the bodies
that once they were, or out of
the brains that bore them;

                                    (11)

This is not a syntax of disjunction but of conjunction, wherein the motion of word and phrase across line breaks mimics in its form the perpetual coming into sense and form that the long sentence describes. Andrew Crozier writes that

> *A Furnace* involves extended reflection on the nature of signs and of cognitive enquiry: how signs are produced from sense perception but have significance that is modified as enquiry is pursued; how this variation divides signs from the contexts in which they arise, from the general cases of both the perceptual field and conventional significance. The sign "rides over intention" and its singularity is multiple. It accomplishes its own identity and meaning and is at the same time invested in the world as our access to it. . . . Mind and world are not homologous, but occur as a particular conjunction through which signs travel thick and fast, "many modes/funnelling fast through one event." . . . If Fisher is not philosophically realist no more is he nominalist; he is not

concerned with real existences as such but with the signs they make and by which they can be evoked. (30–31)

A Furnace might be said to take as its occasion the transformations and metamorphosis of Fisher's native Birmingham and its surrounding areas, of other cities in Europe, and, more broadly, of civilizations, cultures, and meanings. As Peter Barry has noted, unlike the earlier poem *City,* where the "over-riding concern" was with "a specific locale and its citizenry," the concerns of *A Furnace* involve "energy, change, transformation, superimposition, and process *as* such, viewed as transcendent entities" (3–4). In his own preface Fisher speaks of the "equivocal ways in which time can be thought about," and suggests that the poem's larger structure is modeled after the "ancient figure of the double spiral, whose line turns back on itself at the centre and leads out again, against its own incoming curve" (vii–viii). This figure, in turn, might suggest the structure of the basic genetic material of DNA. Signs and their cognition, the transfiguration of history and myth — these are the concerns of this meditative poem, which begins in a deictic modernist mode describing the impressions and sensations of a bus trip across the city as they allow the intuition of "more dimensions than I can know" (3), the self evidently present in the poetry, as Lawson notes, "only as an absent cause, discoverable among its effects" (415).

Fisher's work is categorized by Lawson as an "abridged romanticism, a truncated theology," as a "polytheism without gods," as a "modernism that . . . attempts to keep faith with the past as a temporality imbued with at least the semblance of meaning" (418). If we quote the rest of the long, unravelling sentence begun above, we can understand the grounds for that last claim:

> but trapped into water-drops,
> windows they glanced through
> or had their images
> detained by and reflected
> or into whose molten glass the coloured oxides
> burned their qualities;
>
> *like dark-finned fish embedded in ice*
> *they have life in them that can be revived.*
>
> (12)

What Fisher is describing here is not merely a matter of the existence of traces of residual cultural practices and formations that might, if we wish, be re-animated. Fisher's references to "timeless flux" and "timeless identities" prompts Crozier to write, "What is imagined—the timeless identities entering nature—might yet give even well-disposed readers pause. And I think we should at least pause to ask if *A Furnace* does not arrive, finally, at a heterodox mysticism" (32). This is a fair question: in what sense do Fisher's "timeless identities" invoke the transcendent? On the one hand the poem will indeed acknowledge "the sense of another world / not past, but primordial, / everything in it simultaneous, and moving / every way but forward" (14). Fisher's apprehension of the primordial is figured most powerfully in the image of an old peasant woman in Birmingham who might have been beamed back from the nineteenth century: "No imaginable / beginning to her epoch, and she's / ignored its end" (15). She represents the persistence of an identity otherwise anomalous in her surroundings.

The writing that authority performs "records" identities, Fisher thinks, in order to limit them, making them "traceable" but only so that they might be ignored: "and as if it were a military installation / specialize and classify and hide / the life of the dead" (17). Fisher writes of "the dead" that "they come anyway / to the trench, / the dead in their surprise, / taking whatever form they can / to push across. They've no news. / They infest the brickwork" (18). The dead exist as material forms and practices whose meaning the present is called upon to identify. Poetry might participate in that identifying but also, when "thrown" or sprung like Fisher's lines across their line breaks, in the breaking down of known identity. Later in the poem, Fisher writes of "The true gods, known only / as *those of whom there is never news*" (42). So we do not have access to the "true gods," in this polytheistic absolute, except as pure negativity, only to their traces, their "signs"—those sites of human interaction with "it." Heraclitus, who is mentioned in the poem's preface, writes in a famous fragment that "the lord whose oracle is at Delphi neither speaks nor conceals, but gives signs" (70).

Thinking about the last passage of Fisher's poem, in which we are presented with an image of snails reduplicating half of the poem's own motion by spiralling up fennel stalks "together and upward; / tight and seraphic" (48), Crozier writes that "the stress on human agency may seem light but the statement is major: the signs that encode identity and culture originate in the same human desire, and by that desire we are attached to the world" (32). This is certainly a credible reading of the poem, identifying as it must "the true gods" with a felt lack which in turn animates the productive processes of cultural metamorphosis which are the result of human struggle. But the question of Fisher's mysticism will not be easily resolved. In the "Core" section of the poem, the central section, we read of a "dead acoustic" space, the intersection point of the two spirals, death and life, a "total stillness" which is "as if inside the world but nowhere / continuous with it" (29). The "as if" locates the timeless within the reaches of the imagination and desire but it also names a possibility. Surely the question itself, like Fisher's focus on metamorphosis, helps us situate Fisher's project within the field of modernist rather than postmodernist poetics, the latter having mostly rejected even the semblance of the kind of continuity with the past that Fisher imagines in favor of what Lawson calls a "decathected and derealized present" (417).

I have largely given over this last discussion of Roy Fisher to several English critics for much the same reason as I gave over the end of this chapter's first section to Cris Cheek. The critical writing on Fisher's poetry is of an extraordinarily high quality. There are a number of his British peers about whom we could say the same thing. In part this gives the lie to the idea that there has been a "convention of critical silence" at work in Britain with regard to the poetries I have briefly surveyed here—except, alas, that this criticism itself is hardly more visible to the institutions of the public sphere than the poetry itself.

7. Edward Kamau Brathwaite's *X / Self* and Black British Poetry

In the third book of Edward Kamau Brathwaite's second poetic trilogy, the volume *X / Self* (1987), there is a poem entitled "X / Self's Xth Letters from the Thirteen Provinces." Following a poem lamenting the slaughter of children in Soweto and preceding another contrasting "the wasteful Byzantine poverty of opulence" witnessed at a Kingston art exhibit with the "opulence of poverty" evident elsewhere in Kingston, "X / Self's Xth Letters from the Thirteen Provinces" is a two part epistolary poem in the patois, in what Brathwaite himself calls "nation-language."[1] Ostensibly a speaker's casual discourse to his mother about various subjects including his decision to write using a word processor, the poem also presents an interlude wherein Brathwaite questions his work in *X / Self*. At the end of the poem, the speaker asks his mother—and we might also think that Brathwaite asks himself and us, each of his readers—what it means that he is sitting before his computer "Chipp/in dis poem onta dis tablet // chiss / ellin darkness writin in light / like i is a some/ is a some // body / a // x // pert or some // thing like moses or aaron or one of dem dyaam isra // lite."[2] A speaker, or, more exactly, a writer—humble, respectful of his mother, self-consciously awkward among "experts"—asks what it means that he is writing a poem that reaches for the force and significance of the Pentateuch, of Torah. Considering the epic scope and the political intensity of much of *X / Self*, this poem's unpretentious, even self-deprecating voice, this one brief glimpse of that collective identity in search of definition which is "X / Self," is, for me at least, the most surprising among the book's thirty poems. After hearing the voices of decadent Romans and New World conquerors, after poems concerned with Hannibal and Charlemagne, we are suddenly in the West Indies overhearing a letter written by one contemporary "subject" of all this epochal history, who turns out also to be its "author." In my discussion of Brathwaite's work I want to think about what Brathwaite might be accomplishing by offering meta-discourse about the book in this voice, this persona.

Brathwaite is an ambitious poet, nowhere more global in his concerns than in *X / Self,* and his two trilogies together with his *Barabajan Poems* (1994) might be said to aspire to the status of foundational narratives for the anglophone West Indies. Ideally, *X / Self* should be read as a part of the second trilogy, which begins with *Mother Poem* (1977) and continues with *Sun Poem* (1982), Brathwaite's most "autobiographical" volumes. The critic Gordon Rohlehr has described *X / Self* as an "intellectual autobiography," a poem "telling us that to understand where I am coming from you have to understand all of those things."[3] Complete with nineteen pages of footnotes and references to historical persons and events spanning some four thousand years, the book can be as demanding as the work of Pound and David Jones. It has a thesis about history to argue, which is encapsulated in a phrase repeated often in the narrative poems interspersed between dramatic monologues and lyrics: "Rome burns / and our slavery begins."[4] Brathwaite explained the import of the phrase to Nathaniel Mackey as follows:

> What I'm saying there is that Rome created some kind of law, order, structure, for the ancient world and with Rome's fall mercantilism, commercialism and materialism, unbridled materialism, rushed in to fill that gap. And that included eventually the alterRenaissance, the business of selling us, selling people, selling Africans, the slave trade. That is how the thing works out. The Roman Empire, the *civus* of Rome, gives way to the mercantilism of western Europe. The death of Rome signals the beginning of western expansion, which includes slavery and the slave trade and resultant disequilibriums throughout the world and within, therefore, the word. As Mt. Blanc rises, Lake Chad and Kilimanjaro sink and the desertification of Africa begins (45).

As Rohlehr points out, identifying this account of "the desertification of Africa" as central to the poem is quite different from "trying to look at how he worked that vision out in the poetry." That is, if we focus too narrowly on the content of the historical narrative abstracted from its mode of presentation in the poem, we miss something essential to the poem, what Rohlehr calls "a fun which tends to reduce the grandeur." We miss the "punning which reduces, which cuts down, which tries to see this thing in a new way" (115–16). In short, we miss what makes *X / Self* a poem rather than a treatise by Walter Rodney or by Brathwaite himself.

In X / Self's letter we have one instance of this "reduction of grandeur" that shows itself in so many different ways throughout the poem. Beginning his notes to the book, Brathwaite writes:

> The poetry of *X / Self* is based on a culture that is personal—i-man / Caribbean—and multifarious, with the learning and education that this implies. Because Caribbean culture has been so cruelly neglected both by the Caribbean itself, and by the rest of the world (except for spot / check and catch-ups via cricket and reggae), my references (my nommos and icons) may appear mysterious, meaningless even, to both Caribbean and non-Caribbean readers. So the notes . . . which I hope are helpful, but which I provide with great reluctance, since the irony is that they may suggest the poetry is so obscure in itself that it has to be lighted up; is so lame, that it has to have a crutch; and (most hurtful of all) that it is bookish, academic, "history." Which therefore makes my magical realism, the dub riddims and nation language and caliban-isms appear contradictory: *how could these things come from a learned treatise?* The impression, in other words, is that I write the poems from the notes, when in fact I have to dig up these notes from fragments, glimpses, partial memories (it would take a lifetime to track them all down), and the only satisfaction I get is the fascination of watching the counterpoint emerge of "fact" versus the "fiction" of the poetry (113).

Poetry and history in "counterpoint": just as important as the historical thesis the poem offers is the fact that this thesis itself is articulated in a fragmented form, creolized by myth and fiction and by "magical realism" of the sort that finds "Richard Nix" (Nixon) crossing the Rubicon in a "red catallac" ("Nix," 14). The persona of X / Self—subject of history and fictional author of this text—must be made to seem to be struggling with the "meaning" of his poem—piecing it together, inventing it, explod-ing received histories—because the meaning of the African diaspora and Caribbean experience is anything but settled. The poem is about begin-nings rather than endings, about finding the word as much as establishing it or corroborating it—testifying to the "facts." Because West Indian identities are still emerging from the experience of colonialism, and because the African, Amerindian, and Creole traditions that are worth retrieving or preserving in the construction of these identities have been and continue to be most powerfully present in the folk and popular culture of the West Indies, X / Self's written language must be a language of uncertainty and improvisation that is faithful to a spoken language, a language of the people whose everyday life bears traces of traditions with meaning sometimes "mysterious" to them. A persona, then, perhaps representative of the larger culture, whose discourse is set apart from a range of parodic, historical, and religious discourses that surround "him" in the book.

X / Self is conscious of writing at the beginning of a postcolonial existence, self-aware but not self-assured: "but it is like we still start // where we start / in out start / in out start / in out start / in // out since menelek was a bwoy & why // is dat" (85). This can be understood as his response to Brathwaite's desire to give Barbados and the West Indies "the cup of my word" ("Citadel," 99) — here the seriousness of the task at hand is gathered in another idiom. It will not be easy, of course, to offer "the cup of my word" because of the pressure of European and colonial narratives, and of previous histories of the African diaspora such as that authored by M. J. Herskovits. X / Self wonders, "& what is de bess weh to seh so / so it doan sounn like // brigg // flatts nor hervokitz // nor de pisan cantos nor de souf sea // bible // not like ink. le & yarico & de anglo saxon // chronicles" (85). The Bajan phrase "since menelek was a bwoy," which Brathwaite explains means "for ages" or "for as long as I can remember," offering in his notes as well brief biographies of Menelek I (1000 B.C.) and Menelek II (1896), is representative of the difficulties and opportunities of Brathwaite's project. An "inexplicable Bajan expression," as he calls it in his notes, it is an element of that folk culture which carries traces of an ancestral history in need of further definition. X / Self must learn the significance of the repressed content of this and like "expressions" as he confronts the possibility of a postcolonial aesthetic. He must become self-conscious of his own tradition.

In his study of Caribbean modernism, Simon Gikandi argues that the kind of cross-fertilization or creolization that such a phrase represents is typical of Caribbean modernism:

> Caribbean writers cannot adopt the history and culture of European modernism, especially as defined by the colonizing structures, but neither can they escape from it because it has overdetermined Carib-

bean cultures in many ways. Moreover, for peoples of African and Asian descent, the central categories of European modernism—history, national language, subjectivity—have value only when they are fertilized by figures of the "other"imagination which colonialism has sought to repress. (3–4)

Gikandi's description goes a long way toward explaining how history is present in Brathwaite's poem. What Brathwaite calls "magical realism" is constituted not just by a rejection of the content of European history, but also by a rejection of the form of such history and the ideas of reason, language, teleology, progress, and, perhaps especially "realism" such forms sustain. In its diction, *X / Self* breaks the word into parts, constructing oppositional meaning out of the ruins of a "standard" diction and rhythm. As narrative history it contests linearity, collapses and juxtaposes historical events and personages in historical rhymes. Myth and history are interwoven in an effort to "deny these histories"—European and English histories—in a manic dance summoning the collapse of Western dominance and celebrating its forewarnings: "london bridge is fall // en down fall // en down fall // en down fall // en down" ("Song Charlemagne," 23–25).

As Gikandi knows, the Caribbean writer is often ambivalent about modernity, for "the West is modern, the modern is the West. By this logic, other societies can enter history, grasp the future, only at the price of their destruction" (5). It might equally be argued that any project attempting to extract a Caribbean or diasporic black culture from modernity ignores the extent to which modernity itself is already inconceivable except as a racially and culturally hybrid phenomenon—thus "ambivalence." Ambivalence is figured in Brathwaite's book in X / Self trying to convince his "mamma" of the benefits of writing with a word processor. Obviously, for Brathwaite, the word processor makes possible a refined scoring of the rhythms that drive his poems, allowing readers to better imagine for themselves what the effect of their performance might be and thereby keeping the poetry as close as possible to oral traditions. At the level of diction, the word processor also assists Brathwaite in fashioning and calling attention to the "puns, malapropisms, odd spellings, neologisms, and strained meanings" which "speak of disturbances outside as well as inside the language, social distempers the word is made to carry," as Nathaniel Mackey puts it (202). But, since the word processor is crucial to global information systems which some say are westernized or even Americanized, the most pressing concern of X / Self's letter is convincing his "mamma" that this technology can be used for his own ends, that using the word processor does not mean that he has decided to "jine de mercantilists": "but is like what i trying to sen/ seh & // seh about muse / // in computer & // learnin prosepero linguage & // ting // not fe dem / not fe dem // de way caliban // done // but fe we // fe a-we // for not one a we should responsible if prospero get curse // wid im own // curser" (87). In *Barabajan Poems* Brathwaite writes of a "new Middle Passage . . . flowing out across Atlantic now not to factories of cotton sugar flash but to new industries of . . . computer processes" (80). He adds that "the forces that created the computer are very similar to our gods of the Middle Passage" (378). X / Self must reconfigure the computer, so to speak, in order to seize its possibilities.

As Brathwaite told Mackey, the lines from *X / Self* quoted above offer a critique of the Caliban who is a "primitive rebel" and fails because he never connects with his "mother," Sycorax, source of local traditions (46). In asserting the integrity and independence of one's own traditions and one's own community, one must not simply speak back to oppression. One must also speak *for* one's own traditions. Brathwaite is not reluctant to don the mantle of the national poet, to speak the Word—and this distinguishes him, I think, from nearly all contemporary American, British, and European poets. But while the community Brathwaite would speak for ideally would be rooted in knowledge of folk traditions and an African past, it cannot afford to simply repeat old stories, nor can it be content with traditional means of cultural transmission—storytelling for instance—for these encourage isolation and an easy submission to the past: "say // what? / get on wi de same ole // story? // okay // okay // okay // okay // if yu cyaan [can't] beat prospero // whistle?" (80). The modern or postmodern Caribbean writer, in his or her hopefulness, must be prepared to appropriate current technologies for Caribbean ends. Brathwaite calls new style developed in the years immediately following the publication of the book under discussion a "Sycorax video style." In books such as *Barabajan Poems* and *Middle Passages* (1993)—which includes a revised version of the poem at the center of this discussion—Brathwaite explores the resources of multiple fonts and experiments with representations of computer effects such as the "window." The video style seems to involve a search for new forms; now our conventions of the printed page and its typefaces will be made visible too—resisted, "defamiliarized" and "denaturalized," transformed. But not altogether rejected—as difficult to do that as to erase Sycorax from *The Tempest*. Increasingly, Brathwaite seems interested in the visual aspects of poetry equally as much as the oral, and this is, one assumes, because it is for him part of the intellectual's responsibility to define the word and to offer it in all its capacities. The semipermanence of writing must be confronted and challenged on the very surfaces of the page. The modern Caribbean writer finds the word very much under construction and must show himself to be actively freeing himself from the weight of its past, which includes its past in Brathwaite's own books. Few poets have so actively revised and re-presented their own works.

Let me pause for a moment to offer a sample of the look of Brathwaite's poetry on the page in the Oxford University Press version of X / Self's letter, which is rife with the nation language and the calibanizations Brathwaite wrote of in his note to the book:

> a fine
> a cyaan get nutten
>
> write
>
> a cyaan get nutten really
> rite
> while a stannin up here in me years & like i inside a me shadow
> like de man still mekkin i walk up de slope dat e slide
> in black down de whole long curve a de arch
>
> i
> pell
> ago
> long
> long
> ago
> like a
> tread
> like a
> tread
> like a tread
> mill

> (85–86)

The effects are multiple. A political pun rewrites "back" as "black," recasting Sisyphus as a slave. A fracturing of "archipelago" into its syllables begins to establish a short line used earlier in "Negus" and "Caliban" from

Brathwaite's first trilogy—Brathwaite has always liked this short, pounding, single-stressed, then syncopated line:

> And
> Ban
> Ban
> Cal-
> iban
> like to play
> pan
> at the Car-
> nival;
> pran-
> cing up to the lim-
> bo silence
> down
> down
> down

(192)

As Brathwaite's work has matured, he has come to be able to use more and more cadences *within* poems as well as among them, and, increasingly, the jazz and blues and dub rhythms are accompanied by wordplay that is most effective when "visual" as well as audible. All of this is evident in the distance between this fragment of "Caliban" and the fragment from X / Self's letter that precedes it. American readers schooled in the logopoeic techniques of modernist and postmodernist poetry might want to understand Brathwaite's wordplay as part of that tradition, but wordplay in Brathwaite emerges from different concerns. It is both more overtly politicized and less ironic than the kind of wordplay one finds in, say, John Ashbery's poetry, where one idiom after another is tried on and found to be inadequate, an abundant and necessary but flawed human resource. In Ashbery all the words are intact, if their uses can seem both debased and surprising. Brathwaite more actively distorts the word, breaking it up in order to insert meaning; the point is not so much to question conventions of discourse or particular idioms as it is to interrupt the word by assembling a new (often politicized) one from its parts.

Brathwaite's modernism is a Caribbean modernism, but it has been and continues to be instructive for a few British and American readers.

For obvious reasons his poetry has been especially important to black British poetry, a richly diverse and growing body of work which finds itself confronted by problems specific to the political and cultural realities of a Britain, which, since World War II, has seen what the Jamaican poet Louise Bennett once called "colonisation in reverse" (32). Stewart Brown, reviewing Brathwaite's *Sun Poem* for the Arts Council's poetry magazine *Poetry Review*, writes that "arguably Brathwaite is technically the most daring poet currently published by a major British firm" (72) — the Oxford University Press. High praise indeed, and thus it is surprising, as Eliot Weinberger has noted, that the poetry is not better known in America, though American interest is increasing with New Directions's commitment to the work and Brathwaite's recent academic appointments in the United States. Innovative poetry has typically fared better in the United States than in Britain, but the more "traditional," European-influenced poetry of Derek Walcott has mostly carried the day here. In Britain Brathwaite has been reviewed in a wide range of magazines and newspapers, including the conservative *PN Review* and the eclectic *London Magazine,* and he is regarded as Walcott's equal.[5]

In the introduction to his Bloodaxe anthology of Caribbean and black British poetry, E. A. Markham writes in remembering the 1960s and the effect of the publication of the first volume of Brathwaite's first trilogy that "the explosive force of the Brathwaite eruption is hard to imagine. The impact on the normally non-poetry-reading Caribbean youth was immediate. . . . Brathwaite made records and that helped" (28). A few pages later he adds, more critically, that "a main difference between Brathwaite and his imitators is that his music isn't external to the lines but contained within them" (30). Such a remark shows Markham intent on preserving forms and values he understands as specifically literary. One of the paradoxes of Caribbean and black British poetry in England is that, while a few poets who are backed up by musicians attract large audiences in live performances and via radio, television, and recordings, the publication and distribution of much black British poetry has met with the usual, predictable problems and a poetry extraordinarily popular and powerful in performance continues to struggle for recognition in the academy and other "established" cultural institutions, as is indicated by the press reaction to Benjamin Zephaniah's application for a fellowship at Cambridge University. John La Rose's New Beacon Press and the poet-musician Linton Kwesi Johnson's publisher Bogle-L'Ouverture (which takes its name from Jamaica's Paul Bogle and Haiti's Toussaint l'Ouverture) have published

Caribbean and black British writers, and more recently Bloodaxe has contributed, but these presses face the same difficulties as most small press publishers, such as the regular collapse of alternative distributors who must compete in a marketplace that regularly swallows them.[6] Johnson has toured Europe and America and played to audiences numbering in the thousands so we should not be surprised to hear him speak of an audience of three hundred, large for a poetry crowd in the United States or Britain, as "small" (255). For an academic such as Markham, Johnson's success within a "mass culture" must be understood beside the fact that such work still too rarely intersects with most of poetry's other performance sites, or publications. Caribbean and black British poetry must be represented in the poetry anthology and the academy—by all forms of cultural exchange—in order for its full potential to be realized. To think otherwise would be to reflect a naïveté about the power of elite institutions.

Houston Baker Jr. has berated the American academy—literature departments, cultural and black studies programs—for ignoring rap music, and his attack is motivated not only by his knowing that rap has much to tell us about contemporary African-American culture but also by his belief that popular forms are the future of poetry. He writes enthusiastically of graduate students at an elite university who tell him that "the function of poetry belongs in our era to a telecommunal, popular space in which a global audience interacts with performative artists. A link between music and performance—specifically popular music and performance—seem determinative in their definition of the current and future function of poetry" (94). One might juxtapose these remarks with remarks made by Linton Kwesi Johnson in the interview included in Markham's anthology. There Johnson seems to be uneasy about being characterized too narrowly as a "musician" or "mass culture" performance poet. Playing with a band has deprived him, he says, of time to devote to poetry; moreover, he feels "the strict parameters of the reggae form" can be "limiting" to the point where he finds himself "getting drawn closer to the music" and away from the poetry (260). Johnson's popularity, as he knows, is largely due to his music, but he also very much wants to be recognized as a poet apart from his music. This is also clear in his performances, which often include the solo recitation of one or several of his poems.

Distinctions among genres and the limits as well as possibilities of mixed genres and mass genres are part of the point here, but so is prestige. In his introduction to Benjamin Zephaniah's *City Psalms* (1992), Bob Mole compares Zephaniah's "modern urban songs, ballads, raps, rants and poems" to the poems of "tribal bards in Africa, the Gawain poet in Cheshire, Dunbar and Henryson in Scotland," thereby asserting cross-cultural continuities with several bardic traditions recognized by British canons. He quotes nothing less than the *Oxford History of English Literature* (on Henryson) in describing poems that read like this: "As an African a plastic bullet hit me in Northern Ireland, / But me children overstood and dey grew strong, / As an African I was woman in a man's world, / A man in a computer world, / A fly on de wall of China, / A Rastafarian diplomat,/ An a miner in Wales. / I was a red hot Eskimo, / A peace luvin hippie" (28). Just as Zephaniah's poem links the diasporic African community with other oppressed or marginal communities, Mole's introduction seeks alliances with literary "nation-languages" opposed to the homogenizing power of standard English. With Zephaniah (unlike, say, Jean Binta Breeze) the examples can stretch the rhetoric toward absurdity, but the point is that Mole's tactics are very different from Baker's. Baker would have the academy incorporate rap because it *is* popular and contemporary; Mole feels obliged to gesture towards the past and the authority of standards of taste perpetuated by institutions traditionally concerned with literary value. The difference perhaps bespeaks greater openness in the elite institutions in the United States.

If we are to believe such a credible witness as Paul Gilroy, the British musicologist and cultural critic, one of the most noteworthy developments in black British culture since 1981 has been the search among black artists for "a means to position themselves relative to [British] society and to create a sense of belonging which could transcend 'racial,' ethnic, local and class-based particularities and redefine England/Britain as a truly plural community" (196). Pluralizing identifications, resisting ghettoized categories—these seem to be the order of the day, as the children of immigrants from the Caribbean and Africa (and also the Indian subcontinent, whose peoples are too often lumped in the "black British" category and whose work is beyond the boundaries of this chapter) grow up more removed from Caribbean experience. The need to identify with Britain does not supplant ties to the African diaspora but it does open up avenues beyond "identity politics," which Rastafarianism had promoted in the seventies. Markham's refusal to enter into discussions of the "Carribean *versus* the Caribbean diaspora" is akin to the younger British poet Fred D'Aguiar expressing a need "to state categorically that it is nonsense to pretend that what black writers are doing in Britain is so unlike what their white compatriots in craft are practicing that it merits a category entirely of its own.

. . . The reality is that poets of a particular age, class, and locality, often have more in common in terms of their craft and themes, whatever racial definitions may obtain, than poets of the same race who belong to a different generation and class and live at opposite ends of the country" (70).

Brutal dichotomies of style as well as cultural and racial identification have their cost, as David Dabydeen asserts succinctly in speaking of the double-bind black British writers are forced into when deciding whether to write in a version of "nation language" or in "standard English":

> Either you drop the epithet "black" and think of yourself as a "writer" (a few of us foolishly embrace this position, desirous of the status of "writing" and knowing that "black" is blighted)—that is, you cease dwelling on the nigger/tribal/nationalistic themes, you cease *folking* up the literature, and you become "universal"—or else you perish in the backwater of small presses. . . . This is how the threat against us is presented" (12–13).

One way out of this double-bind is to move between and among modalities, between performance and writing, nation-language and "standard" English, refusing to be pinned down in one or the other. D'Aguiar, whose own work, like that of many of his contemporaries, resists old and easy dichotomies between so-called "standard English" and the patois, writes that "Although some poets are best heard in performance rather than read solely on the page, I would be hard pressed to confine a poet to one realm or the other. At the level of composition many poets are working towards a coalition of the two" (3–4).

Such a "coalition" of the oral and the literary, of page and performance, does not necessarily imply an abandonment of "nation-language" or popular or "folk" rhythms and forms, though it sometimes does in D'Aguiar's work and in poems such as Dabydeen's "Turner" (1994), which begins as follows: "Stillborn from all the signs. First a woman sobs / Above the creak of timbers and the cleaving / Of the sea, sobs from the depths of true / Hurt and grief" (10). As a theorist of nation-language and a poet explicitly invested in recovering, uncovering, and inventing (again and again) Caribbean identity, Brathwaite might seem to have little interest in strategies of plural identification resembling D'Aguiar's or in poetic forms and idioms such as those of "Turner" (Dabydeen's "Coolie Odyssey" is another matter.) His work would seem to lend itself easily to discourses of transnational, diasporic identity politics such as those D'Aguiar wants partly to disperse with his emphasis on class, generation, region, and British specificity. A contrast of D'Aguiar and Brathwaite would have value, then, but only up to a point. At one point in *X / Self* we encounter Thomas of Celano's Latin hymn "Dies Irae" converted to "Dies Irie," "irie" being a Rasta phrase for "high" or "happy":

> Day of sulphur dreadful day
>   when the world shall pass away
>   so the priests and shamans say
>
> what gaunt shadows shall affront me
>   my lai sharpeville wounded knee
>   ho chi marti makandal
>
> to what judgement meekly led
>   my lai harlem wounded knee
>   fedon fatah sun yat sen
>
> life and death shall here be voice
>   less rising from their moist
>   interment hoist
>
> ing all their flags before them
>   shall men gather trumpeted
> by nyabingeh from the dead
>   ("Dies Irie," 37)

Brathwaite can occasionally work in Western canonical forms so long as the content these carry is transformed. His debt to T. S. Eliot is also noteworthy. But Brathwaite is not Derek Walcott and one can carry this line of argument too far: there is no question that the single most important development in both Caribbean *and* black British poetry over the last twenty five years has been the exploration of the rhythms and traditions of "nation-language," and there is no getting around Brathwaite's influence in discussing this phenomenon. Dabydeen has said, in "On Not Being Milton: Nigger Talk in England Today," that "Brathwaite and others rescued us from [a] cascade of nonsense-sounds," pointing to weak imitations of Milton in a Guyanese poet.

It is surely true, as Charles Bernstein has argued in an essay on "ideolect," that Brathwaite's idea of "nation-language" is "as much a new standard to rally national spirit as it is a break from standardization." Nation-language, Bernstein continues, "has a centripetal force, regrouping often denigrated and dispirited language practices around a common center; ideolect, in contrast, suggests a centrifugal force moving away from normative practices without necessarily replacing them with a new center of gravity, at least defined by self or group" (7). But this contrast is a little too neat: when Brathwaite's nation-language enters British (or American) contexts it inspires ideolectical, nonnormative practices. Moreover, as "Dies Irie" shows, nation-language does not describe the whole of Brathwaite's poetic practice; it names one way to read specific practices within a Caribbean context.

Brathwaite is capable of writing in many different idioms and forms and with reference to many traditions — not all of them Caribbean or African — because it is also the case, as Markham argues, that

> We are multi-national; cosmopolitan — some of us multi-lingual in ways that encompass and extend beyond the standard-English nation-language debate and have residences on earth which defy the makers of treaties and the laws of immigration. . . . We who represent the First, Third, and Fourth Worlds (some of us live in the First, we are grounded in the Third and we have sympathies with those of the Fourth seeking a homeland) have lost the luxury of those who, once claiming to be on the margins of society, celebrated disintegration at the center. Suddenly (or gradually) our margins have become the "front line" and so we have to shed early assumptions of what the center holds. The centre holds us. (19)

I would imagine that there is some irony in that last sentence. Does "holds" mean "contains" or "includes"? In context, Markham's remarks here amount to a plea for international consciousness, for assuming responsibility and resisting marginalization. His views are seemingly shared by Brathwaite, for whom Caribbean isolationism is nearly as great a problem as the legacy of British colonialism (56), but it will not do simply to speak of Brathwaite's "internationalism." One way to combat isolationism is to raise consciousness of solidarity with enemies of Western imperialism from around the world — Ho Chi Minh, for instance — but such solidarity is largely a rhetorical one. Even the effort to identify African forms and traditions which persist in or influence literature around the world must be alert to particular contexts and locations: Brathwaite's *Barabajan Poems* is perhaps the most powerful testament to his understanding of his project as a local one. A local one declaring international affiliations and influences, a national poetry mingling with the impure cultures of the world in search of something approaching integrity and identity.

Formally, Brathwaite's work is at odds with much British and American postmodern poetry of the last fifteen years in its pursuit of a marriage of oral traditions and literary experimentalism, of speech and visual text. He is closer to the New Americans with the strongest bardic tendencies—to Allen Ginsberg and Nathaniel Tarn—than he is to Tom Raworth or Charles Bernstein. As I will explain below, his poetry is also at odds with much of British and American modernist poetry in its combining of deconstructive and logopoeic wordplay with a reverence for the almost "magically" creative power of "naming" and poetry itself. Most significantly, it differs from much of modernist and postmodernist practice in its pursuit of synthesis, its discomfort with cultural fragmentation. While much modernist poetry reflects a nostalgia for cultural homogeneity only to bemoan contemporary fragmentation, and while much postmodernist poetry seems intent on furthering the dispersal of identity and authority to the point where the idea of a center itself becomes undesirable, Brathwaite is in search of a creole synthesis that will permit an acceptance of an ancient and ongoing cross-fertilization of cultures the West has too often tried to limit. Brathwaite shows little interest in modernist American poetry, Pound's especially, for, as he explained to Nathaniel Mackey, "I've never found Pound able to reconstitute elements. . . . Whereas, you see, as a Caribbean person, we start with the ruins and our responsibility is to rebuild those fragments into a whole society" (52). But it is Pound's failure that he is rejecting, not his intentions, at least as I understand them, which do involve synthesis. Of course, Pound's totalizing ambitions are very different from Brathwaite's insofar as they are driven by a politics that would repel him, but it is also true that some readers will find in *X / Self* (more so than in *Barabajan Poems* or in other books) a totalizing that will make them uncomfortable, an insensitivity to local differences and contingencies, a mixing of Ho Chi Minh, Castro, Africans, and Native Americans in a global victim pool sullied by the same evil. It is exactly because I am skeptical of such a *demonization* of the West that I find the stumbling, humble persona of X / Self so significant. There, Brathwaite seems to secure a distance from monumental history by appropriating a local voice anything but aggressive and totalizing.

Since I have mentioned Ezra Pound, I should note that Brathwaite has confessed a relative ignorance of—even a lack of interest in—American poetry. When he speaks of one American poet who has influenced him, he speaks not of Pound or Williams or Stein or Crane or Olson, but of Eliot, the very poet so many recent American experimentalists have set up as a whipping boy. While Eliot too is, for Brathwaite, a poet of the ruins, and therefore not finally an acceptable model, the "voice" in Eliot's poetry remains attractive to him (Markham, 52). I suspect this is because its seductive rhythms and archetypal figures often carry traces of the same biblical texts that are an important part of Caribbean traditions and Brathwaite's own work. We can hear echoes of Eliot regularly throughout *X / Self,* nowhere more self-conscious than they are in "Shaman," which begins

> So don't say i didnt warn you
> but you scorned me in mein rags
> with my clutch of doves with my leprous nipple
>
> by the waters
>
> there was a nibble of faith
> and in the morning i woke up dreaming of surgeons
> by the waters

and ends

> i see the towers rising russian red beyond the dungle
> and i have heard the names of the strange architects you plaster
> paris on them crying each to each
>
> by the waters by the waters where i sit down to reap
> ("Shaman," 65–68)

The rhythms of Eliot are appropriated, and then his despair is parodied—the cultural fragmentation Eliot lamented cannot be separated from the spread of global capitalism. There are wastelands greater than England.

When obliged to locate himself within a poetic lineage, Brathwaite names Aimé Césaire, Nicolás Guillén, and Léon Gontran Damas, while insisting that because of the partly self-willed isolation of Caribbean life he came late even to Césaire's *Cahier d'un Retour au Pays Natural,* one of the most influential poems in modern Caribbean poetry. Such a lineage constructs a Caribbean poetic modernism with continuities across the borders of nations and languages, continuities that include folk rhythms and speech patterns but also more significantly a view of the word Brathwaite believes is common "in all folk cultures," an idea of language as "a creative act in itself," of the "secret power" of the word [*nommo,* or "name"] (90–91). In his *Cahier,* Césaire has a passage Clayton Eshleman and Annette Smith have translated as follows:

> I would rediscover the secret of great communications and great combustions. I would say storm. I would say river. I would say tornado. I would say leaf. I would say tree. I would be drenched by all rains, moistened by all dews. I would roll like frenetic blood on the slow current of the eye of words turned into mad horses into fresh children into clots into curfew into vestiges of temples into precious stones remote enough to discourage miners. Whoever would not understand me would not understand any better the roaring of a tiger. (43–44)

In "The African Presence in Caribbean Literature," Brathwaite reads this passage as a kind of "conjuration / divination," tracing it to the "same magical /; miracle tradition as the conjur-man" (91). And he echoes it in *X / Self*'s "Sunsong," a poem that represents this "conjuring" as a summoning of spirit, as a prayer for redemption:

> i would still say with cesaire. spark
> i would say. storm. olodumare's conflagration
> i would speak sperm. and twinkle
>
> spirit of the fire
> red river of reflection
> vermilion dancer out of antelope
>
> i summon you from trees
> from ancient memories of forests
> from the uncurling ashes of the dead
>
> that we may all be cleansed
>
>   ("Sunsong," 98)

In what is surely far from the best writing in the poem — "twinkle" borders on the ludicrous — Brathwaite is not quite up to the penultimate sentence of the older poet, where the word made blood paratactically accumulates a dazzling series of images constructing a world. It is worth noting Brathwaite's sense of belatedness here, of having "still" to say with Césaire. With his lineation, which breaks what Césaire heaps together into paced and parallel lines, this passage is more self-consciously pastoral, less violent, than Césaire's, less angry than reverent in a melancholy but also hopeful way.

Brathwaite's "conjuration / divination," his sense of the power of "nommo" and word, distinguishes him from one tradition in modernism that invokes an Adamic myth of language only to despair of the loss over time of an original correspondence of word and referent. In the work of Geoffrey Hill, for instance, the poet no longer has the ability to "make" meaning so much as he must guard against the possibilities of meaning being "taken" from him in the ambiguities of interpretation. Underlying Brathwaite's efforts to summon a tradition of Adamic language is a sense of history few British poets can share. Gikandi argues that

> while European modernists would posit history as a nightmare from which the aesthetic imperative was going to rescue the artist, Caribbean literature has often been haunted by the projection of the Caribbean colonial subject as either an ahistorical figure of European desire or simply a victim of the history of conquest and enslavement. Caribbean writers simultaneously represent colonial history as a nightmare and affirm the power of historicity in the slave community. (5–6)

Consider this stanza from the British late modernist Geoffrey Hill's *The Mystery of the Charity of Charles Péguy* (1983):

> History commands the stage wielding a toy gun,
> rehearsing another scene. It has raged so before,
> countless times; and will do so, countless times more,
> in the guise of supreme clown, dire tragedian.
>
> (13)

Hill's description of history as tragic farce, though it echoes Marx's remarks in *The Eighteenth Brumaire of Louis Bonaparte,* reflects what is in his case a conservative's suspicion of narratives of progress and technological advance. As Donald Davie has written, Hill's poem, published at the time of the Falklands war, was read as both an endorsement of patriotism and "martial valour" and as a polemic against them. Readers miss the point, Davie thinks, if they do not realize that the poem itself in its post-symbolist techniques almost guarantees such confusion, for "the upshot of the poem was a monumental uncertainty, or ambivalence, about both of them" (210). But ambivalence about colonial or neocolonial aggression is something the West Indian writer obviously cannot afford, and while he or she may want to dismiss *particular* narratives of history or even "progress," history itself cannot be written off as "farce." "History is law" (25) Hill writes elsewhere in his poem, but, as the above passage demonstrates, he reserves the right to stand apart from it in ironic judgment. For one hundred quatrains he meditates upon the responsibility of the French poet Charles Péguy to his word, pondering this question: "must men stand by what they write / as by their camp-beds or their weaponry / or shell-shocked comrades while they sag and cry?" (13). The question is not new—Yeats and many others have asked it during or after their forays into political poetry. But it is not a question that causes much anguish in Brathwaite or any other Caribbean poet.

Brathwaite is neither above politics nor especially tortured by the potential consequences of his language as these might be unintended. There is no separating aesthetics and politics in his work, and he more often runs the risk of shrill and blunt rhetoric than irony. Here are a few passages from "The Fapal State Machine," a polemic against the state and religion in the West, or the state *as* religion—the title being, I think, one of Brathwaite's politicized neologisms, combining "fatal" and "papal":

general patton and archbishop rommel   tri
umphant in their tanks   the softest centre
is always surrounded by helots by pawns by hedgehogs and by

phalanxes

in rome

god and his armies have become identified with each other
. . . . .
this word is

writ
ten soon and known as holy writ and later holly

wrood

be
stowed on all for all for ever or on some

select / elect

how/ man how /many few how / furious
how / black how/ brown how/ byzantine

. . . . .

without this apparat this parthenon
this fapal state machine

these sleepless shears
these lookout crucifixions on the cliff

there will be
scabbard legions clashing in the night

there will be
riots fires insurrections nkrumah's heedless statue broken down

the universal sun eclipsed by man and time and chaos
ships slipping past the pillows of hesperides

to where there should have been no wind no water hoof of
world no word

towards
where marco polo could not walk

towards
young caliban howling for his tongue

towards
algonquin pontiac discovering his arrows were on fire

(17–21)

This has the rhythm of some Baptist pulpits, though Brathwaite is not afraid to plunder (and pun on) chestnuts from the canons of English poetry with phrases such as "clashing in the night." What sustains this writing—what makes it interesting as poetry—is its rhythms as they are combined with the visual effects of breaking a word like "bestowed" so that we can see that what was offered as a benevolent gift—the Word of the Roman church cum imperial state cum Hollywood—is really smuggled aboard. The risk such poetry takes is preaching to the converted, but one feels that this is a risk Brathwaite is prepared to take.

It is because of passages like this, which are numerous in *X / Self,* that the brief appearance of X / Self is so important to this poem—or he is to me at least, to a reader less prepared to discuss the West in sweeping, abstract terms like *mercantilism,* less prepared to accept a "magical realist" reductionist narrative of history that makes Mont Blanc symbolic of evil and Kilimanjaro of good. History can't be very persuasive in such evidently moralized terms, Hollywood's black hat and white hat. But poetry sometimes can be, especially when it is made to seem to inhabit a particularized "voice." And, just as, for me, Allen Ginsberg's most effective political poems are those which include self-deprecating humor and admissions of his fallibility, the introduction of a bewildered West Indian persona humanizes the rage of *X / Self,* anchors it in an individual:

> dear mamma
>
> i writin you dis letter / wha?
> guess what! pun a computer o/kay?
> like i jine de mercantilists!
>
> well not quite!
>
> . . . . .
> a fine
> a cyaan get nutten
>
> write
>
> a cyaan get nutten really
> rite

$$(85)$$

"Write" slides into "rite" here (noting but bypassing "right"), one supposes, because X / Self's inability to write is also simultaneously an inability to speak confidently a West Indian culture—this utopian vision remains to be fulfilled, the word translated into "custom" or "rite." Like Ginsberg's more theatrical persona, Brathwaite's here acknowledges the frustration and powerlessness from which he speaks, which makes one all the more ready to listen to him. This is an advantage—though that is a curious way to put it—that a Geoffrey Hill does not have. The weight of English history upon Hill leaves him only an ironic distance from the ambiguities of the word. Next to that poetry Brathwaite's rage can be understood as emanating from a troubled amazement at the very opportunity to speak.

Notes

Introduction

1. Andrew Duncan edits and writes much of the criticism for *Angel Exhaust,* at this writing one of the most pointedly polemical poetry journals in Britain. Drew Milne edited the recently discontinued journal *Parataxis.* Both have written an evaluative criticism seeking to outline and compare alternative poetries in Britain. Two recent books also might be singled out here as promising signs: Hampson and Barry 1993, and Riley 1992.

2. "Sign that empties itself at each instance of meaning, and how else to reinvent attention"; see Palmer 1981, 5.

3. Davie points to "the conversational quality of Bunting's verse in *Briggflatts*" and, contrasting the poem's procedures with the "series of disjunct phrases" to be found in poems by Ezra Pound and George Oppen, claims that "Bunting, though he strenuously condenses his sentences, never abandons the subject-verb-object structure of the English sentence." Davie concludes that "Bunting wore his modernism with a difference, an English or British difference," thereby linking a "conversational" poetry, a more or less "standard" syntactic practice, and generic English/British poetic identity. Peter Quartermain, who elsewhere links Bunting's work with Whitman's and Pound's parataxis, writes that "Bunting is both outside and inside the culture/the koiné at the same time, using what he subverts, subverting what he uses. But it is not an ironic relationship, and his linguistic, syntactic and formal stance is not finally satiric. It is compositional. The Northumbrian writer insofar as he nourishes his difference, his distinctness, his Northumbrian-ness, like any outcast views society politically, yet at the same time — if he is to write at all, if he is to be heard or to be read — he is obliged to work within the culture too, presenting himself perhaps as apolitical. Prefiguring subversion, his work equally signifies order. Which is why there are so many apparent contradictions, conflicts, and inconsistencies in Bunting's work — between the private personal verse, individual, and the public; between the strictly local and the koiné, between the insistence on the primacy of sound and the demand that the poem have matter." Much of Bunting's long poem is hard to imagine as conversation; Quartermain reads one passage that he finds "strongly reminiscent" of the Welsh cynghanedd and notes that "these lines break a lot of rules — they don't even make a 'correct' sentence"; see Davie 1989, 41–42; Quartermain 1990, 15–16.

4. See, for instance, Robert Sheppard, a younger poet, critic, and publisher, writing of the interaction of British and American experimental poets in "Recognition and Discovery in the 1980s" (1990, 60–61). Noting that "it seems important to me to stress the British context for this work [the poems published

in *Floating Capital,* an anthology of British poetry published by Potes and Poets Press, a small American press], Sheppard explains that he is "concerned that a crude form of cultural imperialism that has dogged previous British poets does not take hold." Sheppard refers to accusations leveled against poets such as those associated with the events of what Eric Mottram called the British Poetry Revival, which I discuss in more detail in chapter 1.

5. See Perloff 1991. Perloff remains the one American academic critic of her generation willing and able to engage varieties of innovative writing from all nations. Britain has no equivalent: an academic critic with her reputation still discovering new writing.

6. Many have noted that Poggioli fails to distinguish between avant-gardism and modernism. Fewer have remembered the climate of opinion concerning activism and experimentalism in art and literature within which he wrote the following: "As a negative and hypothetical assertion, we could say that avant-garde art is destined to perish only if our civilization is condemned to perish, that is, if the world as we know it is destined to fall before a new order in which mass culture is the only form of admissible or possible culture, an order that inaugurates an uninterrupted series of totalitarian communities unable to allow a single intellectual minority to survive, unable even to conceive of exception as valid or possible. But if such a transformation is not imminent or unavoidable, then the art of the avant-garde is condemned or destined to endure, blessed in its liberty and cursed in its alienation" (109).

7. "The avant-garde dies in discourse, as discourse, perhaps all discourse on the avant-garde is its death; it was never distinct from its death, indeed death was always its most abiding force; it sought death in order to reflect it better, to become the reflection of a reflection, to conclude nothing but to go on articulating its exhaustion. What we witness today is not a terminus, since advanced art appears in ever greater profusion, but the becoming-(death-) discourse of the avant-garde within an economy in which nothing is more vital than death" (40). For Huyssen's discussion of Bürger's book, see 191–95. For Hal Foster's, 1–32. For Marjorie Perloff's, see 1989, 193–203.

8. Writing of the poetry of John Ashbery and C. K. Williams, Altieri says that "I do not think any philosopher gives us as fully developed a rendering of subjective agency immanent to the indexical uses of language, yet thereby capable of establishing long-term aspects of identity for the agents" (220). Middleton writes that "Recent British poetry shows that there are complexities to subjectivity, especially political complexities, which are not fully accounted for in mainstream theory" (132). For Bernstein's remarks on "tone-lock," see 1993.

9. See *Under Briggflatts:* "In Gunn's development this [Gunn's book *Moly*] represented a penetration, behind the ambiguous and magnetic figure of John Donne who had fascinated him from the start, into the Renaissance poetic out of which Donne sprang, and from which he diverged. In particular it represented

a creative penetration of Shakespeare" (85). High praise indeed. Leaving aside Davie's metaphor for influence, who in the United States would think to compare a living poet with Shakespeare?

10. After a brief survey of recent literature on shamanism and its understanding in modern Western societies, Duncan writes that "a broad sector of contemporary Creative Persons doesn't at all mind dressing up as witches and wizards and proclaiming their closeness to Primal magic. How far is it from sha-persons to sword-and-sorcery novels? . . . or even from [Ted Hughes's] *Crow* to *In the House of the Shaman?* . . . Shamanism in Western art has got about as much to do with Siberia and the Paleoarctic as Aladin has to do with China. But the exoticism, the supernatural, the fine song and dance, offer a superb opportunity for a coup de théâtre" (*Angel Exhaust* 12 [1995]: 110).

Chapter I

1. In his long review of the essays collected in Homi Bhabha's *Nation and Narration,* Ian Baucom discusses Simon During's description of an English "civil imaginary": "The civil imaginary is a sort of simulacral rearguard, a defensive reproduction of the genteel and the everyday. The architecture of the civil imaginary is the closed house of the middle-class man of letters. It is reproduced most perfectly by the novels of Scott and Austen and is canonized by a critical practice intent on preserving the subjective experience of the English bourgeoisie from the onslaughts of a nationalist practice informed by Enlightenment theory, and this, to During's mind, is precisely the problem. The civil imaginary is a sort of pre-Leavisite reification of England, their England. Adjacent to the space of the nation, it allies literature and criticism to a politics predicated upon a refusal of the modern nation and egalitarian notions of individual liberty." Baucom notes that "this argument enables During to condemn literature's extranational positioning and to plead for a literary engagement with the nation" but goes on to argue that "During's essay signals a refusal to recognize that the discourse of nationalism is able to imprint onto itself both the radical politics of the Enlightenment and the conservative cultural practice of the counterrevolution, that the space of the nation is neither that of culture nor of anarchy but of both at once, and, at once, in-between" (144–53). One would not want to claim that any modern literary practice, or appeals to "internationalism" or a "republic of letters," would be free of the traces of local contexts or the nation itself, and I am not interested in whether or not Hall's essay speaks an overt "nationalism" but rather in exploring the ways in which rhetoric of this sort too easily allows us to abandon the necessity that one literature pursue contacts and crossings with another. Writing as he does of "American tradition" it appears that Americans reading British poetry will absorb nothing but syntax because Americans already are (and will

apparently remain) what they are. In the words of Robert von Hallberg, "literary texts rightly desire another world" (1996, 116). In chapter 6, I mention Allen Fisher's effort to define the poetics of a so-called Cambridge school as gathered in *A Various Art*—an anthology of alternative British poetry—as "civic production," a term related to "civil imaginary" as used here and naming a poetics adjacent to (and implicated in) the political without being overtly politicized. As is evident with the poets of that anthology, a "civil imaginary" is a site in need of defining and contesting like any other and need not forever be shaped by genteel customs.

2. See Hill, 23. In *The Force of Poetry* and elsewhere, Christopher Ricks discusses commas in Hill's poetry.

3. "Clutching's opposite, which would be the most handsome part of our condition, is I suppose the specifically human form of attractiveness—attraction being another tremendous Emersonian term or master-tone—naming the rightful call we have upon one another, and that I and the world make upon one another. Heidegger's term for the opposite of grasping the world is that of being drawn to things." See Stanley Cavell, 86–87. If one hopes to encourage an understanding of identity as what we are drawn to rather than what we grasp—or what we think we are or think we mean—as well as cultural practices that allow for multiplicity and hybridity, then Ashbery's poetry is probably a better place to go than Hill's.

4. See the survey of "New Generation" poets in *Poetry Review* 84 (Spring 1994).

5. See especially Golding and Rasula.

6. See Sinclair, xiv. For another account of Mottram's tenure at the *Poetry Review,* see Görtschacher.

7. From a letter to the author by Andrew Crozier.

8. See Forbes. The allusion to an early song by The Who seems right for this poetry. Robert Sheppard and Cris Cheek are two among contemporary alternative poets who have tried reviewing for "mainstream" papers—*The New Statesman* and *The Times,* respectively.

9. From a letter to the author by Andrew Crozier.

10. Not to end entirely on a note of pessimism, I want to mention that, in England itself, there are some encouraging signs—innovative efforts to build community and audiences for vital poetries and arts. At the rural Dartington College of the Arts, for instance, a new "performance writing" program has been initiated. Here students are obliged to study "sonic" and "visual" values in writing, to work cooperatively with artists in various media, to read "theory" in its various forms, and to produce texts and installations best understood, in the wake of Fluxus, as "intermedia." One practical way to challenge the marginalization of poetry in contemporary culture is to bring it into contact with other arts. It is too often the case that disciplinary boundaries still intact within universities also persist outside their boundaries, so that for instance visual artists can proceed in ignorance of poetries—the work of Susan Howe, Hannah Weiner, Caroline Bergvall—that

might otherwise be of interest to them. Traditionally, avant-gardes have been constituted by dialogue among the arts, but this has been less and less the case lately. Dartington is one institution that seeks to remedy this state of affairs.

Chapter 2

1. I owe this phrase to Rasula, who early on in the chapter he gives this title professes a desire to "develop here a sense of poetry in America as a matrix of lives lived, not a Jurassic Park of spectacular behemoths" (58).

2. Tomlinson accuses many of the poets of Conquest's anthology of "a suburban mental ratio" and "a singular want of vital awareness of the continuum outside themselves" (209).

3. One of the best readings of models of subjectivity on view in various "confessional" poetries is Paul Breslin's.

4. The "statements on poetics" included in Allen's anthology challenge contemporaneous belletristic and academic orthodoxies in their form as well as their content, ranging as they do from Olson's manifesto "Projective Verse" to excerpts from the journals of Michael McClure and John Weiners.

5. See Whittemore, esp. 263, where he discusses his trip to a southern women's college where sonnet writing was taught as one of the "graces": "As I say all this I recall vaguely some of H. L. Mencken's caustic remarks about Southern Writing as all decorum and flowers (he was speaking of the literature before the Fugitives and our other modern Southern celebrities); and I recall also the contempt which some of the Fugitives themselves — no friends of Mencken — have expressed about the empty literature of the Old South. I recognize and sympathize with these criticisms, and think that the word 'empty' is the critical one here; but I think that in our various contemporary efforts to produce the opposite, that is, a literature that is in one way or another 'full,' we have got ourselves into a position where we tend to neglect one of the great traditional sources of strength in literature. As a result we have not even a contemporary vocabulary to deal with the qualities I am struggling to refer to. I am positively embarrassed to be talking here about 'grace' and 'elegance' and 'finish'; I feel I should be talking instead about 'technical skill' or 'precision' or 'a sense of structure,' or perhaps not talking at all about these peripheral matters but concentrating instead on our writers' capacity really to deal with life. My embarrassment, I feel, is produced by a literary situation in which the academics as well as the anti-academics have played a part. Both sides keep trying to justify literature in a world where literature's power is no longer taken for granted. All is therefore purposefulness; all must be clearly directed toward some social or spiritual or emotional end. The earnest literary functionalism visible in the proliferation of various academic writing schemes is thus just one manifestation of this." From a contemporary perspective it is interesting to

see the opposition here between belletrism and functionalism and to note that the New Criticism and writing programs are linked with the latter where, today, more often they are linked (if not in histories of literary criticism then in the everyday life of literature departments) with the former.

6. See Rasula, 158: "The post-war education boom gradually confronted critics with the fact that the arts were not efficient delivery systems for humanist values. Teaching Shakespeare, Milton, and Arnold did not ennoble the mind and humanize the sensibility, except haphazardly. High culture could not, apparently, be transmitted through universal education. The G. I. college graduate still preferred Gunsmoke to The Iliad." Rasula replaces the naive idealism of fifties educators with a totalizing cynicism.

7. See Perkin, 419. Perkin means to defend the welfare state against its dismantling by Thatcherism, so, while he dutifully records the arguments of those who would offer a more pessimistic analysis of class structures in postwar England, he makes the most optimistic comparisons possible. The same pertains to his remarks on race in England: "Whether the English were more xenophobic than the French towards their Algerian, the Germans towards their Turkish and Yugoslav, or even the Swiss towards their Spanish and Portuguese 'guestworkers,' none of whom, unlike the British immigrants, were granted full citizenship, may well be doubted, but Britain acquired a race problem which took it by surprise" (420). As if such comparisons excused anybody.

8. For Davie on Hughes, see *Under Briggflatts*, 165.

Chapter 3

1. For a reading of Pound's "Patria Mia" discussing its two (imagined) audiences in England and Progressive-era America, see Tuma 1990.

2. "There is among the younger writers a certain movement to Americanize. The tendency is to isolate America from Europe, and to produce an art that shall be starkly American, for the Americans." See Lewis, 8–9. Much of Lewis's evidence in this argument with American nativist modernism comes from the work of Sherwood Anderson, but his real targets seem to be Bergson, Spengler, and especially D. H. Lawrence: "Mr. D. H. Lawrence, an English writer, supplies the most important evidence in the review of the contemporary american 'consciousness.' But, first of all, many American and English books are read almost equally on both sides of the Atlantic; Sinclair Lewis is as much at home here in England as he is in America, and Mr. Lawrence is, I believe, more widely read in the United States than in England" (6–7).

3. "Gertie Gitana's Hymn to Waltzing" is part of *Caveat Emptor: Poems by Basil Bunting*, unpublished typescript dated 1935 in the Beinecke Rare Book and Manuscript Library, Yale University. It was first published in Bunting 1991.

4. "*Façade* was performed for the first time on 24 January 1922 in the drawing room of 2 Carlyle Square, the home of Osbert and Sachverell [Sitwell]. William Walton conducted the straggly band of musicians, who had to be sustained by sloe gin, and the rather bewildered audience was gratefully revived with hot rum punch afterwards in the dining-room. The following year, after much consultation and substitution of poems, the first public performance took place at the Aeolian Hall. It caused such an immediate reaction of hostility or rage, that the Sitwells knew they had made a mark on the arts in some form or other. While Edith, dressed in her customary 'Gothic' style, was basking in the limelight at the party afterwards—her friends around her playing charades—the newspaper reviewers were preparing their attack which would create the scandal establishing the Sitwell 'cult' image for the rest of their lives. In the light of her first volumes of poetry, for which Edith had been unanimously hailed as a serious poet of great promise (although her controversial annual periodical *Wheels,* 1916–21, where she championed various poets as well as writing herself, caused no little discussion among critics), these *Façade* poems, more nonsense than sense, bouncing along to popular ditties, foxtrots and tangos, must have seemed a strange deviation" (Hunter 1987).

5. Pound wrote to Harriet Monroe on 27 March 1931: "My idea of a Brit. number was that it shd. give 'em the best show possible, but that it was bound to be American chauvinism, because the best Brit. show would be very much inferior to Zuk's number" (Pound 1950, 232).

6. See the letter from "Reginald" (Peter Riley) in *Parataxis* 4 (Summer 1993). Riley names Macleod, Hugh Sykes David, Charles Madge, Nicholas Moore, Lynette Roberts, Rosemary Tonks, Nigel Heseltine, Charles Wrey Gardiner, Thomas Good, J. F. Hendry, Henry Treece, Stephen Coates, and W. G. Archer as "lost precursors," though it must be added that his enthusiasm for these poets, and for various works by them, varies greatly. Though I have recently been told that interest in Macleod—first on Riley's list—extends to Andrew Duncan, J. H. Prynne, Tony Lopez, and others, finding Riley's letter was for this writer both a surprise and an indication that he was onto work that might have some significance in the near future.

7. Joseph Gordon Macleod to Ezra Pound, 23 Mar. 1936. Beinecke Rare Book and Manuscript Library, Yale University.

8. Ezra Pound to Joseph Gordon Macleod, 28 Mar. 1936 (?). Beinecke Rare Book and Manuscript Library, Yale University.

9. Joseph Gordon Macleod to Ezra Pound, 23 Mar. 1936. Beinecke Rare Book and Manuscript Library, Yale University.

10. Iain Sinclair's Picador anthology of recent "alternative" British poetry, *Conductors of Chaos* (1996), includes introductions to and selections from the poetry of David Gascoyne (Jeremy Reed), David Jones (Drew Milne), Nicholas Moore (Peter Riley), W. S. Graham (Tony Lopez), and J. F. Hendry (Andrew Crozier).

Chapter 4

1. It is tempting to blame the paucity of scholarly and critical attention to Loy in Britain on the hostility to modernism now longstanding there. In recent years, Thom Gunn has been her only persistent advocate there. Denise Levertov, also an Englishwoman who, like Loy, came to live in the United States, has also been for some years an important advocate of the poetry. Before Levertov and Gunn (among poets) there was Basil Bunting. More recently, Peter Nicholls, in his book *Modernisms,* has discussed Loy's work within an international frame, and there are other indications that the work in general and "Anglo-Mongrels and the Rose" too might soon receive more attention. Loy's work has been nearly invisible in the United States until recently too, and that fact, together with Loy's long exile from England and apparent apathy about her reputation there (or anywhere) must be considered before one begins criticizing British scholars for ignoring work that might be claimed (at least in part) for Britain. In "Wyndham Lewis, Blast, and Popular Culture," *ELH* 54.1 (Spring 1987), 403–19, I have compared Loy's earliest mature poetry with the prose of Wyndham Lewis's "Enemy of the Stars" (1914), and Loy's debts to Blake and Dante Gabriel Rossetti, whom she credited with her awakening in poetry, deserve an extended discussion I cannot offer here.

2. All references to "Anglo-Mongrels and the Rose" are from Loy 1982.

Chapter 5

1. Enoch Powell as quoted in Nairn, 259.

2. I take this phrase from John Peck (170), whose reading of Bunting's poem is extended here.

3. Basil Bunting as quoted in Makin, 94–95.

4. For Cuthbert's importance to Bunting, see Makin, 190–215.

5. For a more formalist discussion of Bunting and Lucretius, see Gilonis.

6. Aristotle's text is reprinted in Klibansky, Panofsky, and Saxl, which remains an invaluable resource for students of the history of melancholy.

7. On Bunting's religious beliefs, see Reagan. Two excerpts from interviews with Bunting seem especially pertinent here: "I'm a Quaker by upbringing, and fortunately it is a religion with no dogma at all"; and "I have no use for religion conceived as church forms or as believing as historical fact what are ancient parables, but I do believe that there is a possibility of a kind of reverence for the whole creation."

8. In Louis Zukofsky's short novel *Ferdinand,* the narrator says of an Englishman who is likely modeled after Bunting that "a decent British empire, he believed, could be the best government in the world." An amusing scene follows

when Ferdinand (Zukofsky?) introduces the Englishman to a "frankly unsubmissive subject of the Empire," a Hindu activist. The two do not quarrel but instead end up discussing the Persian poet Firdosi (38–40). It should be noted that Bunting, who did great service to England in Iran during World War II and after, was extremely knowledgeable of and sensitive to the various indigenous cultures there and resisted most contemporary pseudo-justifications of imperialism. Compare his remarks on imperialism in "Yeats Recollected." Bunting's wartime and postwar experience in Iran cannot be underestimated in any reading of his later poetry. The war marked for him the collapse of the dreams of civilization propounded by his friends Eliot, Pound, and Yeats; it also introduced him to nonwestern cultures which he would periodically argue offered the West a potential source of renewal. Bunting's diagnosis of various concerns of the region—from problems involving the ownership of oil fields and American behavior in them to local tribal customs—are remarkably prescient and perceptive, but they are the subject of another essay.

9. See Rosenthal and Gall, where it is suggested that the opening of section 2 is the poem's worst, written in a "recognizable, even trite, poetic mode" (292).

10. See, for instance, Forde, 147–50; Makin, 239–65; and Gordon.

11. For biographical information concerning Bunting, see Makin, 3–125; and Victoria Forde, 15–69.

12. Makin identifies "Hastor" as Hugh Astor of the *Times* (147).

13. Bunting as quoted in Quartermain 1990, 10.

Chapter 6

1. *Conductors of Chaos,* together with reviews in small journals such as *Object Permanence,* received attention in publications such as *Poetry Review, The Observer,* and *TLS.* The reviews were far from uniformly positive. In *The Observer* for 28 July 1996, New Gen poet Don Paterson claims that the book "left me with some of my prejudices reinforced. A few others are under serious threat." In the *TLS* for 20 September 1996, Robert Potts writes, "Some of the poets in Sinclair's volume probably deserve, and may well receive, a wider readership on the back of this enterprise. The rest will no doubt be satisfied that their work is simply too good for most readers, and return to their worthy isolation." The venomous ascription of elitist arrogance in that last sentence is truly remarkable, but on the theory that no publicity is bad publicity it is possible that this rare appearance in a widely available book published in a comparatively cheap edition by a press such as Paladin will result in more readers for some of the poets published therein.

2. Neil Corcoran's survey of recent British poetry, *English Poetry since 1940,* accords the Movement one chapter, Larkin a chapter by himself, and squeezes

Christopher Middleton, Roy Fisher, and J. H. Prynne into one chapter entitled "Varieties of Neo-Modernism." The "Martian" poetry of Craig Raine and Christopher Reid gets equal space. That said, Corcoran's book serves fairly well its function as an overview of recent poetries and is instructive in its apportioning of space; this is the field of contemporary British poetry from a fairly representative academic perspective. Tom Raworth is mentioned twice in passing; his poems are not discussed. Allen Fisher, Peter Riley, and Eric Mottram—among many others—are not mentioned. Several other books have appeared too recently to be integrated into the discussion here. Clive Bush's *Out of Dissent* contains lengthy and useful readings of five poets long a part of the "alternative" scene: Thomas Clark, Allen Fisher, Eric Mottram, Barry MacSweeney, and Bill Griffiths. Ian Gregson's *Contemporary Poetry and Postmodernism* argues that recent British "mainstream" poets such as Craig Raine, Paul Muldoon, and Carol Ann Duffy have absorbed modernist techniques; they are among Gregson's "dialogic poets" whose work demonstrates a "promiscuous mingling of materials, an enjoyment of hybrid forms and images, a conflating of voices and perspectives" (10). Gregson's modernists are primarily Roy Fisher, Christopher Middleton, and Edwin Morgan; his effort is in part to show that the boundaries between "mainstream" and other practices are eroding and to urge that further erosion will be productive. Finally, the essays collected by Romana Huk and James Acheson in *Contemporary British Poetry* offer a broad and significant survey of various contemporary British poetries and issues pertinent in it.

3. From a post by Cheek to the Buffalo Poetics listserv <poetics@ubvm.cc. buffalo.edu.> on 8 February 1995.

4. Among the various attempts to reinvent the social space of poetry and writing in performance one might mention the "preter-millenial audience rumble" of "The Night of the Living Tongues," parts 1 and 2, events curated by Cheek. The second of these brought together the "site performance" of Brian Catling, the cybertexts of John Cayley, experimental film and music and writing—even a trick cyclist. A new cabaret isn't the sole answer, of course, but it's one way to get poetry out of the several boxes it has too long lived in. Much as in the poetry slam culture of the United States and elsewhere (a much more limited and genre-specific performance typically) such initiatives will breed their fair share of dreadful, posturing work. But so does academic and print culture.

5. Contrasting the map of the city as seen from atop the Empire State Building (his figure for knowledge as surveillance) with pedestrian views of the city (his figure for everyday knowledges and practices eluding administration), Michel de Certeau writes, "Rather than remaining within the field of a discourse that upholds its privilege by inverting its content . . . one can try another path: one can try another path: one can analyze the microbe-like, singular and plural practices which an urbanistic system was supposed to administer or suppress, but which have outlived its decay; one can follow the swarming activity of those pro-

cedures that, far from being regulated or eliminated by panoptic administration, have reinforced themselves in a proliferating illegitimacy, developed and insinuated themselves into the networks of surveillance, and combined in accord with unreadable but stable tactics to the point of constituting everyday regulations and surreptitious creativities that are merely concealed by the frantic mechanisms and discourses of the observational organization" (92, 96).

6. Drew Milne writes that "a corollary of the oxygen of privacy is hesitancy and embarrassment about public pronouncement, programmes and manifestoes, indeed a full scale retreat before the notion of a collective avant-garde. Modes of evasive or transcendent hermeticism seem less vulnerable. This suggests a hostility to collective criticism. There is a desperate absence of successful mode of mediation between the expertise of the initiated and the naivety of the ignorant. Most of all this is exemplified by an embarrassment and lack of interest in description or criticism which might seek to support or refine creativity" (27).

7. On the traditions of the "visible word," see Drucker, especially the distinction between "marked" and "unmarked" texts: "In general, the split between marked and unmarked texts corresponds to the split between commercial and literary uses of typography, reflecting the distinction in linguistic modes of enunciation by which these domains are frequently distinguished from each other. . . . The basic distinction between marked and unmarked typography occurred simultaneously with the invention of printing. Gutenburg printed two distinctly different kinds of documents, which embodied the characteristic features of what evolved into the two distinct traditions. On the one hand he printed bibles, with their perfectly uniform grey pages, their uninterrupted blocks of text, without headings or sub-headings or any distraction beyond the occasional initial letter. These bibles are the archetype of the unmarked text, the text in which the words on the page 'appear to speak themselves' without the visible intervention of author or printer. Such a text appears to possess an authority which transcends the mere material presence of words on the page, ink impressions on parchment. By contrast, the Indulgences which he printed displayed the embryonic features of a marked typography. Different sizes of type were used to hierarchize information, to create an order in the text so that different parts of it appear to 'speak' differently, to address a reader whose presence was inscribed at the outset by a complicity with the graphic tools of a printer who recognized and utilized the capacity of typographic representation to manipulate the semantic value of the text through visual means" (94–95).

8. See for instance Sheppard 1990, 60–61. Writing of his work in coediting *Floating Capital,* an anthology of British poetry published in America and introduced by the American language poet Bruce Andrews (who writes that "everything begins with graftings"), Sheppard acknowledges the influence of related American poetries but then says, "It seems important for me to stress the British context for this work."

9. These remarks appear on the inside front cover of Riley and James, *Collection Seven*. They are uncredited but it seems more than likely that Riley had a hand in writing them.

10. Examples of the propositions resisted by several Cambridge poet-critics would include the following, the first from McCaffery and the second from Bernstein 1986: "Language Writing involves a fundamental repudiation of the socially defined functions of author and reader as the productive and consumptive poles respectively of a commodital axis. The main thrust of the work is hence political rather than aesthetic, away from the manufacture of formal objects toward a frontal assault on the steady categories of author and reader, offering instead the writer-reader function as a compound, fluid relationship of two interchangeable agencies within sign production and sign circulation" (15); "we find ourselves in the grip of—living out—feeling—the attitudes programmed into us by the phrases, &c, and their sequencing, that are continually being repeated to us—language control=thought control=reality control: it must be decentered, community controlled, taken out of the service of the capitalist project. For now, an image of the antivirus: indigestible, intransigient" (60). It would seem to be the case that Prynne's pessimism altogether rejects the utopian elements of such discourse.

11. Prynne's remarks were first made in a letter to Steve McCaffery and have since been published in *Language Issue* #1 as addressed to "Ashley Hales."

12. I should also note Geoffrey Ward's useful monograph *Language Poetry and the American Avant-Garde,* one of the more temperate, mixed responses to "language writing" by a British critic.

13. In "Optimism and Critical Excess (Process)" Bernstein writes, "In other words, I think that activities such as this one have to be understood as situational. . . . The positions you may be disputing may have arisen because it was, at one time, necessary to emphasize a term or process or mode to combat a prevalent, but poetically disenfranchising, view. Poetics is all about changing the current poetic course. Putting on a dress, not strapping yourself into a uniform" (1992, 156–57).

14. Quoted from a letter to the author by cris cheek.

15. See Reeve and Kerridge.

16. See for instance Powell 1991, 145–78. The phrase in quotation marks is Powell's, as is the translation from Rilke quoted below in the text.

17. Quoted from a manuscript version of the essay supplied by Fisher. A shorter version was published by Fisher's press Spanner.

18. See Barry 1993, 200–201: "It might be useful to have a name for poetry of this kind, poetry which explores highly specific materials and data with heuristic intent and as implicit metaphor. A useful analogy is with the kind of art known as 'site-specific' work."

19. See Conte, 3.

20. See Wills, 35; Kinnahan; and Kidd.

21. Quoted in Kinnahan, 639.

22. Noting among many other affinities Wittgenstein's and Gertrude Stein's interest in "grammar," Marjorie Perloff makes the most extensive case to date for a "Wittgensteinian poetics" in her *Wittgenstein's Ladder*.

Chapter 7

1. See the notes to "Nam" and "Twoom" in *X / Self*, 126–28. "Nation language" is a phrase used regularly in studies of Caribbean aesthetics and culture both by and about Brathwaite. See for instance Brathwaite's "The African Presence in Caribbean Literature": "In 'William Saves His Sweetheart,' the folk imagination is again concerned with water, but this time its expression is entirely in intransigent non-English or, as I prefer to call it, nation-language, since Africans in the New World always referred to themselves as belonging to certain nations (Congo, Kromantee, etc.)." If "nation language" is "intransigent non-English" (the phrase preserves "English" in negating it) it is also "survival rhythm" (84). A good place to begin an examination of Caribbean aesthetics is Brathwaites's "The Love Axe (1)": "Our new native art, our own home-blood aesthetics will have its devastations and disfigurements. But this is saying little more than that like all 'whole' cultural expressions, it must be rounded, complex, paradoxical, uncertain, despairing at times, tragic and ironic as well as optimistic. But never negative. Not negative because the aesthetic expectations of an emerging culture cannot be in the same way that a growing child or planet or constellation cannot be. So that although we may lose the individuals, we cannot lose the individual contribution to the collective vision or our now revealing selves. For there is too much complexity of history to understand, of cultures to understand, of local tree and bird and places to know, of local language to command. There might be slavery, yes, but liberation also; it might be schistomiasis, dungle, the kiss of alcohol: but nevertheless growth: process out of that: a constant transformation. So that my own formulation for ourselves begins with rhythm: survival rhythm, emancipation rhythm, transfiguration rhythm" (26). The optimism of this passage I try to find in *X / Self*.

2. *X / Self*, 87. When quoting Brathwaite's poems within a sentence, I use a double slash to indicate Brathwaite's line breaks.

3. See the transcript of Rohlehr's conversation with Markham included in *Hinterland*, 115–16.

4. "Rome burns" appears in three poems in *X / Self*—"Salt," "Mont Blanc," and "Ice/Nya"—and six times in all: 5, 8, 31, 102, 103, 104.

5. See for instance John Figueroa's review of *X / Self* and Walcott's *The Arkansas Testament*.

6. On the difficulties confronting the publishing of black British writing in England, see Saakana.

Works Cited

Abse, Dannie, ed. *The Hutchinson Book of Post-War British Poets*. London: Hutchinson, 1989.

Acheson, James, and Romana Huk. *Contemporary British Poetry: Essays in Theory and Criticism*. Albany: State University of New York Press, 1996.

Agamben, Giorgio. *The Coming Community*. Trans. Michael Hardt. Minneapolis: University of Minnesota Press, 1993.

Aiken, Conrad. *Scepticisms*. New York: Alfred A. Knopf, 1919.

Allen, Donald, ed. *The New American Poetry*. New York: Grove, 1960.

Altieri, Charles. "Contemporary Poetry as Philosophy: Subjective Agency in John Ashbery and C. K. Williams." *Contemporary Literature* 33.2 (1992): 214–42.

Alvarez, A. "The New Poetry; or, Beyond the Gentility Principle." *The New Poetry: An Anthology*. Ed. Alvarez, 21–32. Harmondsworth: Penguin, 1962.

Amis, Kingsley. "Masters." In *New Poets of England and America,* ed. Donald Hall, Robert Pack, and Louis Simpson, 13. New York: Meridian Books, 1957.

Andrews, Bruce. Introduction to *Floating Capital: New Poets from London,* ed. Adrian Clarke and Robert Sheppard, i–v. Elmwood, Conn.; Potes and Poets, 1991.

Antin, David. "Modernism and Post-modernism: Approaching the Present in American Poetry." In *The Avant-Garde Tradition In Literature,* ed. Richard Kostelanatz, 216–47. Buffalo, N.Y.: Prometheus Books, 1982.

————. *What It Means to Be Avant-Garde*. New York: New Directions, 1993.

Armitage, Simon. *Zoom!* Newcastle upon Tyne: Bloodaxe, 1989.

Ashbery, John. *Houseboat Days*. New York: Penguin, 1977.

Auden, W. H. "American Poetry." *The Dyer's Hand and Other Essays*. New York: Vintage, 1968.

————. *The English Auden: Poems, Essays and Dramatic Writings 1927–1939*. Ed. Edward Mendelson. London: Faber and Faber, 1977.

Averill, Gage. "Global Imaginings." In *Making and Selling Culture,* ed. Richard Ohmann, 203–23. Hanover, N.H.: Wesleyan University Press, 1996.

Axtmann, Roland. "Collective Identity and the Democratic Nation-State in the Age of Globalization." In *Articulating the Global and the Local: Globalization and Cultural Studies,* ed. Ann Cvetkovich and Douglas Kellner, 33–54. Boulder, Colo.: Westview, 1997.

Baker, Houston, Jr. *Black Studies, Rap, and the Academy*. Chicago: University of Chicago Press, 1993.

Barker, George. "Poet as Pariah." *Essays*. London: Macgibbon and Kee, 1970.

Barrell, John. "Subject and Sentence: The Poetry of Tom Raworth." *Critical Inquiry* 17 (Winter 1991): 386–410.

Barry, Peter. " 'Fugitive from All Exegesis': Reading Roy Fisher's *A Furnace*."
Dutch Quarterly Review of Anglo-American Letters 18.1 (1988): 1–19.

———. "Allen Fisher and 'Content-Specific' Poetry." In *New British Poetries:
The Scope of the Possible,* ed. Robert Hampson and Peter Barry, 198–215.
Manchester: Manchester University Press, 1993.

Baucom, Ian. "Narrating the Nation." *Transition* 55 (1992): 144–53.

Baudrillard, Jean. *America.* Trans. Chris Turner. London: Verso, 1988.

Bedient, Calvin. *Eight Contemporary Poets.* London: Oxford University Press,
1974.

Bennett, Louise. "Colonisation in Reverse." In *The Penguin Book of Caribbean
Verse in English.* Ed. Paula Bennett. Harmondsworth: Penguin, 1986.

Bergvall, Caroline. *Éclat.* Lowestoft, England: Sound and Language, 1996.

Berman, Russell. *Modern Culture and Critical Theory: Art, Politics, and the Legacy
of the Frankfurt School.* Madison: University of Wisconsin Press, 1989.

Bernstein, Charles. "The Dollar Value of Poetry." *Content's Dream: Essays
1975–1984.* Los Angeles: Sun and Moon, 1986. 57–60.

———. *A Poetics.* Cambridge, Mass.: Harvard University Press, 1992.

———. "What's Art Got to Do with it? The Status of the Subject of the
Humanities in the Age of Cultural Studies." *American Literary History* 5.4
(1993): 597–615.

———. "Leaking Truth: British Poetry in the '90s." *Sulfur* 35 (1994): 204–12.

———. "Poetics of the Americas." *Modernism/Modernity* 3.3 (1996): 1–23.

Betjeman, John. *Collected Poems.* Boston: Houghton Mifflin, 1971.

Blanchot, Maurice. *The Gaze of Orpheus and Other Literary Essays.* Trans. Lydia
Davis. Barrytown, N.Y.: Station Hill, 1981.

Booth, Martin. *Driving through the Barricades.* London: Routledge and Kegan
Paul, 1985.

Bowers, Edgar. *Collected Poems.* New York: Alfred A. Knopf, 1997.

Brathwaite, Edward Kamau. *The Arrivants.* Oxford: Oxford University Press,
1973.

———. "The African Presence in Caribbean Literature." *Daedalus* 103 (1974):
73–109.

———. "The Love Axe (1): Developing a Caribbean Aesthetic 1962–1974." In
*Reading Black: Essays in the Criticism of African, Caribbean, and Black
American Literature,* ed. Houston Baker, Jr., 20–36. Ithaca, N.Y.: Cornell
University Press, 1976.

———. *X / Self.* Oxford: Oxford University Press, 1987.

———. *Barabajan Poems.* Kingston, Jamaica. Savocou North, 1994.

Breslin, James E. B. *From Modern to Contemporary: American Poetry 1945–1965.*
Chicago: University of Chicago Press, 1984.

Breslin, Paul. *The Psycho-Political Muse: American Poetry since the Fifties.*
Chicago: University of Chicago Press, 1987.

Brooks, Cleanth. *Modern Poetry and the Tradition.* Chapel Hill: University of North Carolina Press, 1939.

Brown, Stewart. Review of Edward Kamau Brathwaite's *Sun Poem. Poetry Review* 72.4 (1983): 60–62.

Brownjohn, Alan. "We are going to see the rabbit. . . ." In *A Group Anthology,* ed. Edward Lucie-Smith and Philip Hobsbaum, 19–21. London: Oxford University Press, 1963.

———. "A View of English Poetry in the Early Seventies." In *British Poetry since 1960,* ed. Michael Schmidt and Grevel Lindop, 240–49. Oxford: Carcanet, 1972.

Bruce, George. "Joseph Gordon Macleod." *Contemporary Poets.* 3d ed, 961–63. New York: St. Martin's Press, 1980.

Bunting, Basil. "English Poetry Today." *Poetry* 39.5 (1932): 264–71.

———. "Yeats Recollected." *Agenda* 12.2 (1974): 36–47.

———. "Eighty of the Best." Interview with Jonathan Williams. *Paideuma* 9.1 (1980): 121–39.

———. *A Note on Briggflatts.* Durham: Basil Bunting Archive, 1989.

———. *Uncollected Poems.* Ed. Richard Caddel. Oxford: Oxford University Press, 1991.

———. *Complete Poems.* Ed. Richard Caddel. Oxford and New York: Oxford University Press, 1994.

Bürger, Peter. *The Theory of the Avant-Garde.* Trans. Michael Shaw. Minneapolis: University of Minnesota Press, 1984.

Burke, Carolyn. *Becoming Modern: The Life of Mina Loy.* New York: Farrar Straus Giroux, 1996.

Bush, Clive. *Out of Dissent: A Study of Five Contemporary British Poets.* London: Talus, 1997.

Caddel, Richard, ed. *Sharp Study and Long Toil.* Durham: Durham University Journal Special Supplement, 1995.

Cavell, Stanley. *This New Yet Unapproachable America: Lectures after Emerson after Wittgenstein.* Albuquerque: Living Batch Press, 1989.

Césaire, Aimé. *The Collected Poetry.* Trans. Clayton Eshleman and Annette Smith. Berkeley: University of California Press, 1983.

Chénieux-Gendron, Jacqueline. *Surrealism.* Trans. Vivian Folkenflik. New York: Columbia University Press, 1990.

Conquest, Robert. *New Lines.* London: Macmillan, 1956.

Conte, Joseph M. *Unending Design: The Forms of Postmodern Poetry.* Ithaca, N.Y.: Cornell University Press, 1991.

Corcoran, Neil. *English Poetry since 1940.* London: Longman, 1994.

Crozier, Andrew. "Thrills and Frills: Poetry as Figures of Empirical Lyricism." In *Society and Literature 1945–1970,* ed. Alan Sinfield, 199–233. New York: Holmes and Meier, 1983.

————. "Signs of Identity: Roy Fisher's *A Furnace.*" *PN Review* 18.3 (1992): 25–32.

Crozier, Andrew, and Tim Longville, eds. *A Various Art.* Manchester: Carcanet, 1987.

Dabydeen, David. "On Not Being Milton: Nigger Talk in England Today." *The State of the Language.* Ed. Christopher Ricks and Leonard Michaels. Berkeley: University of California Press, 1990.

————. *Turner.* London: Jonathan Cape, 1994.

D'Aguiar, Fred. Introduction to *The New British Poetry,* ed. Gillian Allnut, Fred D'Aguiar, Ken Edwards, Eric Mottram, 3–4. London: Paladin, 1988.

————. "Have You Been Here Long? Black Poetry in Britain." In *New British Poetries: The Scope of the Possible,* ed. Robert Hampson and Peter Barry, 51–71. Manchester: Manchester University Press, 1993.

Davie, Donald. *Articulate Energy: An Inquiry into the Syntax of English Poetry.* London: Routledge and Kegan Paul, 1955.

————. "Homage to William Cowper." In *New Poets of England and America,* ed. Donald Hall, Robert Pack, and Louis Simpson, 52–53. New York: Meridian, 1957.

————. *Thomas Hardy and British Poetry.* New York: Oxford University Press, 1972.

————. "Remembering the Movement." In *The Poet in the Imaginary Museum,* ed. Barry Alpert, 72–75. New York: Persea Books, 1977.

————. "Ezra Pound and the English." In *Trying to Explain.* Ann Arbor: University of Michigan Press, 1979.

————. "My Americas." *London Review of Books,* 16 Sept. 1981. 3–4.

————. *Under Briggflatts: A History of Poetry in Great Britain, 1960–1988.* Chicago: University of Chicago Press, 1989.

Deane, Patrick. *At Home in Time: Forms of Neo-Augustanism in Modern English Poetry.* Montreal: McGill-Queen's University Press, 1994.

de Certeau, Michel. *The Practice of Everyday Life.* Trans. Steven Rendall. Berkeley: University of California Press, 1984.

Dorn, Edward. *The Collected Poems 1956–1974.* Bolinas, Calif.: Four Seasons, 1975.

Doyle, Brian. *English and Englishness.* London: Routledge, 1989.

Drucker, Johanna. *The Visible Word: Experimental Typography and Modern Art, 1909–1923.* Chicago: University of Chicago Press, 1994.

Duncan, Andrew. "The Cambridge Leisure Centre: Traits." *Angel Exhaust* 8 (1992): 5–14.

————. Review of Bill Griffiths, *Selected Poems 1969–89;* David Harsent, *News from the Front;* and Maggie O'Sullivan, *In the House of the Shaman. Angel Exhaust* 12 (1995): 107–22.

Easthope, Anthony. "The Impact of Radical Theory on Britain." In *The Arts in the 1970s: Cultural Closure?* Ed. Bart Moore-Gilbert, 57–77. London: Routledge, 1994.

Eliot, T. S. *To Criticize the Critic and Other Writings.* Lincoln: University of Nebraska Press, 1991.

Ellis, R. J. "Mapping the UK Little Magazine Field." In *New British Poetries: The Scope of the Possible,* ed. Robert Hampson and Peter Barry, 72–103. Manchester: Manchester University Press, 1993.

Empson, William. "A London Letter." *Poetry* 49.4 (1937): 221–22.

Figueroa, John. Review of Edward Kamau Brathwaite's *X / Self* and Derek Walcott's *The Arkansas Testament. London Magazine* 28.5–6 (Aug.–Sept. 1988): 116–19.

Fisher, Allen. "Necessary Business: A Text Regarding the Poetry of New Pertinence Produced from the Works of Cris Cheek, Eric Mottram and J. H. Prynne." Typescript, 36 pp.

———. *Unpolished Mirrors.* London: Reality Studios, 1985.

———. "Towards Civic Production." *Reality Studios* 10 (1988): 66–88.

———. *SCRAM: or The Transformation of the Concept of Cities.* London: Spectacular Diseases, 1994.

Fisher, Allen, and Drew Milne. "Exchange in Process." *Parataxis* 6 (1994): 28–36.

Fisher, Roy. *A Furnace.* Oxford: Oxford University Press, 1986.

———. *Poems 1955–1987.* Oxford: Oxford University Press, 1988.

Forbes, Peter. "Talking About a New Generation." *Poetry Review* 84 (Spring 1994): 25–28.

Forced Entertainment. "Speak Bitterness." *Language Alive* 1 (1995).

Forde, Victoria. *The Poetry of Basil Bunting.* Newcastle upon Tyne: Bloodaxe, 1991.

Foster, Hal. *The Return of the Real: The Avant-Garde at the End of the Century.* Cambridge, Mass.: MIT Press, 1996.

Freud, Sigmund. "Mourning and Melancholia." *The Standard Edition of the Complete Psychological Works of Sigmund Freud.* Trans. and ed. James Strachey, vol. 14, 243–58. London: Hogarth, 1961.

Geyer, Michael. "Multiculturalism and the Politics of General Education." *Critical Inquiry* 19 (Spring 1993): 499–533.

Gikandi, Simon. *Writing in Limbo: Modernism and Caribbean Literature.* Ithaca, N.Y.: Cornell University Press, 1992.

Gilonis, Harry. "The Forms Cut Out of the Mystery: Bunting, Some Contemporaries, and Lucretius's 'Poetry of Facts.'" In *Sharp Study and Long Toil,* ed. Richard Caddel, 146–62. Durham: Durham University Journal Special Supplement, 1995.

Gilroy, Paul. *"There Ain't No Black In The Union Jack": The Cultural Politics of Race and Nation.* Chicago: University of Chicago Press, 1991.

Gioia, Dana. *Can Poetry Matter? Essays on Poetry and American Culture.* St. Paul, Minn.: Graywolf, 1992.

Goacher, Denis. "Denis Goacher Talks About Bunting." In *Sharp Study and Long Toil,* ed. Richard Caddel, 197–200. Durham: Durham University Journal Special Supplement, 1995.

Golding, Alan. *From Outlaw to Classic: Canons in American Poetry.* Madison: University of Wisconsin Press, 1995.

Gordon, David. "The Structure of Bunting's *Sonatas.*" In *Basil Bunting, Man and Poet,* ed. Carroll F. Terrell, 107–23. Orono, Maine: National Poetry Foundation, 1980.

Görtschacher, Wolfgang. "Inside the Whale of Britain's Literary Establishment." In *Alive in Parts of This Century: Eric Mottram at Seventy,* ed. Peterjon and Yasmin Skelts, 51–56. Twickenham: North and South, 1994.

Gregson, Ian. *Contemporary Poetry and Postmodernism.* New York: St. Martin's, 1996.

Griffin, Jonathan. *Collected Poems.* Orono, Maine: National Poetry Foundation, 1989.

Grigson, Geoffrey. "A Letter from England." *Poetry* 49.2 (1936): 101–2.

Grossman, Allen, with Mark Halliday. *The Sighted Singer: Two Works on Poetry for Readers and Writers.* Baltimore: Johns Hopkins University Press, 1992.

Gunn, Thom. "What the Slowworm Said." In *The Occasions of Poetry: Essays in Criticism and Autobiography,* 148–58. San Francisco: North Point, 1985.

———. "A Sketch of the Great Dejection." *The Man with Night Sweats.* New York: Farrar Straus Giroux, 1992.

Hall, Donald. "Reading the English: The Continental Drift of the Poetries." *Parnassus* 7.2 (1979): 24–43.

Hall, Donald, Robert Pack, and Louis Simpson, eds. *New Poets of England and America.* New York: Meridian, 1957.

Hall, John. Review of Peter Riley, *Lines on the Liver* and *Tracks and Mineshafts and Two Essays. The Many Review* 2 (1985): 12–18.

Hall, Stuart. "Introduction: Who Needs Identity?" In *Questions of Cultural Identity,* ed. Hall and Paul du Gay, 1–17. London: Sage, 1996.

Hampson, Robert, and Peter Barry, eds. *New British Poetries: The Scope of the Possible.* Manchester: Manchester University Press, 1993.

Harrison, Tony. "A Good Read." *Selected Poems.* Harmondsworth: Penguin, 1985.

Heaney, Seamus. "Sounding Auden." *The Government of the Tongue.* New York: Farrar Straus Giroux, 1988.

Heraclitus. "Fragments." *The Presocratics.* Ed. Philip Wheelwright. New York: Macmillan, 1966.

Heseltine, Nigel. "Microcosmos." In *New British Poets,* ed. Kenneth Rexroth, 97–98. New York: New Directions, 1949.

Hill, Geoffrey. *The Mystery of the Charity of Charles Péguy.* New York: Oxford University Press, 1984.

Hodder, Ian. "Architecture and Meaning: The Example of Neolithic Houses and Tombs." In *Architecture and Order: Approaches to Social Space,* ed. Michael Parker and Colin Richards, 73–86. London: Routledge, 1994.

Horovitz, Michael, ed. *Children of Albion: Poetry of the Underground in Britain.* Harmondsworth: Penguin, 1969.

Hulse, Michael, David Kennedy, and David Morley, eds. *The New Poetry.* Newcastle upon Tyne: Bloodaxe, 1993.

Hunter, Pamela. Introduction to Edith Sitwell, *Façade,* 9–18. London: Duckworth, 1987.

Huyssen, Andreas. *After the Great Divide: Modernism, Mass Culture, and Postmodernism.* Bloomington: Indiana University Press, 1986.

James, John. *Berlin Return.* Liverpool, Engl.: Grosseteste, Ferry, Delires, 1983.

———. "Good Old Harry." In *A Various Art,* ed. Crozier and Longville, 156–57.

———. "Sister Midnight." In *A Various Art,* ed. Crozier and Longville, 158–60.

Kaplan, Amy. "Left Alone with America: The Absence of Empire in the Study of American Culture." In *Cultures of United States Imperialism,* ed. Kaplan and Donald E. Pease, 3–21. Durham, N.C.: Duke University Press, 1993.

Kennedy, David. *New Relations: The Refashioning of British Poetry 1980–1994.* Bridgend, Wales: Seren, 1996.

Kenner, Hugh. *A Sinking Island: The Modern English Writers.* New York: Alfred A. Knopf, 1988.

Kermode, Frank. "Remembering the Movement, and Researching It." *London Review of Books,* 2–18 June 1980, 6–7.

———. "The Common Reader." *An Appetite for Poetry.* Cambridge, Mass.: Harvard University Press, 1989.

Kidd, Helen. "The Paper City: Women, Writing and Experience." In *New British Poetries: The Scope of the Possible,* ed. Robert Hampson and Peter Barry, 156–80. Manchester: Manchester University Press, 1993.

Kinnahan, Linda A. "Experimental Poetics and the Lyric in British Women's Poetry: Geraldine Monk, Wendy Mulford, and Denise Riley." *Contemporary Literature* 37.4 (1996): 620–70.

Klibansky, Raymond, with Erwin Panofsky and Fritz Saxl. *Saturn and Melancholy: Studies in the History of Natural Philosophy.* London: T. Nelson, 1964.

Koethe, John. "The Tension between Poetry and Theory." *Critical Inquiry* 18 (Autumn 1991): 64–75.

Kouidis, Virginia. *Mina Loy: American Modernist Poet.* Baton Rouge: Louisiana State University Press, 1980.

Kristeva, Julia. *Black Sun: Depression and Melancholia.* Trans. Leon S. Roudiez. New York: Columbia University Press, 1989.

Kuhn, Reinhard. *The Demon of Noontide: Ennui in Western Literature.* Princeton, N.J.: Princeton University Press, 1976.

Larkin, Philip. *Required Writing: Miscellaneous Pieces 1955–1982.* London: Faber and Faber, 1983.

———. *Collected Poems.* New York: Farrar Straus Giroux, 1989.

Lawson, Andrew. "Life after Larkin: Postmodern British Poetry." *Textual Practice* 3.3 (1990): 413–25.

Leavis, F. R. *New Bearings in English Poetry.* London: Chatto and Windus, 1932.

———. "English Letter." *Poetry* 44.2 (1934): 264–65.

Lechte, John. "Art, Love and Melancholy in the Work of Julia Kristeva." In *Abjection, Melancholia and Love: The Work of Julia Kristeva,* ed. John Fletcher and Andrew Benjamin, 24–41. London: Routledge, 1990.

Leonard, Tom. "The Locust Tree in Flower, and Why It Had Difficulty Flowering in Britain." In *Invisible Shivers: Selected Work 1965–1983.* Newcastle upon Tyne: Galloping Dog Press, 1984.

Lewis, Wyndham. "Paleface." *The Enemy* 2 (1928): 5–137.

Lopez, Tony. "Under Saxon the Stone: National Identity in Basil Bunting's *Briggflatts.*" In *Sharp Study and Long Toil,* ed. Richard Caddel, 114–22. Durham: Durham University Journal Special Supplement, 1995.

Lowell, Robert. *Life Studies.* New York: Farrar, Straus, Giroux, 1959.

Loy, Mina. *The Last Lunar Baedeker.* Ed. Roger L. Conover. Highlands, N.C.: Jargon Society, 1982.

———. "Notes on Religion." Ed. Keith Tuma. *Sulfur* 27 (1990): 13–16.

———. *Insel.* Ed. Elizabeth Arnold. Santa Rosa: Black Sparrow Press, 1991.

———. "Modern Poetry." *The Lost Lunar Baedeker.* Ed. Roger L. Conover. New York: Farrar Straus Giroux, 1996.

Lucie-Smith, Edward. *British Poetry Since 1945.* Harmondsworth: Penguin, 1970.

Lucretius. *On the Nature of the Universe.* Trans. R. E. Latham. London: Penguin, n.d.

MacCabe, Colin. Review of Tom Raworth's *Writing. Times Literary Supplement* 30 Dec. 1983: 1455.

Mackey, Nathaniel. Review of Edward Kamau Brathwaite's *Sun Poem. Sulfur* 4.2 (1984): 200–205.

———. "An Interview with Edward Kamau Brathwaite." *Hambone* 9 (1991): 42–59.

Macleod, Joseph Gordon. *The Ecliptic.* London: Faber and Faber, 1930.

———. "Poet and People." In *Little Reviews Anthology,* ed. Denys Val Baker, 116–29. London: Metheun, 1949.

Makin, Peter. *Bunting: The Shaping of His Verse.* Oxford: Clarendon, 1992.

Mann, Paul. *The Theory-Death of the Avant-Garde.* Bloomington: Indiana University Press, 1991.

Markham, E. A. "Random Thoughts." In *Hinterland: Caribbean Poetry from the*

West Indies and Britain, ed. E. A. Markham. Newcastle upon Tyne: Bloodaxe, 1989.

Marrriott, D. S. "Signs Taken for Signifiers: Language Writing, Fetishism and Disavowal." *Fragmente* 6 (1995): 73–83.

Matthias, John. "Anthologies of Contemporary British Poetry." In *Reading Old Friends: Essays, Reviews, and Poems on Poetics 1975–1990*, 207–21. Albany: State University of New York Press, 1992.

Matthias, John, ed. *Twenty-three Modern British Poets*. Chicago: Swallow Press, 1971.

Maxwell, Glyn. "Thief on the Cross." *Out of the Rain*. Newcastle upon Tyne: Bloodaxe, 1992.

McCaffery, Steve. "Diminished Reference and the Model Reader." *North of Intention*. New York: Roof, 1986.

Mellors, Anthony. "Out of the American Tree: Language Writing and the Politics of Form." *Fragmente* 6 (1995): 84–91.

Michaels, Walter Benn. "Posthistoricism: The End of the End of History." *Transition* 70 (1996): 4–19.

Middleton, Peter. "Who Am I to Speak? The Politics of Subjectivity in Recent British Poetry." In *New British Poetries: The Scope of the Possible*, ed. Robert Hampson and Peter Barry, 107–33. Manchester: Manchester University Press, 1993.

Miller, David. "Heart of Saying: The Poetry of Gael Turnbull." In *New British Poetries: The Scope of the Possible*, ed. Robert Hampson and Peter Barry, 183–97. Manchester: Manchester University Press, 1993.

Milne, Drew. "Agoraphobia, and the Embarrassment of Manifestoes: Notes Towards a Community of Risk." *Parataxis* 3 (1993): 25–39.

Mole, Bob. Foreword to Benjamin Zephaniah, *City Psalms*. Newcastle upon Tyne: Bloodaxe, 1992.

Monk, Geraldine. *The Sway of Precious Demons: Selected Poems*. Twickenham: North and South, 1992.

Morris, Mervyn. "Interview with Linton Kwesi Johnson." In *Hinterland*, ed. Markham, 250–61.

Morrison, Blake. *The Movement: English Poetry and Fiction of the 1950s*. Oxford: Oxford University Press, 1980.

Morrison, Blake, and Andrew Motion. *The Penguin Book of Contemporary British Poetry*. Harmondsworth: Penguin, 1982.

Mortimer, J. R. *Forty Years' Researches in British and Saxon Burial Mounds in East Yorkshire*. 1905.

Mottram, Eric. *Blood on the Nash Ambassador: Investigations in American Culture*. London: Hutchinson Radius, 1989.

———. "The British Poetry Revival 1960–75." In *New British Poetries: The Scope of the Possible,* ed. Robert Hampson and Peter Barry, 15–50. Manchester: Manchester University Press, 1993.

———. "Poetic Interface: American Poetry and the British Poetry Revival 1960–75." In *Forked Tongues? Comparing Twentieth-Century British and American Literature,* ed. Ann Massa and Alistair Stead, 152–68. Harlow, Engl.: Longman, 1994.

Nairn, Tom. *The Break-Up of Britain: Crisis and Neo-Nationalism.* London: New Left Books, 1977.

Nicholls, Peter. *Modernisms.* Berkeley: University of California, 1995.

Olson, Charles. "Projective Verse." *Selected Writings.* Ed. Robert Creeley. New York: New Directions, 1966.

O'Sullivan, Maggie. *In the House of the Shaman.* London: Reality Street Editions, 1993.

O'Sullivan, Maggie, ed. *Out of Everywhere: Linguistically Innovative Poetry by Women in North America and the United Kingdom.* London: Reality Street, 1996.

Palmer, Michael. *Notes for Echo Lake.* San Francisco: North Point Press, 1981.

Paterson, Don. "Prologue." *Poetry Review* 84.1 (1994): 19.

Peck, John. "Bardic *Briggflatts.*" In *Basil Bunting, Man and Poet,* ed. Carroll F. Terrell, 169–85. Orono, Maine: National Poetry Foundation, 1980.

Perelman, Bob. *The Trouble with Genius: Reading Pound, Joyce, Stein, and Zukofsky.* Berkeley: University of California Press, 1994.

———. *The Marginalization of Poetry.* Princeton, N.J.: Princeton University Press, 1996.

Perkin, Harold. *The Rise of Professional Society: England Since 1880.* London: Routledge, 1989.

Perkins, David. *A History of Modern Poetry: From the 1890s to the High Modernist Mode.* Cambridge, Mass.: Harvard University Press, 1976.

Perloff, Marjorie. "The Two Poetries: An Introduction." *Contemporary Literature* 18 (1977), 263–78.

———. "Music for Words, Perhaps: Reading/Hearing/Seeing John Cage's *Roaratorio.*" In *Postmodern Genres,* ed. Perloff, 193–203. Norman: University of Oklahoma Press, 1989.

———. *Radical Artifice: Writing Poetry in the Age of Media.* Chicago: University of Chicago Press, 1991.

———. *Wittgenstein's Ladder: Poetic Language and the Strangeness of the Ordinary.* Chicago: University of Chicago Press, 1996.

———. "English as a 'Second' Language: Mina Loy's 'Anglo-Mongrels and the Rose.'" In *Mina Loy: Woman and Poet,* ed. Keith Tuma and Maeera Shreiber, 129–46. Orono, Maine: National Poetry Foundation, 1998.

Poggioli, Renato. *The Theory of the Avant-Garde.* Trans. Gerald Fitzgerald. Cambridge, Mass.: Harvard University Press, 1968.

Pound, Ezra. "Cambridge Left." *Poetry* 42.6 (1933): 354–55.

———. "The Prose Tradition in Verse." *Literary Essays of Ezra Pound.* Ed. T. S. Eliot. New York: New Directions, 1935.

———. *The Letters of Ezra Pound.* Ed. D. D. Paige. New York: Harcourt, Brace, World, 1950.

———. "Prefatio Aut Cimicium Tumulus." Preface to *Active Anthology,* in *Polite Essays,* 135–54. Freeport, N.Y.: Books for Libraries, 1966.

———. *Guide to Kulchur.* Rpt. New York: New Directions, 1970.

———. *The Cantos.* New York: New Directions, 1972.

———. "Patria Mia." *Selected Prose of Ezra Pound.* Ed. William Cookson, 100–141. New York: New Directions, 1973.

Powell, Jim. "Basil Bunting and Mina Loy." *Chicago Review* 37.1 (1990): 6–25.

———. "In the Waiting Room." *TriQuarterly* 81 (1991): 145–78.

Prynne, J. H. "Letter." *Language 1.* Cambridge, Engl.: n.d.

———. *Poems.* London: Agneau 2, 1982.

Quartermain, Peter. *Basil Bunting: Poet of the North.* Durham: Basil Bunting Archive, 1990.

———. *Disjunctive Poetics: From Gertrude Stein and Louis Zukofsky to Susan Howe.* Cambridge: Cambridge University Press, 1992.

Rasula, Jed. *The American Poetry Wax Museum: Reality Effects 1940–1990.* Urbana, Ill.: National Council of Teachers of English, 1996.

Raworth, Tom. *Logbook.* Berkeley, Calif.: Poltroon Press, 1976.

———. *Writing.* Berkeley: The Figures, 1982.

———. *Catacoustics.* Cambridge: Street Editions, 1991.

———. "An Anglo-Irish Alternative." *Exact Change* 1 (1995): 315–16.

———. *Clean and Well Lit: Selected Poems 1987–1995.* New York: Roof Books, 1996.

Reagan, Dale, ed. "Basil Bunting Obiter Dicta." In *Basil Bunting, Man and Poet,* ed. Carroll F. Terrell, 229–74. Orono, Maine: National Poetry Foundation, 1980.

Redgrove, Peter. "Rimbaud My Virgil." *Sulfur* 30 (1992): 172–78.

Reeve, N. H., and Richard Kerridge. *Nearly Too Much: The Poetry of J. H. Prynne.* Liverpool: Liverpool University Press, 1995.

Rexroth, Kenneth. *American Poetry in the Twentieth Century.* New York: Herder and Herder, 1971.

Rexroth, Kenneth, ed. *New British Poets.* New York: New Directions, 1949.

Richman, Robert, ed. *The Direction of Poetry.* Boston: Houghton Mifflin, 1988.

Ricks, Christopher. "Donald Davie and the English." *London Review of Books,* 4 June 1980, 19.

———. *The Force of Poetry.* Oxford: Oxford University Press, 1984.

Riley, Denise. *Poets on Writing: Britain, 1970–1991.* London: Macmillan, 1992.

Riley, Peter. "Spitewinter Provocations: An Interview [by Kelvin Corcoran] on the Condition of Poetry with Peter Riley." *Reality Studios* 8 (1986): 1–17.

———. *Distant Points (Excavations Part One Books One and Two).* London: Reality Street Editions, 1995.

———. "The Creative Moment of the Poem." In *Poets on Writing,* ed. Denise Riley, 92–113. London: Macmillan, 1992.

Riley, Peter, and John James, eds. *Collection Seven.* Cambridge, Engl.: n.d.

Robinson, Kit. "Tom Raworth." *Dictionary of Literary Biography* 40. Ed. Vincent B. Sherry, Jr. 459–68. Detroit: Gale Research, 1985.

Rodker, John. *Poems and Adolphe 1920.* Ed. Andrew Crozier. Manchester: Carcanet, 1996.

Rohlehr, Gordon. "Rohlehr on Brathwaite." In *Hinterland: Caribbean Poetry from the West Indies and Britain,* ed. E. A. Markham, 115–16. Newcastle upon Tyne: Bloodaxe, 1989.

Rosenthal, M. L., and Sally M. Gall. *The Modern Poetic Sequence: The Genius of Modern Poetry.* New York: Oxford University Press, 1983.

Rothenberg, Jerome, ed. *Revolution of the Word: A New Gathering of American Avant-Garde Poetry 1914–1945.* New York: Seabury, 1974.

Saakana, Amon Saba. "Out of the Colonial Cocoon." *Washington Post,* 3 July 1988.

Savage, D. S. "London Letter." *Poetry* 50 (Jan. 1938): 277–88.

Schmidt, Michael, and Grevel Lindop. *British Poetry Since 1960.* Oxford: Carcanet, 1972.

Scholem, Gershom. *Major Trends in Jewish Mysticism.* New York: Schocken Books, 1954.

Seed, John. "Hegemony Postponed." *Cultural Revolution: The Challenge of the Arts in the 1960s.* Ed. Bart Moore-Gilbert and John Seed, 15–44. London: Routlege, 1992.

Shapcott, Jo. "Phrasebook." In *The New Poetry,* ed. Michael Hulse, David Kennedy, and David Morley, 204–5. Newcastle upon Tyne: Bloodaxe, 1993.

Sheppard, Robert. "British Poetry and Its Discontents." In *Cultural Revolution: The Challenge of the Arts in the 1960s,* ed. Bart Moore-Gilbert and John Seed, 160–79.

———. "Recognition and Discovery in the 1980s." *Fragmente* 2 (Autumn 1990): 80–81.

———. "The Necessary Business of Allen Fisher." Introduction to Brian Catling, Allen Fisher, Bill Griffifths, *Future Exiles,* 11–17. London: Paladin, 1992.

Shils, Edward. "British Intellectuals in the Mid-Twentieth Century. *The Intellectuals and the Powers and Other Essays.* Chicago: University of Chicago Press, 1972.

Sinclair, Iain. "Infamous and Invisible: A Manifesto for Those Who Do Not Believe in Such Things." In *Conductors of Chaos,* ed. Sinclair, xii–xx. London: Picador, 1996.

Sisson, C. H. "Some Reflections on American Poetry." *The Avoidance of Literature: Collected Essays.* Manchester: Carcanet, 1978.

———. "Place." *Exactions.* Manchester: Carcanet, 1980.

Sommer, Doris. "America as Desire(d): Nathaniel Tarn's Poetry of the Outsider as Insider." *American Poetry* 2.1 (1984): 13–35.

Spender, Stephen. *Love-Hate Relations: A Study of Anglo-American Sensibilities.* London: Hamish Hamilton, 1974.

Steiner, George. "Linguistics and Poetics." In *Extra-Territorial: Papers on Literature and Language.* London: Faber, 1972.

Suter, Anthony. "Musical Structure in the Poetry of Basil Bunting." *Agenda* 16.1 (1978): 46–54.

Tarn, Nathaniel. *The Beautiful Contradictions.* New York: Random House, 1970.

———. "Child as Father to Man in the American Uni-verse" and "The World Wide Open: The Work Laid before Us in This Disunited Kingdom." *Views from Weaving Mountain: Selected Essays in Poetics and Anthropology.* Albuquerque: American Poetry Book, 1991.

Terrell, Carroll F., ed. *Basil Bunting, Man and Poet.* Orono, Maine: National Poetry Foundation, 1980.

Tomlinson, Charles. "The Middlebrow Muse." *Essays in Criticism* 7 (1957): 208–17.

———. *Some Americans.* Berkeley: University of California Press, 1981.

Tuma, Keith. "Ezra Pound, Progressive." *Paideuma* 19 (Spring-Fall 1990): 77–92.

Turnbull, Gael. "Twenty Words, Twenty Days." *While Breath Persist.* Erin, Ontario: The Porcupine's Quill, 1992.

von Hallberg, Robert. *American Poetry and Culture 1945–1980.* Cambridge, Mass.: Harvard University Press, 1985.

———. "Literature and History: Neat Fits." *Modernism/Modernity* 3.3 (1996): 115–20.

Ward, Geoffrey. *Language Poetry and the American Avant-Garde.* Keele, Engl.: British Association for American Studies, 1993.

Weinberger, Eliot. "New in Briefs." *Sulfur* 31 (1992): 231–36.

Whittemore, Reed. "Academic Writing and the Graces." *The Fascination of the Abomination: Poems, Stories, and Essays.* New York: Macmillan, 1963.

Williams, Raymond. "Crisis in English Studies." *Writing in Society.* London: Verso, 1987.

Williams, William Carlos. "Letter to the Editor." *Poetry* 44.3 (1934): 217.

Wills, Clair. "Contemporary Women's Poetry: Experimantalism and the Expressive Voice." *Critical Quarterly* 36.3 (1994): 34–49.

Zabel, Morton Dauwen. "A Dawn in Britain, Part I." *Poetry* 38.1 (1931): 35–41.

———. "A Dawn in Britain, Part II." *Poetry* 38.2 (1931): 101–5.

———. "Obstinate Isles." *Poetry* 41.4 (1933): 214–19.

———. "Recent Magazines." *Poetry* 42.6 (1933): 346–53.

Zephaniah, Benjamin. *City Psalms*. Newcastle upon Tyne: Bloodaxe, 1992.

Zukofsky, Louis. *Ferdinand*. London: Cape, 1968.

Index

Yau, K. W., 224
Yeats, W. B., 68, 167, 173
Yevtushenko, Yevgeny, 50

Zabel, Morton Dauwen, 115–22, 126,
   139
Zephaniah, Benjamin, 212–13, 252–54
Zukofsky, Louis, 29, 41, 48, 55, 107,
   224, 272n